CGI

fast&easy™
web development

Send Us Your Comments:

To comment on this book or any other PRIMA TECH title, visit our reader response page on the Web at **www.prima-tech.com/comments**.

How to Order:

For information on quantity discounts, contact the publisher: Prima Publishing, P.O. Box 1260BK, Rocklin, CA 95677-1260; (916) 787-7000. On your letterhead, include information concerning the intended use of the books and the number of books you want to purchase.

CGI

fast&easy™
web development

Johnnie R. Christenberry, et. al

PRIMA
TECH

A DIVISION OF PRIMA PUBLISHING

A Division of Prima Publishing

Prima Publishing and colophon are registered trademarks of Prima Communications, Inc. PRIMA TECH is a trademark of Prima Communications, Inc., Roseville, California 95661.

Microsoft, Windows, and Internet Explorer are trademarks or registered trademarks of Microsoft Corporation. Mac and Macintosh are trademarks or registered trademarks of Apple Computer, Inc. Netscape is a registered trademark of Netscape Communications Corporation.

Important: Prima Publishing cannot provide software support. Please contact the appropriate software manufacturer's technical support line or Web site for assistance.

Prima Publishing and the authors have attempted throughout this book to distinguish proprietary trademarks from descriptive terms by following the capitalization style used by the manufacturers.

Information contained in this book has been obtained by Prima Publishing from sources believed to be reliable. However, because of the possibility of human or mechanical error by our sources, Prima Publishing, or others, the Publisher does not guarantee the accuracy, adequacy, or completeness of any information and is not responsible for any errors or omissions or the results obtained from the use of such information. Readers should be particularly aware of the fact that the Internet is an ever-changing entity. Some facts might have changed since this book went to press.

ISBN: 0-7615-2938-1

Library of Congress Catalog Card Number: 00-10540

Printed in the United States of America

00 01 02 03 04 DD 10 9 8 7 6 5 4 3 2 1

Publisher:
Stacy L. Hiquet

Marketing Manager:
Judi Taylor

Associate Marketing Manager:
Heather Buzzingham

Managing Editor:
Sandy Doell

Acquisitions Editor:
Melody Layne

Project Editor:
Melody Layne

Copy Editor:
Kezia Endsley

Technical Reviewer:
Angela Denny

Proofreader:
Jessica McCarty

Interior Layout:
Danielle Foster

Cover Design:
Prima Design Team

Indexer:
Johnna VanHoose Dinse

To my wonderful wife, Beth, who is responsible for me being who I am and where I am today. Without your support and continued dedication I would not have achieved all that I have achieved. Johnnie R. Christenberry

To Terry, for giving me the opportunity to stretch myself. Thanks, T.C. Bradley III

To my wife, Stacey, thanks for believing in me - 123! Troy McKenna

Acknowledgments

I want to thank God for blessing me with the abilities and skills necessary to accomplish this task and the many other tasks I have undertaken in my life.

Thanks go to Melody Layne, Kim Spilker, and Prima Tech for giving me the opportunity to write this book, especially Melody whose nerves were tested at every missed deadline. A thank you also goes to Todd Overbeck for introducing me to Melody and Prima Tech. I also want to thank the contributing authors, T. C. Bradley and Troy McKenna, for helping me get this book completed before I gave Melody a nervous breakdown.

A huge THANK YOU goes to Kezia Endsley, the best editor in the world, for finding and correcting the areas of the book where I was obviously asleep or brain-dead. And to my technical editor, Angie Denny, I thank you for keeping me correct in my explanations, descriptions, and code.

Thanks also go to my writing instructors at IUPUI who encouraged me to write and helped me polish my writing skills. Most of them will be shocked that I actually wrote something that was not required for my degree. I thank Sharon Heimansohn, the instructor for my first computer course, for getting me started in the world of programming. Because of you I have become a computer nerd.

I want to thank my sons—Jonathan, Shawn, and Javan—who have shown me that a person can accomplish anything if they want it enough and never give up trying. Thanks go to my parents, Alvin and Phyllis, who always told me, "Anything worth doing is worth doing right the first time." A thank you to my in-laws, Jim and Ann, who believed enough in their daughter to trust her decision to marry me. A very special thank you goes to my wonderful and supportive wife, Beth, who let me put our life on hold for so many weeks, which became months, so that I could write this book. I promise to complete the house remodel before I undertake any new projects.

I also want to thank you, the reader, for purchasing this book. I hope you enjoy using it as much as I enjoyed writing it.

About the Authors

Johnnie R. Christenberry lives in Indianapolis, Indiana with his wife and youngest son. He is a full-time student at Indiana University Purdue University at Indianapolis (IUPUI) and is currently pursuing a B.A. in Religious Studies and a B.S. in Computer Science. Johnnie is the Technical Coordinator/Programmer for the IUPUI TV channel that is supported by the IUPUI Student Life and Diversity Program. He also creates and maintains numerous commercial and educational Web sites through his company Christenberry Enterprises and its subsidiary wbmstr.com.

T.C. Bradley, MCSE, is currently in charge of information systems for the Student Technology Centers at Indiana University-Bloomington. He has been using ColdFusion, Perl CGI and various database systems for the past three years to build integrated intranet applications for IU staff and students. T.C. lives in Bloomington, Indiana with his wife, Lisa, and their cat, Bilbo.

Troy McKenna is a Perl programmer for Command-O Software, Inc., a company located in Jackson Hole, Wyoming that specializes in CGI programming for the Web (http://www.command-o.com). Troy lives in Alpine, Wyoming with his wife Stacey. You can contact him via e-mail at troy@command-o.com.

Contents

PART III
ADVANCED DATA 263

Introduction

This book, CGI Fast & Easy Web Development, is designed to take you from the stage of not knowing what the letters CGI stand for to having the ability to create and modify CGI applications. The applications shown throughout the book are created using Perl, a scripting language commonly used on the Web. It will be helpful for you to have an understanding of basic Web page development; however, the examples provided include the necessary HTML code for creating the forms you will use with your CGI applications.

You can read this book from cover to cover and gain an understanding of CGI and writing applications, or you can use it as a reference tool to look up specific tasks and enhance your current skills. I have included enough theoretical information to assist you in using and modifying the code contained in the book without, hopefully, boring you to death or totally confusing you.

The CD-ROM that accompanies this book contains all of the HTML and CGI code used in every example shown. All of the code is documented, using comments, to allow you to copy and paste it into your application and modify it without referencing the book—you might need to reference the book on the more advanced programs or the lengthy lines of code, as I have kept the comments concise so as not to make the applications unwieldy in length.

What This Book Is About

When I was first introduced to CGI applications, there did not exist the plethora of books that are currently available. I had a choice between two basic types of books. The first type consisted of theoretical explanations of CGI and Perl with very few, if any, usable examples of code. The second type consisted of usable examples of code, but they did not contain enough information to allow me to modify the application or create a more advanced application than what was shown. As I began writing this book I decided that I would create a book that I would have liked to have when I was getting started with CGI: a book that contains usable code and enough information to allow readers to modify the code to fit their needs or create better applications than the examples.

Who Should Read This Book?

This book is a powerful tool for Web developers with little or no previous programming experience. If you are experienced, you will find it extremely useful as a reference tool, and you might gain a better understanding of many of the processes you currently use.

For the novice developer, I have included detailed examples, and I have included extensive comments in the examples contained on the CD-ROM. You can copy and paste the examples directly into a text editor and use them without changing any code; moreover, the comments should allow you to make the changes needed to customize the code to your specific application. You will find it useful to read through the entire book and then use it as a reference guide when you are creating your applications.

For the experienced developer, you will find that the comments in the examples explain the code in a manner that will help you gain a better understanding of CGI and Perl. You will find that you can skip some of the first chapters; however, I recommend that you read them in order to gain any additional knowledge they contain about CGI and Perl.

What You Need to Begin

The only tools you need to begin using the examples in this book are the basic tools needed for Web development. These tools include the following items:

- A text editor program (Notepad, WordPad, etc.) You can use an HTML editor if you like—one is provided on the CD-ROM.

- Access to a Web server on which to store your Web pages and CGI applications (details about this are included in the book).

Conventions Used in This Book

This book contains many helpful comments throughout and includes Tips, Notes, and Cautions to assist you in areas that need extra attention.

Cautions generally tell you how to avoid problems.

Notes provide additional helpful or interesting information.

Tips often suggest techniques and shortcuts to make your life easier.

Author Comments

I hope I have succeeded and you find the book to be as useful as I intended it to be. If you have any questions, or comments about the examples in the book, clarification, or modification tips, please contact me, (jchriste@cs.iupui.edu) and I will assist you or include the suggestions in any future revisions of the book.

I wish you the best of luck with your Web development and I hope you have as much fun creating CGI applications as I had writing this book.

PART I

CGI:
An Introduction

1

CGI and the Web

Before jumping directly into CGI programming, it is helpful to have a general understanding of CGI and how it works. The first ideas presented give you the basic information about CGI and the benefits of using it. This chapter enables you to understand the concepts presented in later chapters of the book. In this chapter, you learn:

- What CGI is
- Why you should use CGI
- Who else uses CGI
- How CGI works
- The CGI server requirements
- How to get started using CGI
- The CGI programming languages

What Is CGI?

You probably know that Web designers use CGI in order to enhance their Web sites, but you might not understand what CGI is or how it works. This section explains what CGI is and introduces you to the basics. CGI is the acronym for *Common Gateway Interface*. Okay, what does that mean? The Common Gateway Interface is the specification that enables Web servers to communicate with programs on the server. Basically, it is a means of adapting one server program to another server program in order to establish a connection between the two.

Essentially, CGI allows different programs, written in different languages, to connect and communicate with each other. CGI programs can be written in any programming language that follows the standards of CGI. Some of the more common languages are C/C++, tcl, Visual Basic, AppleScript, and Perl (the most popular CGI programming language).

This process is similar to an international businessperson using an interpreter while traveling for business. The businessperson does not need to understand the various languages; he or she only needs to be able to communicate with the interpreter. This enables the businessperson to focus on the business at hand and not the language barrier. CGI is similar to this scenario. The browser does not have to understand the programming languages; it only needs to understand the CGI output sent to it by the host server. CGI is how HTML (the *Hypertext Markup Language*) pages are created based on input from the users rather than in advance. CGI is also how forms submit their data and display the results of queries.

Why Use CGI?

You probably purchased this book to find out how to use CGI because you have already decided to use it on your Web site. But, you might not know all the benefits of using it.

The benefit of using CGI as part of your Web site is that it provides interaction between the users and your data.

This interaction can be as simple as signing your guest book.

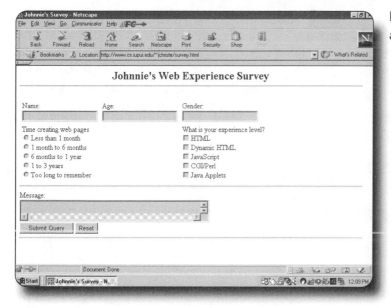

It could be completing a survey.

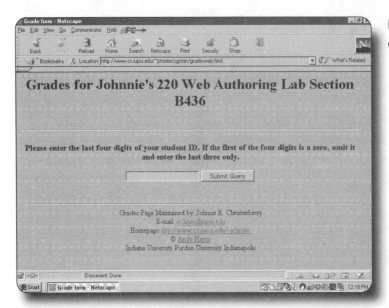

It could be searching your data for information.

Or, it could be to search the Web for specific information.

By using CGI, you can design pages to the users' specifications and generate the pages immediately. The HTML doesn't get created until after the users submit the specifications.

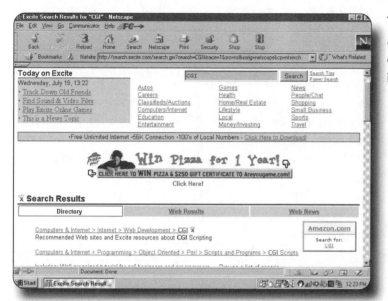

This is how Excite, Yahoo!, and other search engines display the results of each individual search.

Why Is CGI Important to the Web Designer?

The primary problem I have encountered with my Web account is lack of space. Most accounts are allotted a certain amount of space on the server, and it is nearly impossible to get any more. This space constraint poses a problem when you want to create Web pages that interact with your visitors. CGI applications can solve this problem by enabling you to generate multiple pages from a single application. This not only frees up space, it saves you time and effort in creating the individual pages. You might find that creating individual Web pages consumes more time than you expect. With CGI, you create the HTML code one time and include it as the output in your CGI application. The CGI application then creates the individual pages when they are needed (based on input from the users).

Who Uses CGI?

Advanced Web designers who want to include programming on their Web pages use CGI. One advantage to using CGI is that it enables programmers to write the program in almost any programming language. Also, CGI allows the program to be accessed and executed by the server when users activate a call to the program, as opposed to having the program contained in the HTML code.

This is a very important feature, because it gives Web programmers great flexibility when choosing programs to include on their Web site. Many programmers use various scripting languages to perform functions on their sites; however, CGI programs are the most powerful when it comes to using information supplied by the user through the browser.

Sites that have visitor counters, shopping carts, search engines, or any type of forms that create HTML pages based on the users' input, use CGI. CGI allows you to create dynamic Web pages that respond to the users' requests instead of static pages that are created in anticipation of users' input. This reduces the number of Web pages that need to be created and stored in your account.

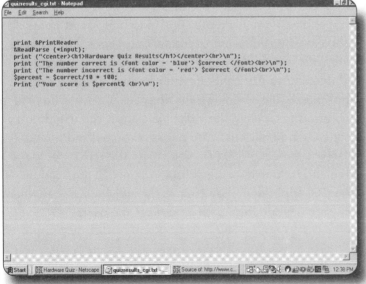

The CGI program creates different pages based upon the information supplied by the users and enables you to create a single basic HTML page format that generates the page based on the data collected from the form.

Wow, a more powerful Web site with less work. You can now see why CGI is so popular with Web programmers.

CGI Basics

CGI is simpler than most people are led to believe. This is promising to Web designers who have very little to no programming experience. However, like any type of programming language, the more advanced the program becomes, the harder it is to design, write, modify, and debug.

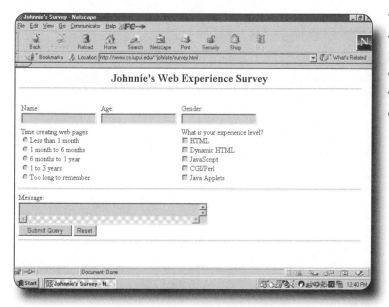

The basic concept of CGI is that the users submit information, generally via a form, from their browser to the server. The server then calls the CGI application.

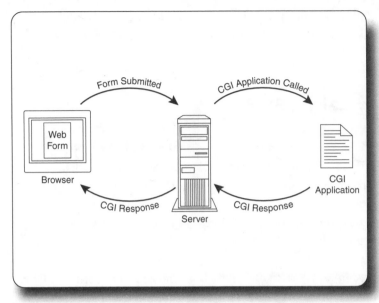

The CGI application then sends a response to the server, and the server sends the CGI response back to the user's browser as an HTML page.

As simple as this process sounds, it is what CGI is all about. Many people expect it to be a more involved process, but it really is this basic. The concept of running programs and applications through your Web site should excite you. The excitement comes from the capability to generate dynamic and powerful Web pages that interact with your users.

What You Need to Run CGI Applications

In order to use CGI applications on your Web site, you must adhere to a few requirements.

NOTE

Check with your server administrator or ISP (*Internet Service Provider*) to determine whether you are allowed to run CGI applications. Many server administrators do not allow just anyone to run CGI applications on their servers because security issues arise when you have access to the files and directories housed on the server.

The first requirement is that CGI applications need to be in a location where the server can locate them.

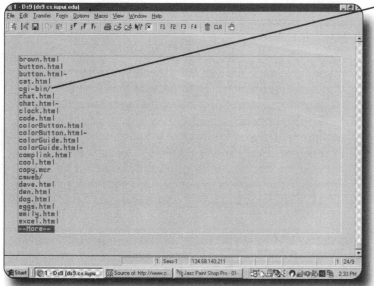

The standard location is in a subdirectory named cgi-bin.

The cgi-bin subdirectory needs to have 7-5-5 permissions in order for the applications to be accessed. Permissions and details about the cgi-bin directory will be explained in the section, "*Establishing Your cgi-bin Directory*," later in this chapter.

Now that you know what CGI is, why you would use it, and how it works, it is time to learn about the server requirements for running CGI applications.

CGI Server Requirements

Because CGI scripts contain separate programs that the server needs to process, they create extra work for the server. This is usually not a problem unless your server is old, slow, or has a small amount of available memory. The problem occurs when multiple users are accessing your CGI programs or other programs housed on the same server. Your best option is to discuss the server requirements with your server administrator. You want to do this for a number of reasons. First, you need to verify that the server is configured to use CGI. Second, you need to verify that you have access to run CGI applications on the server through your account. Finally, you need to know how to gain access to the cgi-bin of the server. Remember, security risks are involved with CGI applications, so most server administrators place restrictions on who can access the cgi-bin.

TIP

If you have used CGI on another server or system, ask that server administrator to provide you with some form of documentation stating that you are qualified to run CGI applications. Basically, this provides testimony that you know what you are doing. I have letters from every server administrator who has allowed me access, stating that they have not had any security issues as a result of my CGI applications.

The amount of time you spend discussing these issues with your server administrator is worthwhile. It is not productive to spend hours writing or modifying script and then find out that you cannot run it on your account. The server administrator also knows which features of CGI and which languages the server supports.

Getting Started with CGI

Before you can start using CGI on your Web site, you need to prepare your account to handle CGI. This is a fairly simple process and does not take much time. A few items need to be incorporated into your account, and you need to set them up prior to running your first CGI application.

Creating Your cgi-bin

The first step in preparing your account for CGI applications is establishing a cgi-bin subdirectory and setting the permissions so this subdirectory can be accessed and can run your CGI applications. This is one of the items you need to discuss with your server administrator prior to preparing your account for CGI.

What Is a cgi-bin?

In order for CGI applications to be executed, they must be placed in a specific directory.

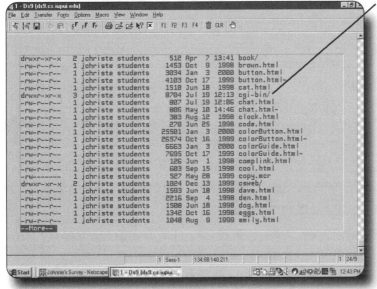

The general directory for CGI applications is the cgi-bin directory.

The reason that the CGI applications are placed in a specific directory is for security purposes. Recall that security risks are involved with CGI applications. If the CGI applications are contained in a specific location, the server administrator has control of them and can monitor them effectively. This is also beneficial to you because you are forced to store all your CGI applications in one directory. Therefore, you eliminate any time and frustration you might otherwise spend trying to locate an application. This might not sound important to you at this time; however, you will discover that time spent searching for a specific file, document, or application is not productive and results in lost revenue.

Establishing Your cgi-bin Directory

In order to create a cgi-bin directory, you need to check with your server administrator as to the exact specifications required. Generally, you need to create a subdirectory within your account.

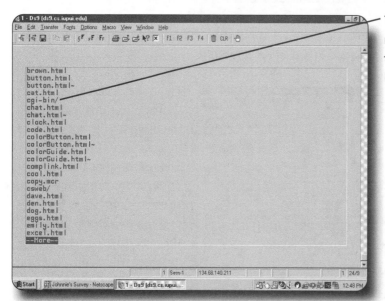

The cgi-bin subdirectory needs to be located within the directory used for your HTML pages.

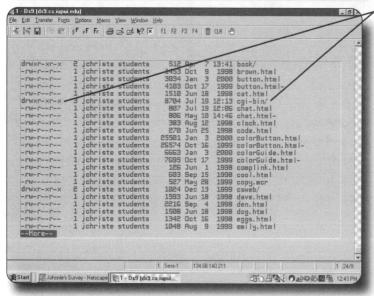

Once you have created the cgi-bin subdirectory, you need to set the permission of the directory to 7-5-5. This can be done using the chmod command as covered in the Chapter 3 section, "Changing the Permissions of Your Application.

The 7-5-5 moniker sets the subdirectory permissions as follows. You have read, write, and execute capability

(7); the group—specific to your organization—has read and execute capability (5); and others have read and execute capability (5). This enables you to write to the directory, whereas others can run the programs contained in the subdirectory but cannot write to it.

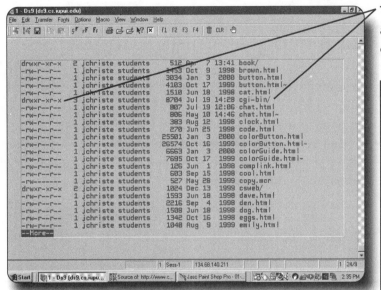

The individual CGI applications need 7-1-1 or 7-5-5 permissions.

NOTE

Permissions are calculated based on a binary number combination. The value associated with the owner having the specified capability is 4, the value associated with the owner's group having the capability is 2, and the value associated with everyone in the world having the capability is 1. These values are added together to produce the individual numbers for the read, write, and execute permissions of a file.

The difference between 7-1-1 and 7-5-5 permissions is that with 7-1-1 others can execute the application; however, they do not have access to read the file. They therefore cannot access the programming code of the applications. This has some security benefits. If you are not certain whether to use 7-1-1 or 7-5-5, you can always set the permissions to 7-5-5.

Recall that this enables you to read, write, and execute the directory, whereas others can only read and execute the directory. Once you have established the cgi-bin directory and set the permissions, you need to decide which language you want to use for your CGI applications.

CGI Programming Languages

One of the best features of using CGI is the number of languages you can use in your applications. The abundance of languages available for building CGI applications can cause some confusion; however, your best option is to stick with a language you understand or a language that has prewritten scripts available.

Your Choices

As mentioned earlier, a number of languages that adhere to CGI standards and protocols are available. These languages are C/C++, tcl, Visual Basic, AppleScript, and Perl. You can use any of these languages to program CGI applications; however, some are more difficult to use than others. For example, C/C++ is a pain when working with strings (text)—strings are discussed in detail in Chapter 2, "Writing Your CGI Application."

The Most Popular CGI Language: Perl

Currently, the most popular CGI programming language is Perl (*Practical Extraction and Report Language*). Larry Wall created Perl in 1986 in order to create reports. Perl has been modified and improved, by Larry and others, into a very powerful programming language that has many uses in addition to a Web-based programming language.

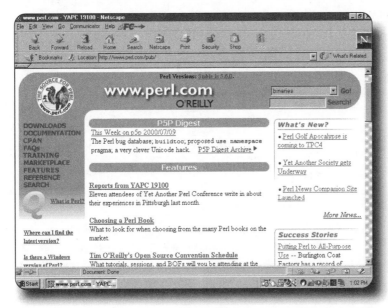

The popularity of Perl as a CGI programming language is due primarily to its ability to manipulate text. Unlike some other languages, Perl allows quick separation of characters into different fields and data that can be used by the program in a variety of ways. Also, Perl provides many ways to accomplish the same task without causing conflicts within the script. One of the powerful features of Perl is that it distinguishes between strings (text) and numbers based on the operator used: therefore, you do not need to spend time converting from strings to numbers and vice versa. This feature will be detailed in Chapter 6, "Scalars." Another popular feature of Perl is its ability to be moved from platform to platform—Windows to UNIX (*Uniplexed Information and Computing System*), UNIX to Windows, and so on—with only a few minor changes to the script. Finally, it is just a cool language to work with and has even sparked a Perl poetry contest.

Now that you understand the language choices you have and why Perl is the most popular language used with CGI, you are ready to look at how you modify your HTML page in order to prepare it for your CGI application.

Preparing Your Web Page for CGI

TIP

For information on creating HTML pages, you can reference Prima Tech's *XHTML Fast & Easy Web Development* by Brian Proffitt and Ann Zupan.

In order to run CGI applications within your Web page, you need to make certain modifications. The first thing you need is a way to get information from your users. This is generally accomplished using an HTML form.

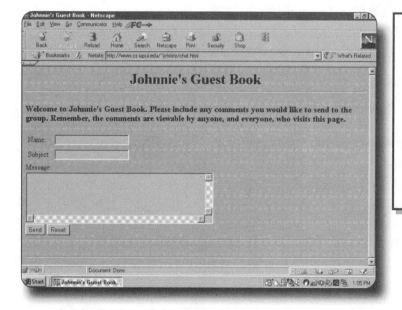

NOTE

Complete details on creating forms and the associated input fields are included in the "Developing Your Form" section of Chapter 4, "Getting the Data From Visitors to Your Web Page."

The HTML code that creates the form includes the `<form>` `</form>` tags, which set up the form.

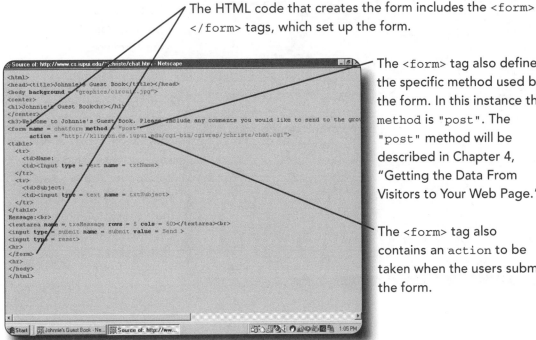

The `<form>` tag also defines the specific method used by the form. In this instance the method is `"post"`. The `"post"` method will be described in Chapter 4, "Getting the Data From Visitors to Your Web Page."

The `<form>` tag also contains an `action` to be taken when the users submit the form.

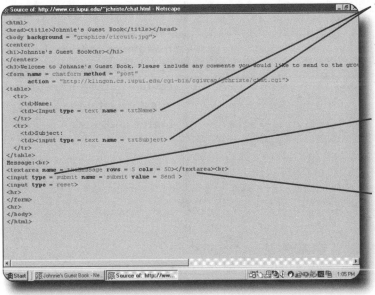

The `<input>` tags perform a couple of different tasks in the HTML code. The first two `<input>` tags create text input fields.

The second two `<input>` tags create the Submit and Reset buttons.

Notice the `<textarea>` tag in the code.

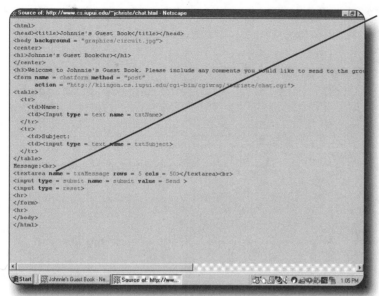

This tag enables the users to input any comments they want to make.

From this example, you probably realized that the `<form>` tag is a major component when using CGI applications within your Web page. The `method` and `action` attributes of the `<form>` tag are actually the most important part of the form.

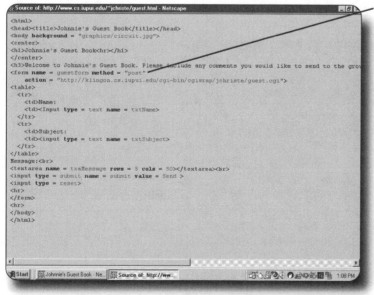

Notice that the `method` attribute tells the form to `"post"` the form contents and the `action` attribute tells the form to go to the URL http://klingon.cs.iupui.edu/ cgi-bin/cgiwrap/jchriste/ guest.cgi after the Submit button is clicked.

> **NOTE**
>
> It is important to note that the URL in the `action` attribute is not a standard Web page URL; it is a CGI program URL. This is an important difference because the `action` attribute is calling an executable program located on the server and not a program contained within the HTML page itself, like occurs with JavaScript. Having the program located on the server instead of being contained in the HTML page reduces the time required for the page to be transferred from the server to the users' browser.

You can see that the changes made to a standard HTML page are not that complicated; however, they are extremely important in order for the CGI application to be accessed correctly. You also can see the value behind thinking through the form and program prior to creating them. Chapter 2, "Writing Your CGI Application," focuses on the importance of planning ahead and the complications that can arise when you do not think about what you are trying to accomplish first.

Summary

This chapter introduced CGI. You learned what CGI is, why you might use CGI, and who uses CGI. You also gained an understanding of how CGI works and what is required to run CGI applications on your Web site. This understanding includes the information you need to establish a cgi-bin in your account, as well as an explanation of why you need to create the cgi-bin.

You gained knowledge about the language choices available for CGI applications and learned why Perl is the language of choice. Finally, you expanded your HTML code writing ability in order to create a form that accesses a CGI application. In the next chapter, you begin the process of designing both the CGI application and the HTML page that connects the users to that application. You are now ready to begin the process of Web programming.

2

Writing Your CGI Application

This chapter introduces you to programming CGI applications with a strong emphasis on the importance of planning ahead. The first sections focus on the planning process and the benefits you receive from this often-overlooked step. The later sections focus on the basic constructs you need to consider when you create your CGI applications. In this chapter you learn:

- The importance of planning ahead
- How to use multiple languages and multiple HTML pages
- Proper form and database design
- How to write pseudocode
- The difference between programs and scripts
- How data is processed in Perl

Planning Ahead Is Important

Novice programmers often overlook the planning step; however, it is the first step employed by successful programmers. The small amount of time you spend planning saves you much frustration and time when programming your CGI application and when creating the HTML pages that correspond to the application. Your first step when planning is to design the HTML pages on paper with notes describing what each page will accomplish.

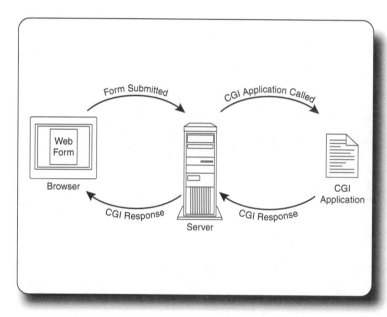

Using Multiple Languages

Programming CGI applications for the Web requires you to use multiple languages—HTML for the Web pages and at least one programming language for the application. The fact that you use two languages does not necessarily create a challenge; the problems arise when you get confused and use one language when you should use the other. I know you are smart enough to keep the languages straight.

```
mail_code_xcomments.txt - Notepad
File  Edit  Search  Help

#get receiver
$receiver = $input{'receiver'};

#get sender
$sender = $input{'sender'};

#get subject
$subject = $input{'subject'};

#get message
$message = $input{'message'};

#send mail
open (MAIL, "|$mailprog $receiver") || die ("couldn't open $mailprog \n");
print MAIL "Subject: $subject \n\n";
print MAIL "Sender: $sender \n\n";
print MAIL 'Message: ';
print MAIL $message . " ";
print MAIL "(sent by Johnnie R. Christenberry's e-mail program: June, 1998.)";
print MAIL " ";
close (MAIL);

#respond to user
#creates HTML output
print &PrintHeader;
print "<html><head><title>Email was delivered</title></head>";
print "<body background = http://klingon.cs.iupui.edu/~jchriste/cgi-bin/firerin\
g.jpg><center><h1>Be sure to check your mailbox for any response!</h1></center>\
<hr>";
print "receiver: $receiver <br> \n"; #uses "receiver" instead of "Send to"
print "sender: $sender <br> \n"; #uses "sender" instead of "From"
print "subject: $subject <br> \n"; #same as form
print "message: <br>  \n $message <br> \n"; #same as form
print "<hr></body></html>";
```

The real challenge, however, occurs when you incorporate the HTML code into the CGI application.

With proper planning, this challenge can be overcome. Your first step in the planning process, as mentioned earlier, is to sketch the HTML pages needed for the application. This might sound elementary; however, every time I have omitted this step, I have made minor mistakes in either the HTML code or the program code. The reason you might make these types of mistakes is likely not due to your lack of knowledge or skill; rather you often make mistakes when you are in a hurry to complete the project, you have deadlines to meet, or other pressing things on your personal agenda. This leads into the next area of possible confusion, which is the result of using multiple HTML pages.

Using Multiple HTML Pages

Most likely, you are familiar with using multiple HTML pages to achieve many different effects on your Web site. A new challenge emerges—not in the creation of the pages, but in the content of the pages. Take a look at the following HTML pages as an example. The first page contains various input fields.

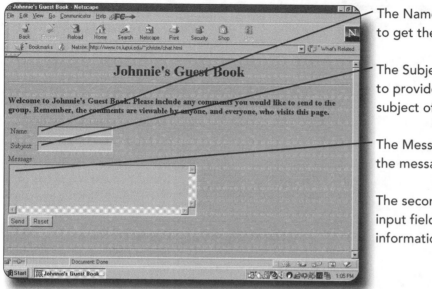

The Name input field is used to get the users' name.

The Subject field is included to provide a place for the subject of the message.

The Message field contains the message to be sent.

The second page contains input fields for different information.

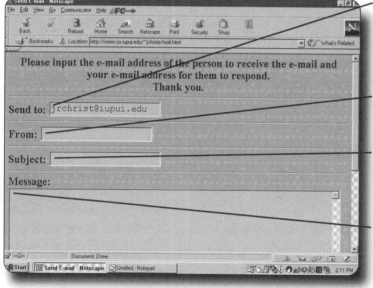

The Send to input field is used to get the e-mail address of the recipient of the message.

The From input field holds the sender's e-mail address.

The Subject input field displays the subject of the message.

And, the Message input field contains the message to be sent.

As similar as these pages are in design, there is a big difference in the content of the input fields. The CGI application uses the input information from these forms to create the output HTML pages, so it is extremely important that you plan the HTML forms and the CGI application with this in mind.

Proper planning will prevent later confusion when designing multiple pages and creating the CGI application. If you are designing multiple HTML pages without having the CGI application generate any of the HTML code, the planning will appear less important; however, you must now consider the CGI application and the HTML code it will generate. The reason this is so important is that the HTML code contained in the CGI application is dependent on the input information derived from the HTML form.

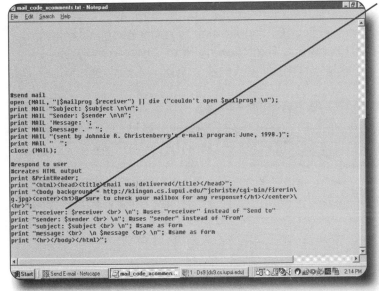

Upon closer inspection, you should notice that the HTML code uses "receiver" and not "Send to," which was the phrase used in the HTML input form.

This change does not create any complications in the CGI application as long as you take it into consideration when creating the program that generates the HTML page. The time you spend planning the HTML pages and the CGI application will decrease any errors that might arise from this minimal difference in terminology. In Chapter 4, "Getting the Data From Visitors to Your Web Page," you are introduced to the process by which the CGI application acquires the input information and how it uses this information. Now that you understand the challenges of using multiple HTML pages with CGI, you can consider the importance of form design.

Adopting Proper Form Design

TIP

For more information on creating HTML forms, you can reference the Prima Tech book *XHTML Fast & Easy Web Development* by Brian Proffitt and Ann Zupan.

If you use forms in your HTML pages, you are already aware of the benefits of proper form design for user convenience. The focus of this section is not on proper form design from the aspect of the users—the focus is on proper form design from the aspect of the designer/programmer.

There are many similarities between user and designer/programmer aspects; however, the differences will be your main concern. When you design a form, you try to make it as user-friendly as you can and generally spend time planning the arrangement of the input fields with usability in mind. As a Web programmer, however, you are more concerned with the content of the form and how you can use it in your CGI application to generate the intended HTML output. The following form is user-friendly and enables users to input several types of information.

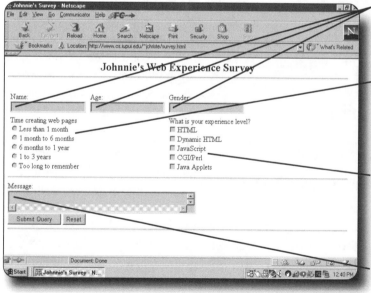

This form includes text inputs in which users can type information.

It contains radio button inputs to allow the users to make a single selection from a set of options.

It also contains check box inputs, which allow the users to make multiple selections from set options.

And finally, it contains a text area input that allows the users to input multiple lines of text.

There is nothing special about this form or its design. The aspects that are important to you as a Web programmer come from the data included on the form and what happens to it within the CGI application. You already realize that the text displayed beside the input fields are of little significance to the CGI application. The important areas of the form are the attributes of the input fields.

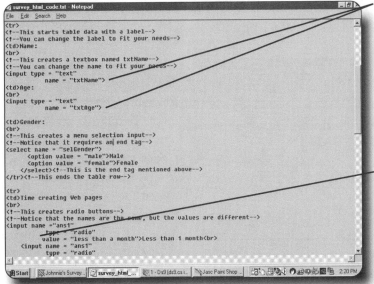

The name attribute will be used by your application to assign a key to the data. Keys will be explained in more detail in Chapter 5, "Getting the Data into Your CGI Application," and Chapter 8, "Hashes."

The value attribute will be the actual data that is used from the form input fields in the application

These attributes are used by the CGI application to generate the HTML pages and other outputs you imbed in the application. The importance of these attributes and how you use them is explained in detail in Chapter 5, "Getting the Data into Your CGI Application." The use of the attributes from the HTML form also has bearing on the files that your CGI application accesses, especially when you use your CGI application to search a database.

Planning the Database Design

Planning ahead becomes extremely important when you are designing a database that will be used in conjunction with your Web page and your CGI application. Again, it is not the physical design of the database that is of the greatest concern but the content of the database and how the CGI application accesses its data.

Recall that the Web page in Chapter 1, "CGI and the Web," shows the form used to access a database containing student grades for a Web Authoring class.

This form has a text field where students input the last four digits of their student IDs.

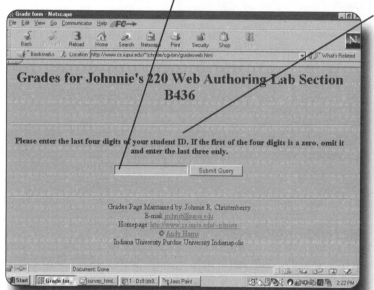

Notice that specific instructions are needed for students whose last four digits begin with a zero.

These special instructions are needed for a reason. When the program was originally written, it did not take into consideration the possibility that this four-digit series might begin with a zero. It took less time to include the textual instruction than to change the program that searched the database. Proper planning, however, would have caught this oversight. Why is it so important to make note of this? The database was designed to list the last four digits of the student ID and did not allow the first digit to be a zero. If the student inputs the last four digits and the first is a zero, the program cannot locate the ID in the database and returns the following HTML page instead.

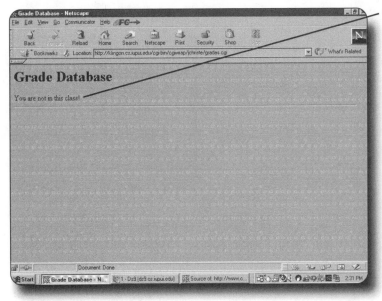

This HTML page informs the students that they are not in the class.

As minor as this oversight appears, it generated tremendous difficulties. Many students could not access their grades, and the problem generated tons of e-mails from confused students. This was not a major problem because I saw the students twice a week and could walk them through the instructions; however, when you create a database that is searched by your CGI application, you might not have the convenience of seeing your users together on a regular basis and therefore do not want your users experiencing problems accessing the data.

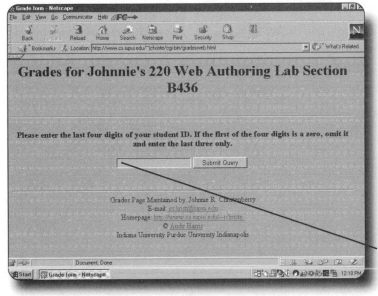

This is especially true when you are creating the HTML page, CGI application, or database for your employer or business. Often you have little or no input into the design of the database. This increases the amount of planning that you need to do in order to create the HTML forms and CGI applications that access the database.

Another problem that occurred with this particular CGI application was the result of a student leaving the input field blank and submitting the data.

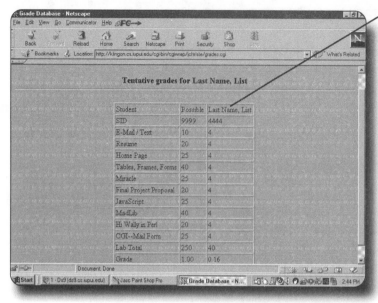

When this happened, the CGI application returned an HTML page for the last student ID in the database.

This creates a very dangerous security problem and can result not only in embarrassment but possible legal ramifications. I have included this information to emphasize the importance of proper planning in CGI applications and to illustrate the difficulties that can arise from lack of planning. Now, you need to learn how to prevent these types of problems from occurring.

Writing Pseudocode

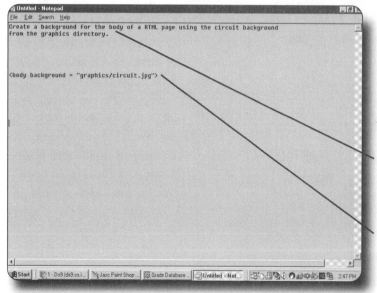

Pseudocode, also known as symbolic code, involves the process of writing the steps and procedures of a program in English instead of the appropriate computer language.

This phrase is an example of pseudocode that represents a simple line of HTML code.

You can use this pseudocode to write your actual HTML code.

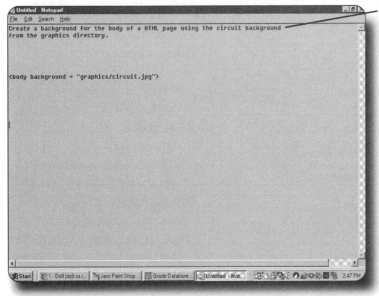

Notice that the pseudocode does not specify the format of the image you are using in your HTML page.

This is because you do not need to include specifics in your pseudocode. The primary reason for pseudocode is to assist you in the design and debugging of your HTML pages and your CGI application. Beginning programmers often want to skip this step and jump right in and start writing the program. You will, however, quickly find that the time you think you are saving by omitting this step is sacrificed when you have to spend more time later figuring out why your program does not work like you want it to.

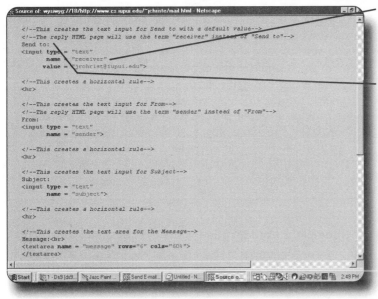

Notice that the name of the text input is "receiver" in the name attribute.

The text input appears as "Send to:" on the HTML form, not as "receiver".

You can easily forget this subtle difference when you create the HTML page, which will cause your CGI application to omit this data from the HTML page it generates. Notice that the sketch of the HTML input form and the HTML page generated by the CGI application show this difference.

HTML Form Page

Text head w/info

Send to: [ ]

From: [ ]

Subject: [ ]

Message: [ ]

[Send] [Clear]

HTML Reply Page

Check your mail box

Receiver:

Sender:

Subject:

Message:

The HTML input form uses Send to: next to the text input box.

The HTML page generated by the CGI application uses receiver.

This sketch is part of your pseudocode—it includes the basic information you need to write your pseudocode and is also where you start the process of writing your pseudocode. You will probably make changes to the sketch and your original pseudocode before you begin writing the HTML code or the CGI application code.

TIP

I cannot stress enough the importance of writing pseudocode and sketching the HTML pages before you start writing the actual code. This is important even as you gain more experience. The biggest mistake you can make is to omit this step once you have some experience because you feel that it's helpful for amateur programmers only. I know because I once felt the same way, and I have written numerous programs in many different languages. However, after spending hours debugging a simple program, I never omit this step!

The complete pseudocode for the mail program shows that during the process of deciding what I wanted to accomplish I realized several important points:

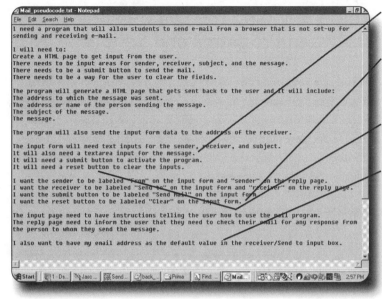

- I needed different input types.

- I would use different terminology in the two HTML pages.

- I needed to change the button names.

- I needed to set a default value for the `"receiver/ Send to"` input.

The process of writing the pseudocode enabled me to think about how I would accomplish the task of getting the input from the users and sending a reply back to them. Now that you have seen the importance of planning ahead and the significance of writing pseudocode, it is time to introduce the CGI application basics.

Learning the Programming Basics

In the "CGI Programming Languages" section of Chapter 1, you were introduced to the variety of languages you can use in CGI applications, including the most popular one: Perl. Based on the popularity of Perl applications and the availability of Perl scripts, this book focuses on using Perl as the primary language for your CGI applications.

Understanding the Difference Between Programs and Scripts

You use a program any time you use a computer—whether it is a word processor, a video game, or a Web browser to access the Internet. These applications are programs that use *code*, commands that are written in a language the computer understands. Each line of code tells the computer what action it is to perform.

For example, when you click on the Back button of a browser, the code tells the browser that it needs to return to the previous URL.

Scripts are lines of code that tell the computer what action to perform. However, scripts are interpreted as they are needed, whereas programs are compiled in advance so they are able to run faster on the computer. Scripts are usually smaller and less advanced than programs.

Learning the Perl Basics

The important thing to note is that you do not need any fancy tools to begin writing scripts in Perl: You only need a basic text editor.

I generally use Notepad for Windows.

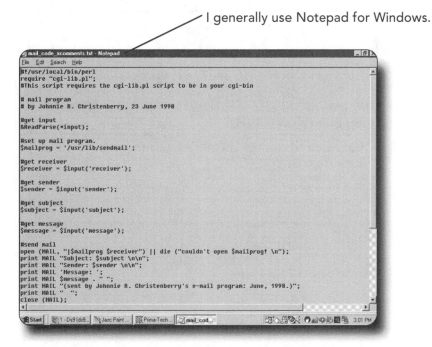

When I am working in UNIX, I use Emacs. You can also use SimpleText, which is the standard text editor found in Macintosh operating systems.

Perl Data

You can think of the data processed in Perl as one of three types. It will either be a string (text) or a number; a variable or constant; or a scalar, array, or hash.

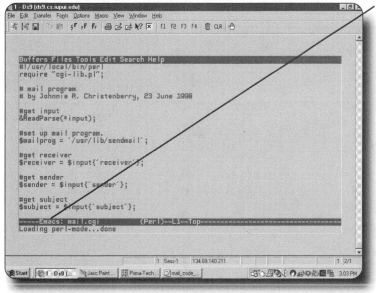

> ## TIP
>
> Comments in Perl begin with the pound sign (#), and comments more than one line long need to have the # at the beginning of each sentence. The multiline comment character you might be used to in HTML does not exist in Perl.
>
> To create a new line in Perl, you use the newline character \n.
>
> A semicolon (;) is used to terminate all simple statements in Perl.

Strings and Numbers

Strings are any letters, numbers, or symbols that correspond to the ASCII (*American Standard Code for Information Interchange*) code from 0 to 255. A string can be:

- a single character

- a word

- a phrase

- an entire sentence

- or even a number

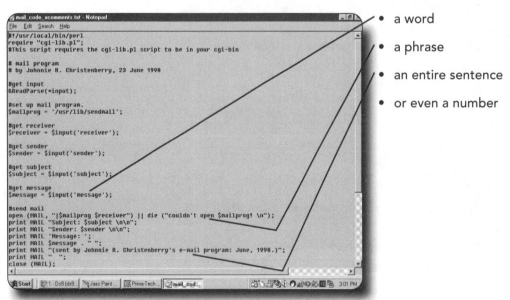

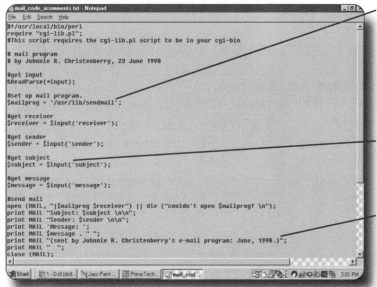

Strings can be constants or variables. When a string is a constant, it is generally enclosed in straight single (') or double (") quotation marks.

You use single quotation marks to mark the start and end of a string.

You use double quotation marks to include special characters, such as hexadecimal codes, tabs, a new line, or returns.

You can leave the quotation marks off; however, it is to your benefit to include them—you will find them extremely useful when you debug your programs. Additional information on quotation marks is included in the "Quotation Marks" section later in this chapter.

Numbers, unlike strings, do not need any special consideration in Perl and do not need to be set apart or be formatted in a special way. They are exactly what Perl expects them to be: digits that represent a specific quantity. The exception to this is if you use a number as a string, in which case the string formatting rule applies.

Variables and Constants

Data in Perl can be specific data or a container that holds data.

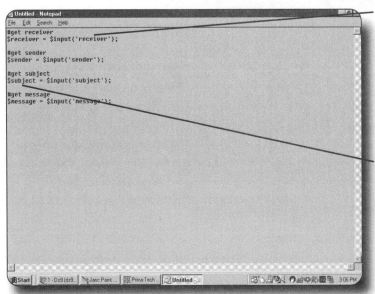

The term constant, or *literal*, is used to refer to specific data. These terms truly describe the data because it does not change and is interpreted exactly as it is seen.

The term *variable* refers to the container that holds data. Variables are used to store data that changes and are useful when the data is controlled by user input.

Using variables saves you from having to create constants for every possible input, which would be nearly impossible to do.

Variable names can consist of any alphanumeric character and the underscore character; however, the common practice is to use lowercase letters that are short, but descriptive. Variable names begin with specific characters for each type of variable

The dollar sign is used for scalars.

The at sign is used for arrays.

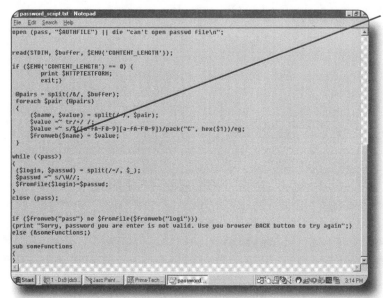

The percent sign is used for hashes.

You are now ready to learn more about the three types of variables just presented.

Scalars, Arrays, and Hashes

Scalars are individual pieces of data and can represent numbers or strings and quoted literals or variables.

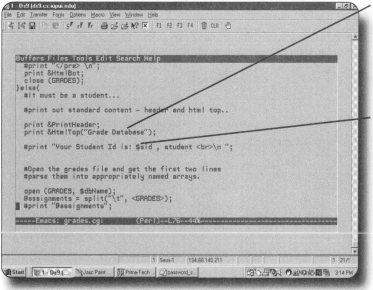

Scalar quoted literals look like regular data. If the scalar is a string you should use quotation marks to identify it.

Scalar variables begin with a dollar sign. The $ shape is a representation for the S in scalar.

Arrays are groups of scalars and can be referred to as *lists*. Arrays can be groups of constants or variables because they consist of scalars, which you know are either quoted literals or variables and numbers or strings. Arrays consist of any number of ordered elements, which are distinct scalar variables each with an independent scalar value. Arrays can contain no elements to as many elements as the available memory will allow. List literals are comma-separated values that you enclose in parentheses and do not have to be constants; they can be variables that are evaluated every time the literal is accessed.

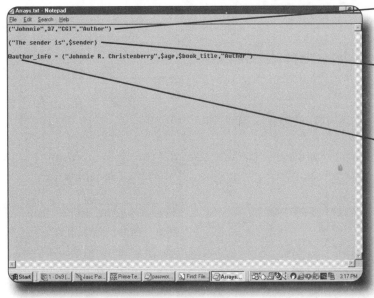

This example is a list literal composed of only constants.

This example is a list literal that contains both constants and variables.

Recall that array variables always begin with the at sign. The @ shape is a representation for the *a* in array.

Hashes are groups of scalars that are in pairs. You will find hashes more useful than arrays in many situations. This is because a hash uses the name and value as a connected pair that can be accessed together.

The key is the first element in each pair.

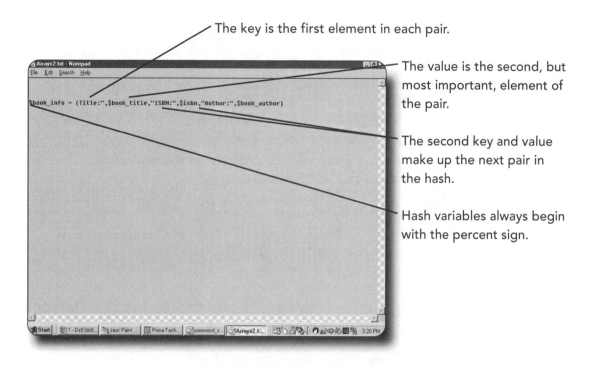

The value is the second, but most important, element of the pair.

The second key and value make up the next pair in the hash.

Hash variables always begin with the percent sign.

Operators and Functions

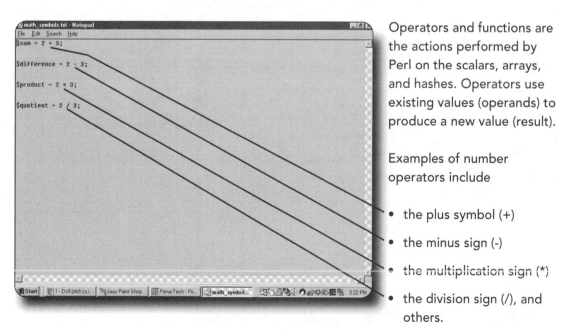

Operators and functions are the actions performed by Perl on the scalars, arrays, and hashes. Operators use existing values (operands) to produce a new value (result).

Examples of number operators include

- the plus symbol (+)

- the minus sign (-)

- the multiplication sign (*)

- the division sign (/), and others.

Perl also allows the use of logical comparison operators that include:

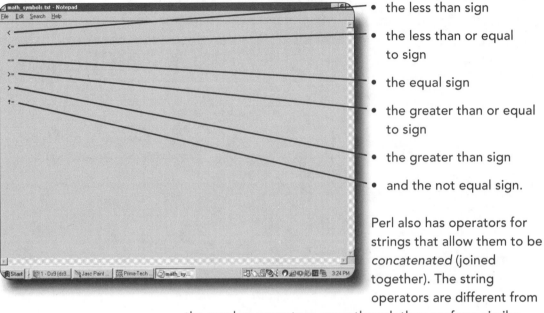

- the less than sign

- the less than or equal to sign

- the equal sign

- the greater than or equal to sign

- the greater than sign

- and the not equal sign.

Perl also has operators for strings that allow them to be *concatenated* (joined together). The string operators are different from the number operators, even though they perform similar operations. These operators consist of:

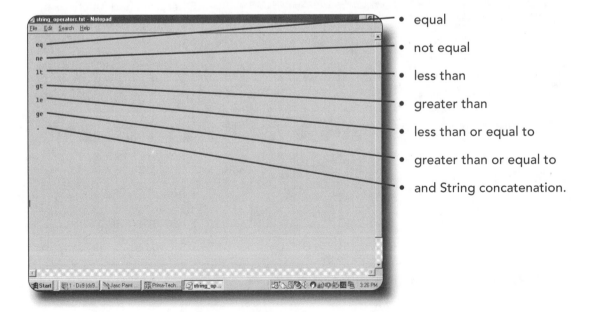

- equal

- not equal

- less than

- greater than

- less than or equal to

- greater than or equal to

- and String concatenation.

This small difference in operators can be a blessing or a hindrance. Perl will automatically convert the string to a number or the number to a string based on the operator you use.

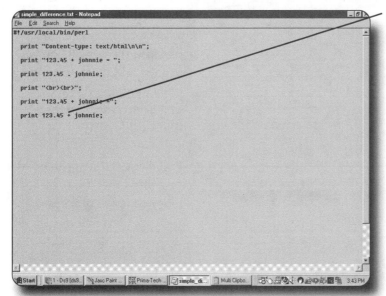

If your code looks like this example...

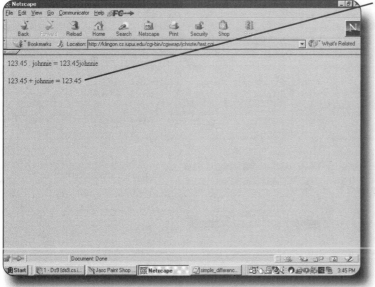

Perl will convert "johnnie" to a zero; thus the code will convert to 12345. This will display as something entirely different from what you anticipate.

This can cause a great amount of confusion if you forget that Perl does this without any warning to you. This is more easily understood if you examine an example of the difference.

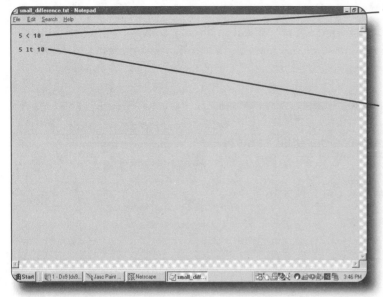

This line of code will return a "`true`" value because the number 5 is less than the number 10.

However, this line of code will return a "`false`" value because the conversion will use the ASCII values of the string, and the ASCII value of 5 is not less than the ASCII value of 1.

Functions are simply named operators that are used for more complex processes.

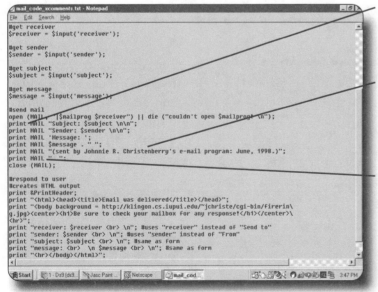

One of the primary functions you will use is the `print` function.

The `print` function sends the data specified (generally in quotation marks) to a specific output.

In this example, the output is MAIL.

You can create functions of your own, known as *subroutines*. This is described in Chapter 11, "Subroutines."

Result and Return Values

Data values can be affected by functions and operators in one of two ways: They either change the data on which they operate, or they return the value to be analyzed by the program.

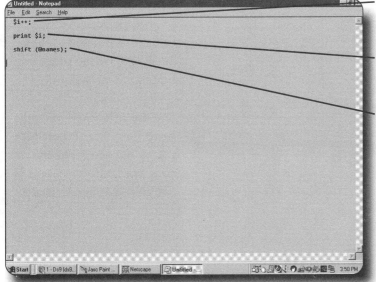

In this case the value is incremented by 1.

This returns the value to be analyzed by the program.

Certain functions will change the variable and produce a specific return value, as is the case with the shift function.

This function removes the leftmost array element and returns the value of the removed element, thus changing the value of the array. For example, if @names contains the names (joe, bob, briggs) the result of the shift function is (bob, briggs) with a return value of joe.

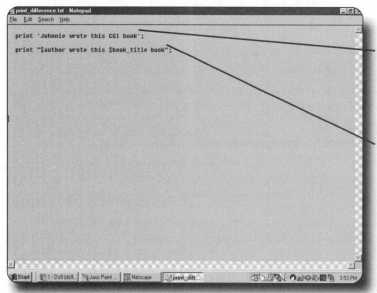

```
print 'Johnnie wrote this CGI book';

print "$author wrote this $book_title book";
```

Quotation Marks

Use single quotation marks to enclose textual information that is taken literally by the program.

Use double quotation marks to enclose data that needs to be interpolated (analyzed) by the program before it is processed.

The use of quotation marks saves you time and enables you to use the same line of code with different users and different input values.

Summary

In this chapter, you learned the importance of planning ahead as it applies to using multiple languages, using multiple HTML pages, proper form and database design, and the essentials of writing pseudocode. You gained knowledge about the differences between programs and scripts. You also learned some basic Perl programming techniques and the different types of Perl data. The data types discussed were strings and numbers; variables and constants; scalars, arrays, and hashes; operators and functions; results and return values; and finally quotation marks. You will use this information in the next chapter, "Your First CGI Application."

3

Your First
CGI Application

You now understand the basics of planning ahead, writing
pseudocode, and using Perl; so it is time to write your first CGI
application. Remember, you only need a simple text editor in order to
accomplish this task. This chapter walks you through the process of
writing your first application by focusing on:

- Creating your application for different platforms
- Transferring your application to the server
- Starting your CGI application using Perl
- Writing your Perl code
- Outputting text to a browser
- Running your application

NOTE

Because this example includes code from a real program currently in use at a university, I have blanked out some lines for security purposes.

Creating Your Application Using Perl

This book focuses on CGI applications using Perl as the primary language. So, you need to understand the process of writing your applications using Perl.

Adding Comments to Your Application

One of the biggest mistakes you can make as a programmer is to omit comments from your program. To add comments in Perl, you need to use the pound sign (#) at the beginning of the code line. This tells Perl to ignore the text that follows.

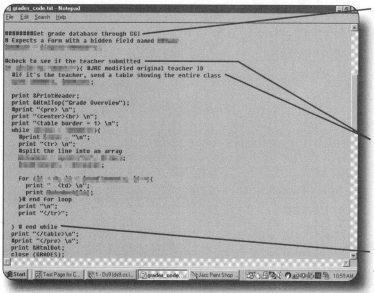

As simple as your code might seem to you now, a week from now you might look at it and ask yourself, "What does this do, and why did I put it here?"

Comments enable you to note what the code is doing. In this case, the comment tells you what the conditional statement is checking.

This comment notes that the conditional statement has ended. This is especially helpful when using nested conditions. Conditional statements are discussed in Chapter 9, "Conditional Statements."

Comments save you from having to write detailed instructions for other programmers who borrow your code. Finally, comments are also of great value when you are debugging your application.

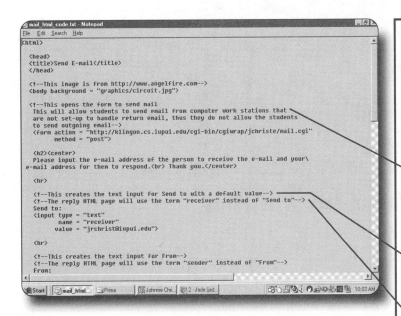

TIP

You will benefit from commenting your HTML code as well. HTML comments are noted by the use of the <!-- and --> characters.

This comment enables you to explain what should happen when you call your application.

Comments can also state what the input fields are used for.

Comments also can note any variations in names from the HTML form to the application or the response HTML page.

To add comments in Perl, you type the pound sign (#) at the beginning of the line. You then type the comment you want to include.

You do not need to end the comment line like you do in HTML. However, Perl does not support multiline comments.

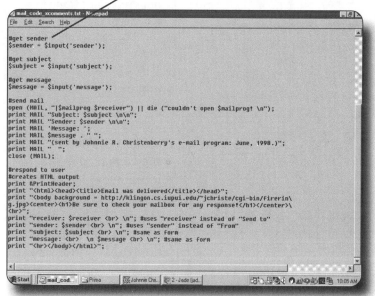

In order to write comments that are longer than a single line, you need to begin each line with #.

You can also include comments at the end of a line of code.

Perl requires you to comment your initial line of code, which is used to locate the Perl interpreter on your server.

This special comment is discussed fully in the section, "Using the Interpreter's Location in Your Application," later in this chapter. With an understanding of the importance of documenting your application with comments, you can now learn how to create your application using different platforms.

Creating Your Application on a PC or Mac

The difference between using a PC and a Mac to create your application is minimal. The major difference between the two operating systems, as it applies to your application, is when you send the application to the server.

Creating Your Application Using a PC

To create your CGI application using a PC, you first open your text editor. The primary choices are Notepad and WordPad—I prefer Notepad because it does very little text formatting.

To begin you click on File, New to open a blank document window.

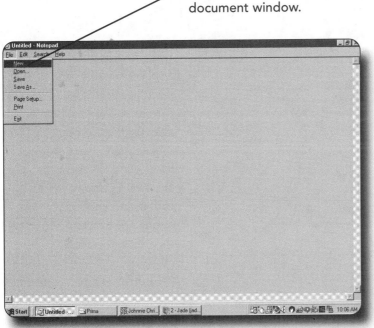

Then you write the code for the application, which is covered in detail in this chapter's section "Writing Your Perl Code."

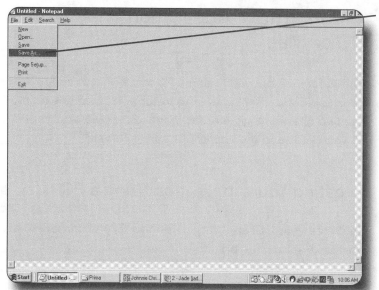

After you write the code for the application, click on Save As.

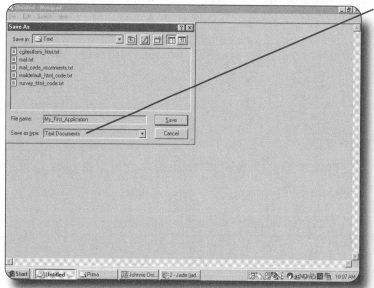

You should save the application as a .txt document. This will eliminate any formatting used by the text editor. The problem with text editor formatting is that it can add line breaks and other formatting characters that might not be understood by the Perl interpreter.

If your text editor does not enable you to change the extension from .txt to .cgi when you save it, you need to rename the file.

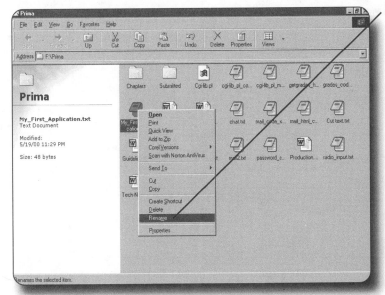

To rename the file, right-click on it, and then click on Rename from the menu that pops up. This will highlight the file.

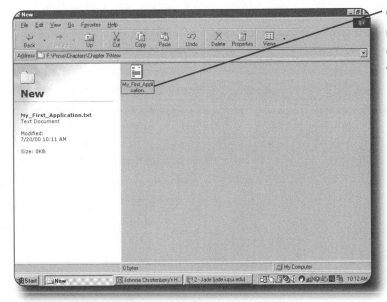

Click at the end of the file name and replace the extension txt with cgi. Press the Enter key.

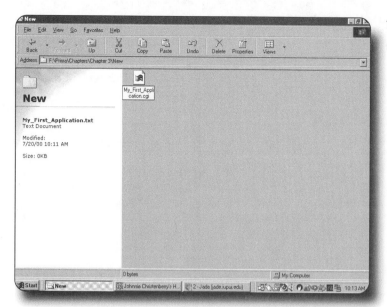

The application now has a cgi extension.

Transferring Your PC Application to the Server

You will use an FTP (*File Transfer Protocol*) program to transfer your application from your PC to the server. If you do not have an FTP program, many freeware and shareware versions are available on the Internet. The CD contains a trial version of CoffeeCup Expresso FTP, which is the FTP program used in the following example. The following steps assist you during the transfer of your application using the CoffeeCup Expresso FTP program.

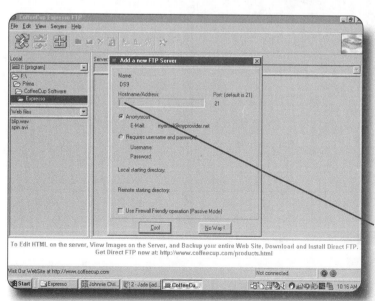

You need to open the FTP program and establish a connection to the server. To do so, you need to enter the name of your server or IP (*Internet Provider*) address in the Hostname/Address field.

Enter your username in the corresponding field.

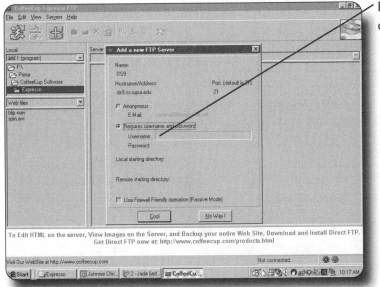

Next, enter your password in the password field.

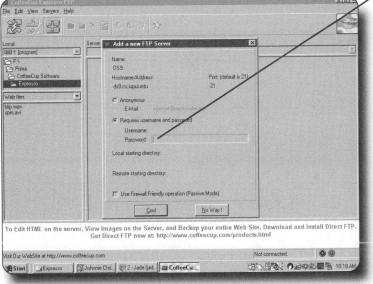

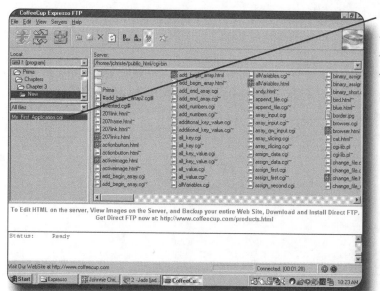

The next step is to locate the file that you want to transfer. Click and drag the file and drop it on to the server window.

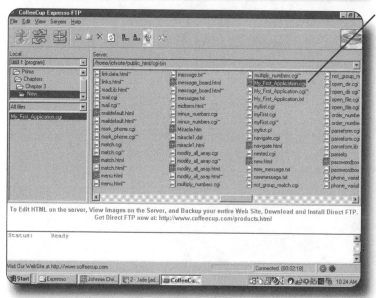

This file has been transferred to the server.

Creating Your Application Using a Mac

To create your CGI application using a Mac, you first need to open your text editor. SimpleText is the Mac text editor of choice, and it is included with most Mac operating systems.

To open a blank document window, click on File, New. Write the code for the application. After you write the code, click on Save As to save your efforts.

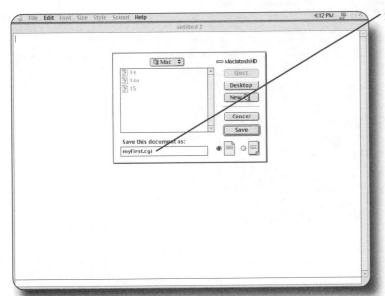

Save the application as a .cgi document so it can be used on the server.

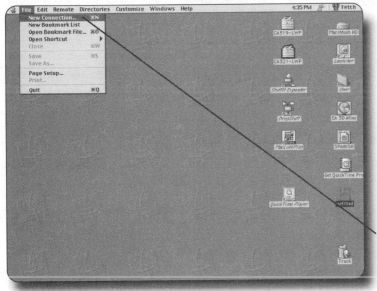

Transferring Your Mac Application to the Server

You will use an FTP program to transfer your application from your Mac to the server. The following steps assist you during the transfer of your application using the Fetch FTP program.

You first need to open the FTP program and establish a connection to the server.

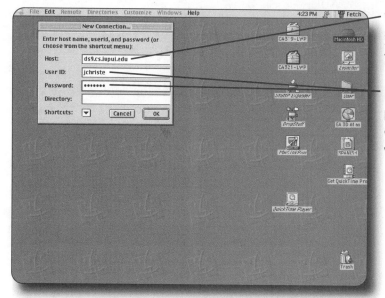

You then enter the name of your server or IP address in the Host field.

Enter your user ID and password in the corresponding fields. This will open the FTP screen.

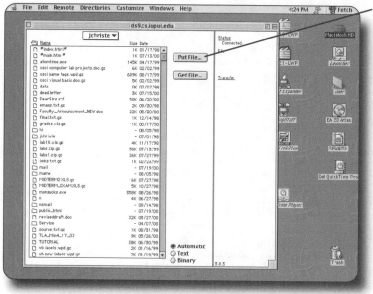

You now have two choices. You can put a file from your computer on the server, or you can get a file from the server and place it on your computer. Because you are sending files to the server, click the Put File button.

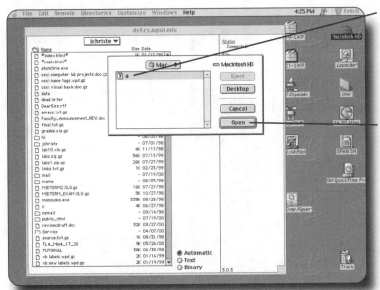

The Open File dialog box will appear. This enables you to choose the file you want to send to the server. Highlight the file you want to send.

Click on Open to prepare to transfer the file to the server.

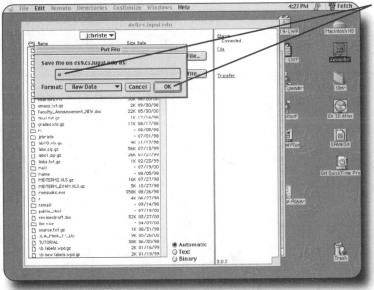

The Put File dialog box prompts you to name the file to send to the server. You need to click on OK after you have chosen the filename. This will transfer the file from your computer to the server.

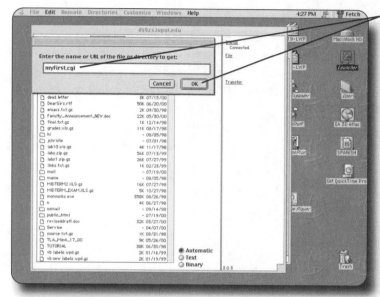

If you transfer a file from the server to your computer, use Get File. The Get File dialog box prompts you for the URL, file, or directory you want to retrieve. Type the URL, file, or directory name in the input field and click on OK.

Creating Your Application on a UNIX Server

To create your application on a UNIX server, you need to use Telnet to go to the server and then find your cgi-bin directory.

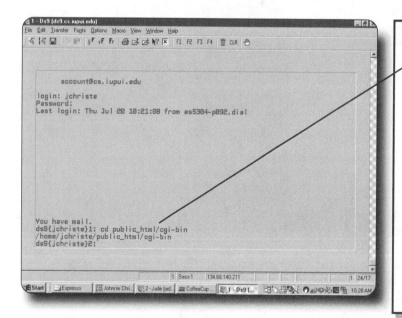

NOTE

To change directories, you need to type **cd directory**, where *directory* is the name of the directory. This move usually requires two directory changes—one to your HTML directory, and one to your cgi-bin directory. You can change multiple directories by separating them with the forward slash (/).

When you get to your cgi-bin directory, you need to open a text editor. The most popular UNIX text editors are Pico, Emacs, and vi. The following example uses Emacs.

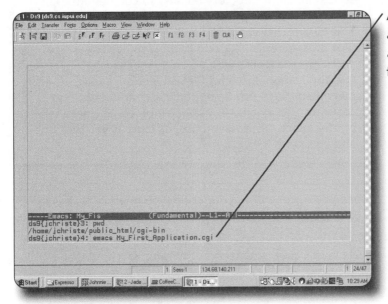

At the prompt, type **emacs application.cgi**, where *application*.cgi is the filename.

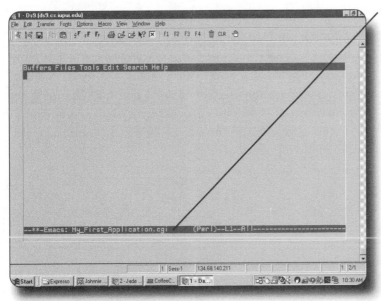

This command will open the *application*.cgi file using the Emacs editor.

> **TIP**
>
> UNIX and Emacs are case-sensitive and do not support spaces in file or directory names, so you need to pay special attention to the way you type these names. This means that cat, CAT, and Cat can all be different files or directories. A good habit is to use lowercase and separate words with an underscore (_)—my_application.cgi. Another convention, called *camelBack*, is to use an uppercase character to separate two words—*myApplication*.cgi. It doesn't matter which method you use, as long as you pick one and stick with it.

Once you have written your code, you need to save it by pressing Ctrl + X, Ctrl + S. To exit the Emacs editor, you will press Ctrl + X, Ctrl + C. You learn more about writing your code in this chapter's section "Writing Your Perl Code."

Changing the Permissions of Your Application

To allow your applications to be executed, you need to change the permissions of your CGI directory and files. By default, UNIX sets the permission of directories to 7-1-1 and files to 6-0-0. You will want your directory set to 7-5-5 and your CGI application files set to 7-1-1 or 7-5-5. Changing the permissions is a simple process on a UNIX server. The first step is to telnet to the server. Next, you want to locate your cgi-bin directory.

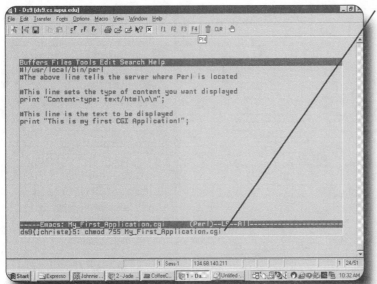

Once you are in your cgi-bin directory, you need to type **chmod 755 *application*.cgi**, where *application*.cgi is the filename, and then press the Enter key.

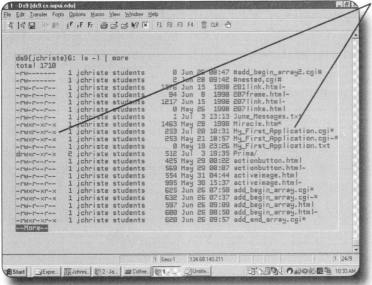

To check the permissions of your files, type **ls –l** and then press the Enter key. This will display all the files in the directory with their permissions. If you have a large number of files in the directory, you might not see the file you are looking for. In that case, type **ls –l l more** (the pipe character (l) is located on the backslash key (\ ), and it requires that you also use the Shift key). This will display the files one screen at a time. You can advance screens by pressing the spacebar.

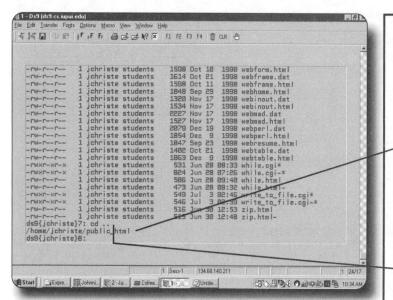

NOTE

If you need to change the permissions of your cgi-bin directory, you should do so from its parent directory.

In the preceding examples, the cgi-bin is contained in the public_html directory, so it is wise to change the permissions of the cgi-bin there.

To back up a directory, type **cd ..** and press the Enter key.

Starting Your CGI Application Using Perl

Now that you know what is required to write your CGI application using Perl, you are ready to learn the steps for actually writing your application. This section introduces the basics needed to write any Perl application for the Web. It also teaches you how to get the server to execute your application.

Finding Perl on Your Server

The first step in writing your Perl application is determining where on your server the Perl interpreter is located.

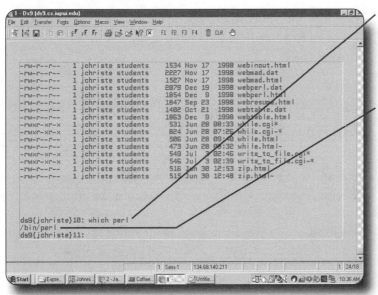

You accomplish this by using Telnet to connect to your server and then typing **which perl**.

The response identifies the location of the Perl interpreter. In this instance it is /bin/perl.

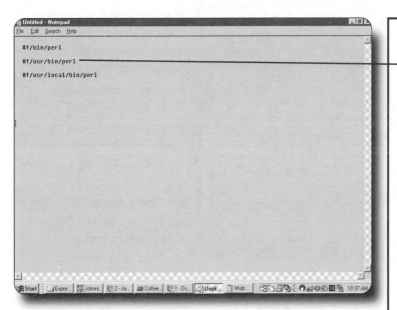

TIP

If you use and modify existing code, you might need to change the Perl location. However, the location can be slightly different and still execute properly. I have found that the UNIX server I use will accept many variations of the location and still execute properly. I can use #!/bin/perl, #!/usr/bin/perl, or #!/usr/local/bin/perl without experiencing any problems.

Now that you know where Perl is located on your server, you need to know how to use the location in your application.

Using the Interpreter's Location in Your Application

Your application needs to know the Perl interpreter's location in order for the server to execute the application.

This location is always the first line in your application, and it must be included in every Perl application you write or use.

Notice that it is actually written as a comment; however, the exclamation mark (!) that follows the pound sign (#) tells the server that this particular comment contains the location of the Perl interpreter. It needs to access this location in order for the code to be executed.

Without this line, the application cannot be executed and your application is useless.

> **TIP**
>
> The location of the Perl interpreter must be the very first line of the application and cannot have any preceding spaces. This is the first item to check if your application does not execute. Many of the examples show the location code on the second line and two spaces from the left border: This was done to allow you to see the code clearly. The example code on the CD-ROM is correct and can be copied and pasted without changing the first line.

Writing Your Perl Code

You are now ready to write the code that will be executed in your application.

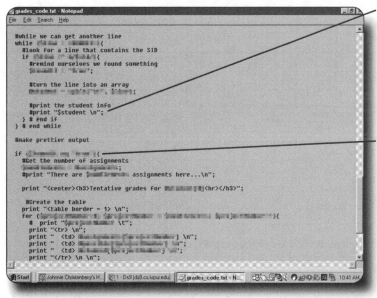

Recall from Chapter 2, "Writing Your CGI Application," that every simple statement in Perl, not including comments, must end with a semicolon (;).

Omission of this semicolon can create numerous problems in your application and is often hard to detect when you debug your application. (Statement blocks are the exception to this rule and are presented in Chapter 9, "Conditional Statements.")

> **NOTE**
>
> The process of debugging your application is covered in detail in Appendix A, "Debugging Your Application." You should mark this appendix, as you will be referencing it many times while writing your first applications.

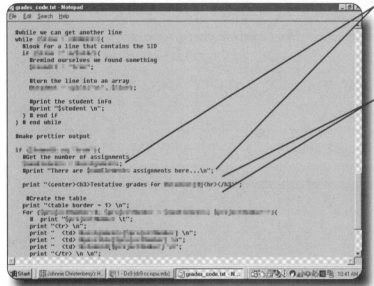

Don't include any spaces between the last character of a line of code and the semicolon.

Good programmers use space between sections of code to help identify separate procedures. This is especially helpful when debugging. You will find that indenting the code in nested conditions, explained in Chapter 9, "Conditional Statements," occurs in layers to help you see where each separate condition begins and ends.

Outputting Text to a Browser

Because this book covers Web programming, you need to understand how to output your application to a browser. Chapter 13, "Outputting Data," covers various ways to do this. This section introduces the basics of outputting to a browser and includes the minimum code required to accomplish this task. It is a good primer before you learn all the nitty-gritty details in Chapter 13.

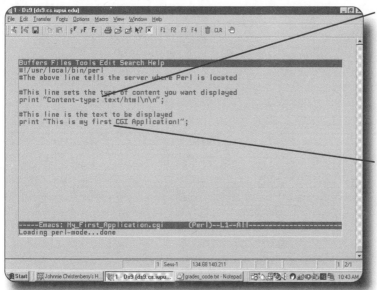

You must first inform the browser that it should expect MIME (*Multipurpose Internet Mail Extensions*) content of the text/html type. In other words, it should expect Web page content.

You then type the code to be displayed on the Web page.

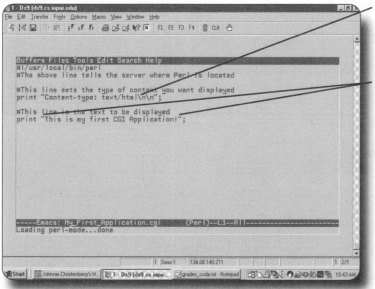

The two newline characters (\n) must be included in this line.

Remember, all content to be displayed, including HTML tags, must be enclosed in quotation marks.

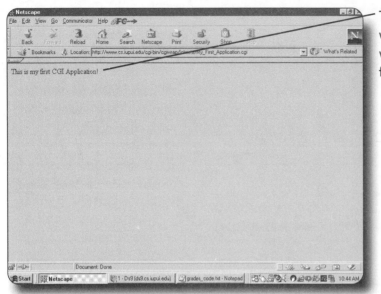

The code that was just written displays this text without any HTML formatting.

In order to have more control of the output, you can include HTML tags within the `print` command.

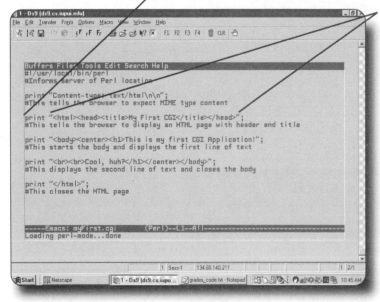

Remember to enclose the HTML tags inside the quotation marks.

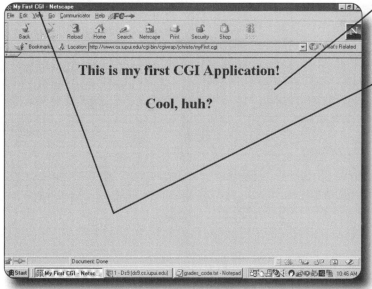

This code generates output that is formatted with HTML tags.

Notice that this page has a title header that was not included in the previous example.

This page looks better than the first page. Also by using HTML tags in your code, you retain control of what the output will look like. Now that you have seen the written code, you need to be able to check it for syntax errors.

Checking the Syntax of Your Application

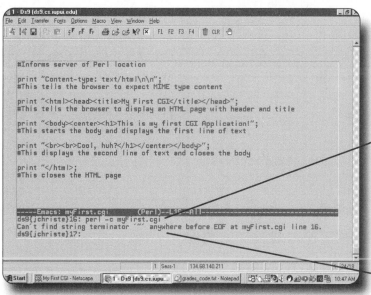

Checking your application's syntax is straight-forward, and this simple step can save you much time and many headaches in your programming endeavors.

To check your syntax, type **perl –c** *application*.**cgi**, where *application*.cgi is the filename, into the command line prompt and press the Enter key.

The response informs you of the status of your application's syntax.

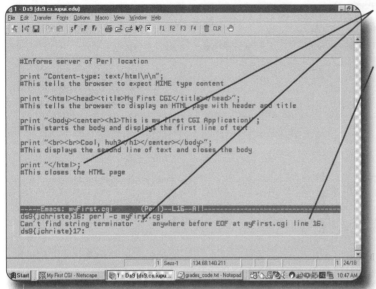

In this case, a quotation mark is missing.

The check tells you which line of code contains the problem syntax.

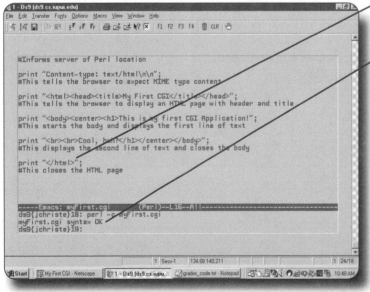

Here, you can see that the error has been corrected.

When you run the check again, the program informs you that there are no syntax errors.

The application is ready and will be executed correctly when you run it.

Running Your CGI Application

Running your application gives you a chance to view it and make certain that it functions the way you want it to. This is the time to redesign and fix any problems that crop up that are not syntax-related, such as displaying incorrect data, or having the text run together (forgetting to include spaces when concatenating strings. There are two methods you can use to run your application. The first is directly by using the URL. The second is to create a test HTML form and use it to run the application.

Using the URL to Run the Application

To run your application using the URL, you need to open your browser and type the URL of the application into the browser.

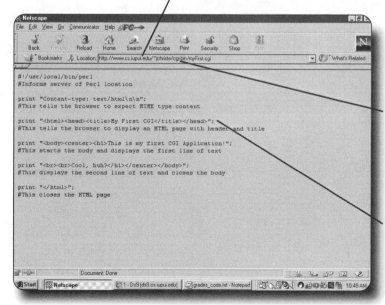

The URL of the application will be different than the URL you normally use to access your files.

Typing your normal URL, with **cgi-bin/*application*.cgi**, where *application*.cgi is the file name, added to the end will execute the application.

Instead of executing the application, this URL will display the application's code in a text format.

To run the application, you need to use the URL that leads to the cgi-bin of the server. This usually includes the words cgi-bin before your username.

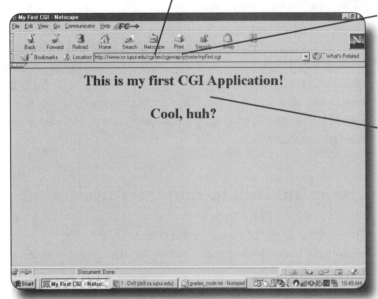

If your server uses a tilde (~) character in front of your username, you will not include it when typing the URL for the cgi-bin.

The application runs correctly and displays the HTML output.

This minor difference between the URL for the code and the URL required to execute the application is why I often use a test HTML form to run my applications.

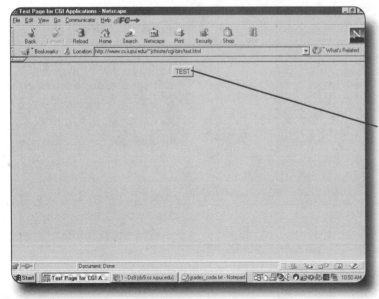

Using a Test HTML Form to Run the Application

To avoid the confusion of entering the previous URLs, you can create a test HTML form to run the application instead. This requires an additional step. However, when you have been up for days writing code or, in my case, this book, it is easy to become frustrated when the application does not run and the browser continues to display the code instead of the HTML output you expect. Therefore, I use a test HTML form that consists of only a submit button. To test my applications, I only need to change the application name at the end of the URL. This eliminates the chance of typing the wrong URL.

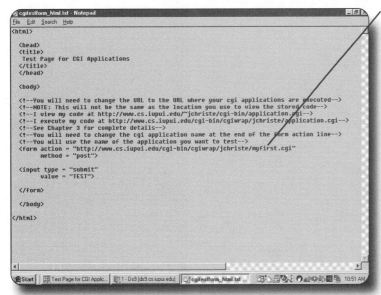

The benefit of using a test HTML form is that you only need to modify the application's file name in the form's action attribute. This requires very little thinking and might save you much aggravation.

Using a test HTML form has often saved me from smashing the keyboard and throwing my computer out the window.

Summary

In this chapter, you learned about the importance of documenting your code. You were taught about the various platforms that you can use to create your CGI applications and the methods for transferring your file to the server. You learned how to change the permissions of your application on the server. Most importantly, you learned how to find the Perl interpreter on your server and how to use this information in your application. You learned how to create your first CGI application using Perl by writing your Perl code, outputting to a browser, and checking your application's syntax. Finally, you learned two techniques for running your application on the browser; they enable you to check for application problems that are not syntax-related.

PART II

Basic Data

4

Getting the Data from Visitors to Your Web Page

With an understanding of what is required to write your CGI application, it is time to consider how you get information from your visitors. You can use many types of input in order to insert visitor data into your application. You will learn how, and why, to use a number of different input types in this chapter, including:

- Data labels
- Text input fields (text boxes, text area boxes, and password boxes)
- Selected choice inputs (radio buttons, check boxes, and menus)
- Action buttons
- Default values
- Links
- Environment variables
- Standard input

Gathering Data from Your Visitors

Getting data from your visitors is usually accomplished using a form on an HTML page; however, you can also gather data by linking to a script. Both of these methods are detailed in this chapter.

Using Data Labels

One of the most important steps to getting visitor data is labeling it so that you know what the information is and how it should be used in the application. You should decide which labels to use and how the data is used by your application. The process of planning ahead, covered in Chapter 2, "Writing Your CGI Application," is starting to pay off.

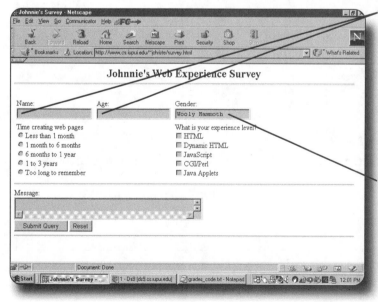

Recall that the survey form included text boxes for name, age, and gender. Unless your application is going to evaluate the data and create a response based on it, you can use these input types for the data labels.

The problem occurs if your visitor inputs a strange value in Gender, such as "Wooly Mammoth." If your application is checking the value to determine whether it is male or female, this data will result in a false analysis.

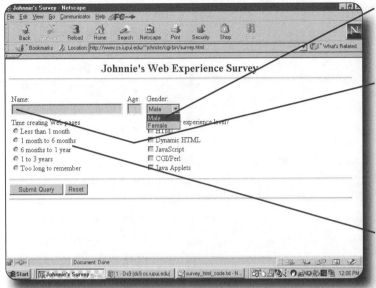

Therefore, you are better off changing the input field to a select type that enables users to choose between male and female.

There are two ways that you can get input from the visitor using a form. You can let users input the data freely by typing in the input field.

You also can allow users to select specific data. The latter requires you to set the `value` attribute and is detailed in the section "Using Selected Choice Inputs," later in this chapter.

Using Name Attributes or HTML Labels

The difference between the `name` attribute and HTML labels can create confusion when you are working with data between your HTML form and your CGI application. As simple as the difference is, it often causes CGI applications to function incorrectly.

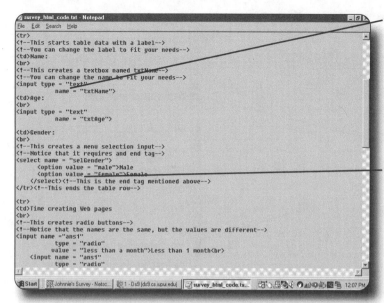

The CGI application uses the contents of the `name` attributes when assigning the form data to scalars, arrays, and hashes. It is also the key of the key-value pair in a hash.

The `value` attributes are also used by the application and become associated with the value of the key-value pair in hashes and the elements in an array.

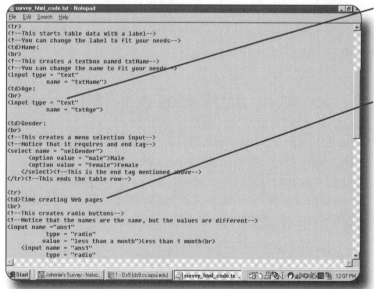

The context of the text fields is also used by the CGI application because it is the `value` of the field.

The CGI application ignores the HTML labels. You do not technically need HTML labels in the application; the HTML labels are used to tell visitors what information they should include in the input fields.

The visitors never see the `value` attributes unless they view the source code of your HTML form, but the information they input is sent to the CGI application when the form is submitted. Now that you have an understanding of which items are important to the CGI application and which are useful to the users, you are ready to learn how to create the form for your CGI application.

Developing Your HTML Form

Recall that the first and most important step in designing your HTML form is planning ahead. This includes writing the pseudocode for your CGI application and the HTML pages that accompany it.

TIP

Do not omit the pseudocode step when designing your HTML form or CGI application! If you think that you will save time by omitting this step, you are mistaken. The small amount of time you spend in the planning stage saves you large amounts of time when you write the actual code, let alone the time you spend debugging your application. I know this from experience. I have written more programs than I can count, and I never write code for a program without having a sketch of what I want and the pseudocode to get me there.

In order to write your pseudocode, you need to understand the different input types you can use in your HTML form.

Using Text Input Fields

Text input fields enable the users to input data by typing it into the field. All data retrieved from text input fields arrives to the application as a string; however, Perl does not require conversion from string to text because the operators control the data type (see the "Operators and

Functions" section of Chapter 2). The three text input fields you learn in this chapter are text boxes, password boxes, and text area boxes.

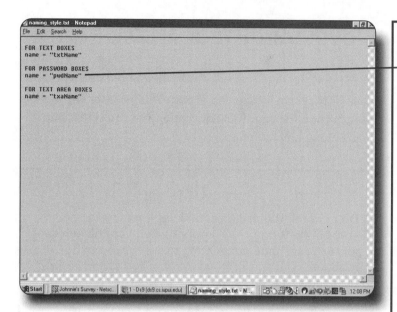

TIP

You will find that consistently naming your input fields (within the `name` attribute, which is detailed in the following sections) is helpful when you write your code as well as when you debug your application. I have found that using a three-letter prefix corresponding to the type of input is a good method. I use `txt` for text boxes, `pwd` for password boxes, and `txa` for text area boxes. You should substitute a name that corresponds to your input field in place of `Name` in the examples. The quotation marks are not required; however, if you start the name with quotation marks you must end with them.

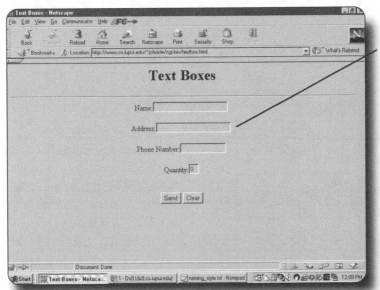

Creating Text Boxes

Text boxes enable users to type one line of text. Text boxes are often used for names, addresses, and phone numbers. Basically, any short text that you want the user to type in manually is fodder for a text box.

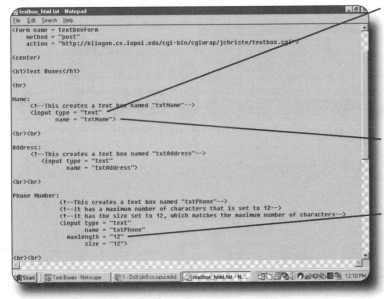

To create a text box, you use the `<input type = "text">` tag. Text boxes have some attributes, such as `maxlength` and size, which are useful.

You must use the `name` attribute to identify the input to your application.

Use the `maxlength` attribute when you want to limit the number of characters the users can enter into the text box.

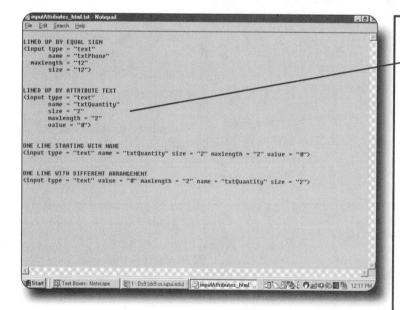

```
textbox_html.txt - Notepad
File  Edit  Search  Help
<form name = textboxForm
    method = "post"
    action = "http://klingon.cs.iupui.edu/cgi-bin/cgiwrap/jchriste/textbox.cgi">

<center>

<h1>Text Boxes</h1>

<hr>

Name:
    <!--This creates a text box named "txtName"-->
        <input type = "text"
            name = "txtName">

<br><br>

Address:
        <!--This creates a text box named "txtAddress"-->
        <input type = "text"
            name = "txtAddress">

<br><br>

Phone Number:
            <!--This creates a text box named "txtPhone"-->
            <!--It has a maximum number of characters that is set to 12-->
            <!--It has the size set to 12, which matches the maximum number of characters-->
            <input type = "text"
                name = "txtPhone"
            maxlength = "12"
                size = "12">

<br><br>
```

You can change the size of the text box with the `size` attribute. `Size` is measured in characters; the default size is 20 characters.

The final attribute you might use is `value`. This attribute contains the default text in the text box. This data is sent to the application if the users do not change it. Using default text is covered in detail in the section "Adding Default Values to Your Forms," later in this chapter.

```
inputAttributes_html.txt - Notepad
File  Edit  Search  Help
LINED UP BY EQUAL SIGN
<input type = "text"
        name = "txtPhone"
  maxlength = "12"
       size = "12">

LINED UP BY ATTRIBUTE TEXT
<input type = "text"
    name = "txtQuantity"
    size = "2"
    maxlength = "2"
    value = "0">

ONE LINE STARTING WITH NAME
<input type = "text" name = "txtQuantity" size = "2" maxlength = "2" value = "0">

ONE LINE WITH DIFFERENT ARRANGEMENT
<input type = "text" value = "0" maxlength = "2" name = "txtQuantity" size = "2">
```

NOTE

The order of the attributes is not important as long as they are within the `<input>` tag. Notice that I usually place my attributes on separate lines with the equals signs lined up. This is a personal preference; however, you should choose one style and be consistent using it. I have included different attribute formats so you can see that they all work.

Creating Password Boxes

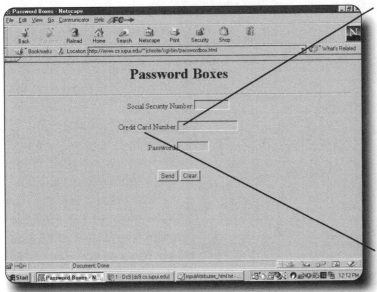

Password boxes are similar to text boxes, but they enable the users to type a password that is not viewable onscreen. Asterisks or bullets appear instead of the text the users type into the password box. Users like password boxes for inputting information they do not want others in the room to view.

Password information can include Social Security numbers, credit card numbers, or as the name implies, passwords to allow access to specific pages or applications.

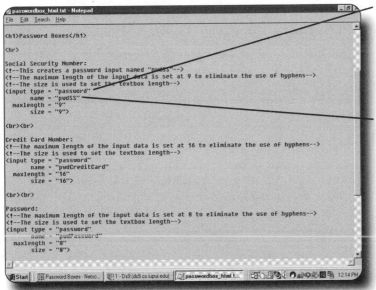

To create a password box, you use the <input type = "password"> tag. Password boxes contain attributes, such as maxlength and size.

You must use the name attribute to identify the input to your application.

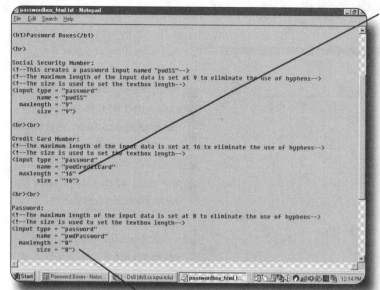

Use the `maxlength` attribute when you want to limit the number of characters the users can enter into the password box. This is especially useful if you do not want users to include hyphens (dashes) in the text. If you want the users to input their Social Security numbers as a long string of numbers, such as 123456789, set the `maxlength` to 9. If they can input it as 123-45-6789, you can use a `maxlength` of 12.

You can change the size of the password box with the `size` attribute. This is a good idea for times when you have set a `maxlength`. `Size` is measured in characters; the default size is 20 characters.

The final password box attribute is `value`. This attribute displays the default text in the password box. There are very few cases where using the `value` attribute in a password box isn't counterproductive, so it's probably best to avoid it here.

CAUTION

Password boxes are not secure input fields. They only prevent other people from viewing the text inserted. They do not send encrypted data to the server; therefore, experienced hackers could access this information.

Creating Text Area Boxes

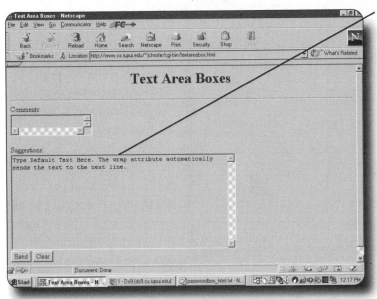

Sometimes you will want users to input a large amount of data that a text box cannot accommodate. In this case, you should use a text area box. The text area box is ideal for soliciting comments and suggestions from the users. Text area boxes are also useful as the message input field in a mail program like the example from Chapter 2.

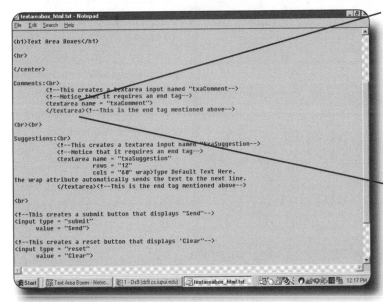

Notice that the text area box does not use the `<input>` tag like the text box and password box do. Instead, the text area box uses the `<textarea>` tag.

NOTE

Unlike the `<input>` tag, which does not require a closing tag, the `<textarea>` tag must be closed with an ending `</textarea>` tag.

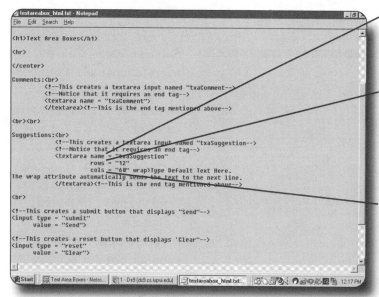

You must use the `name` attribute to identify the input to your application.

Use the `rows` attribute to set the number of rows, which controls the text area height. The default value is four rows tall.

To further control the size of the text area box, you can use the `cols` attribute to set the width of the text area. The width is measured in characters, and the default width is 40 characters wide.

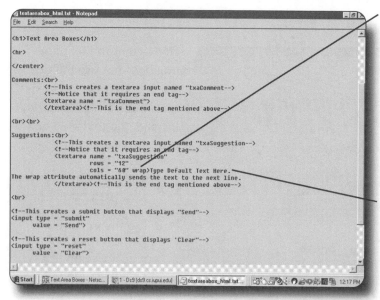

The final attribute you can use with text area boxes is `wrap`. This attribute automatically sends the text typed by the users to the next line when it reaches the edge of the text area box. This gives your text box a more professional look.

You can include default text in text area boxes by placing it between the `<textarea>` and `</textarea>` tags. You do not use the `value` attribute for default text in text area boxes. The maximum number of characters that users can type in the text area box is 32,700, and scroll bars are displayed on the text area box as needed.

Using Selected Choice Inputs

Selected choice inputs give you control over the values that the users can input into your application. You select the values the users can choose from. The options are to allow the users to choose a single value (using radio buttons) or multiple values (using check boxes or menus). You control this option by the selected choice input you use. You use check boxes or menus to allow the users multiple options, whereas radio buttons enable the users to choose only one option from a list. The number of choices included in each type of selected choice inputs is controlled by the number of values you include in the tag's HTML code.

NOTE

If you do not set the `value` attributes of radio buttons, check boxes, or menus, the default value of `on` is sent to your application. This value is usually not the value your application is expecting and can result in application errors.

Creating Radio Buttons

Radio buttons are similar in design to the buttons on the radios of cars in the 1980s. If you are old enough to remember cars with radios like this, you will recall that you chose a station by pushing a button. Pushing a button changed the station to the preset value (the station's call numbers), and any other button that was pressed would pop back up. You were limited to pushing only one button at a time. Radio buttons on forms work the same way, hence the name. The users can select only one of the buttons at a time. When they select a second button, the first button is deselected. This is just like the old car radios.

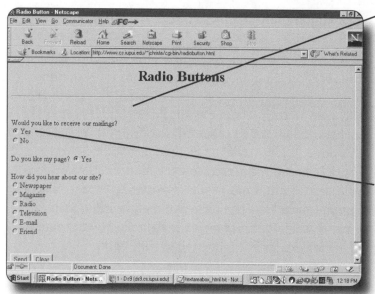

You control the number of choices the users have for each input field, as well as the values they can choose. Unlike the old car radios, the users cannot change the preset values of your radio buttons.

You also can set a particular button as the default for any of the radio button input fields. Using default choices is covered in detail in the section "Adding Default Values to Your Forms," later in this chapter.

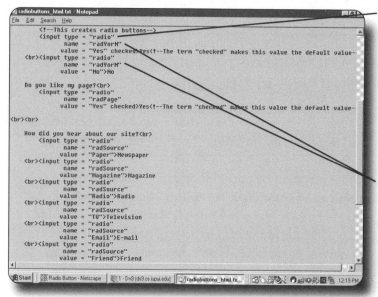

You create radio buttons using the `<input type = "radio">` tag. This tag is basically the same as the tag used to create text boxes and password boxes; however, the `type` attribute is set to `radio`.

The `name` attribute for radio buttons is different from the previous `name` attributes you have been using. The `name` for each button in a set is identical. This is what links the radio buttons together, thus allowing only one choice. You must use the `name` attribute to identify the input to your application.

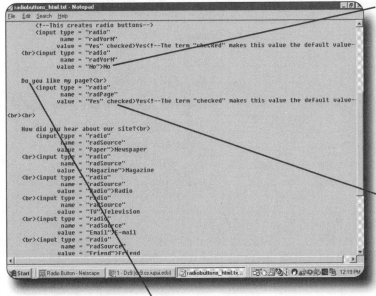

The value attribute differentiates the selections within a set of radio buttons from one another. If the value attribute is not set, the application will receive the value of on, which is usually not the value your application is expecting.

You also can set a default button selection. Use the checked attribute to do so. This attribute is useful when you want to suggest a choice to your users. This also keeps the users from skipping an input field.

You can technically create a radio button list that only contains one choice; however, most users, including myself, find this annoying. If you need to send this information to your application, use a hidden field instead. Hidden fields are described in Chapter 12, "Retaining Visitor Data."

Using Check Boxes

Check boxes are similar to radio buttons in that you determine the choices available to the users. You also set the number of choices. The difference between check boxes and radio buttons is that, with check boxes, the users can check as many of the available choices as they want. This enables the users to input all the relevant data without you having to create numerous input fields to gather it. Just as radio buttons are grouped by the name attribute, check boxes are grouped in sets using the name attribute.

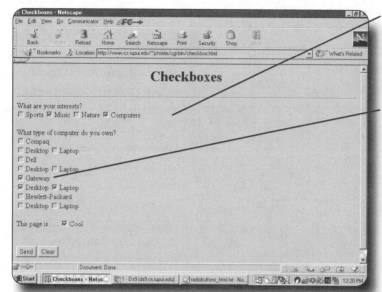

You control the number of choices the users have for each input field, as well as the values they can choose.

You also can set a particular check box as the default for any of the check box input fields.

You create check boxes using the <input type = "checkbox"> tag. This tag is basically the same as the tag used to create text boxes and password boxes; however, the type attribute is set to checkbox.

The name attribute of a check box functions the same way as it does in radio buttons. The name for each check box in a set is identical. This is what links the check boxes together. You must use the name attribute to identify the input to your application.

The value attribute differentiates the selections within a set of check boxes from one another. If the value attribute is not set, the application receives the value of on, which is usually not the value your application is expecting.

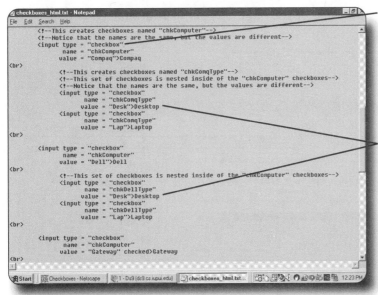

You also can set default check box selections. Use the `checked` attribute to do so. This attribute is useful when you want to suggest a choice to your users.

Check boxes that are part of the same set do not have to be grouped together, although this generally saves confusion. Notice that the Desktop and Laptop check boxes are nested inside each of the individual computer manufacturer names.

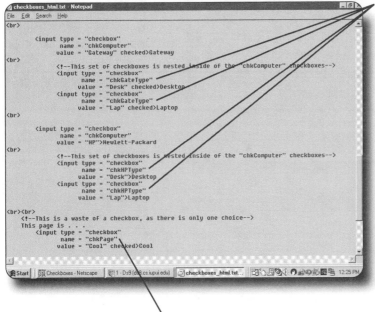

The Desktop and Laptop `name` attributes are different for each of the nested check box sets. Using different `name` attributes for each of the nested sets makes the application less confusing to write and will result in less confusion when debugging the application. Recall that there are many ways to achieve the same results in a Perl application; therefore, the desired result can be accomplished using the same `name` attributes for all the nested Desktop and Laptop check boxes.

You can create a check box list that contains only one choice; however, most users, including myself, find this annoying. If you need to send this information to your application, use a hidden field. Hidden fields will be described in Chapter 12.

Using Menus

Menus are good for allowing your users to choose from a long list of options. Unlike radio buttons and check boxes, menus do not have to show all the choices at once.

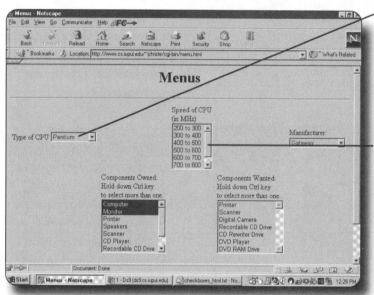

Menus can be designed to appear as text boxes with drop-down menus designated by an arrow on the right side of the input field.

Menus can also be designed to appear as lists of choices. You choose the menu style based on your form design.

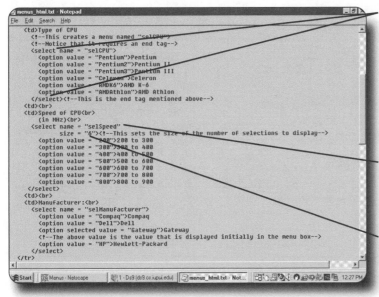

Menus do not use the `<input>` tag. They use the `<select>` tag, which (like the `<textarea>` tag) requires a closing tag. You must use the ending `</select>` tag to end a menu.

As always, use the `name` attribute to identify the input to your application.

Using the `size` attribute enables you to show the menu as a list instead of a text box style drop-down menu. If the `size` attribute is less than the number of choice options, an active scroll bar is displayed. If the `size` attribute is equal to or greater than the options, an inactive scroll bar is displayed.

To enable your users to select more than one choice from the menu, use the `multiple` attribute. In order to select multiple choices, users must press the Ctrl button while clicking on their choices; therefore, it is a good idea to include these instructions on the form.

Place the `<option>` tag between the `<select>` and `</select>` tags to set the value of the menu options.

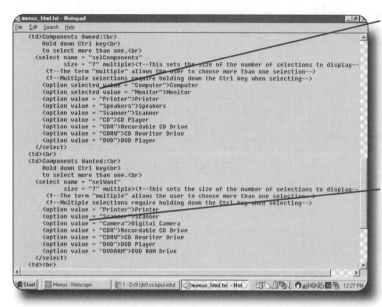

The `selected` attribute of the `<option>` tag contains a default value for the menu list. Default values are explained in detail in the section "Adding Default Values to Your Forms," later in this chapter.

The `value` attribute of the `<option>` tag contains the values displayed by the menu.

Creating Action Buttons

Action buttons enable the users to send the completed form to the server, reset the form to its original settings, or use images to send information to the server.

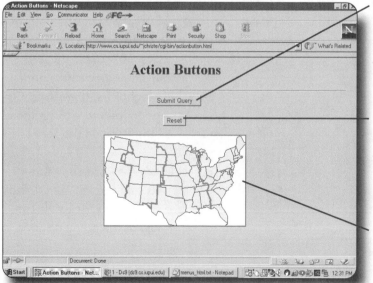

You should always include a Submit button, which enables the users to send their information to the application.

Users appreciate the capability to reset the data with a click of a button instead of deleting each input field separately.

Images are useful when gathering geographical information from users.

The following sections explain how to use these various action buttons on your form.

Using Submit Buttons

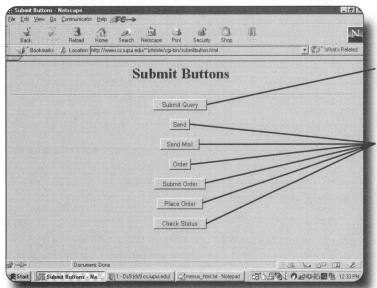

By default, the Submit button displays "Submit Query" as the standard text.

You can change the text displayed on the Submit button so that it corresponds to the form you are using.

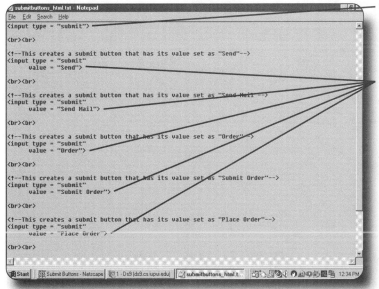

You use the `<input type = "submit">` tag to create a Submit button.

The `value` attribute controls the text displayed in the Submit button. This attribute can be set to the text that best describes the use of the button.

NOTE

The `name` attribute can be used with various Submit buttons to enable different buttons to send different values to your application; however, you can accomplish this same task using radio buttons. Using radio buttons instead of the `name` attribute is less confusing. By eliminating the `name` attribute, the form does not send unneeded information to the application. This superfluous information consists of the name-value for the button, which probably is `"submit, Submit Query"`.

Using Reset Buttons

You can use Reset buttons to enable the users to change the information on the form without having to delete each entry individually. The Reset button resets the form to its original settings—any default values are displayed as they are on the initial form.

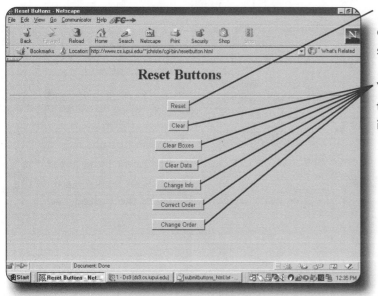

By default, the Reset button displays Reset as the standard text.

You can change the button text to a more useful and instructional value.

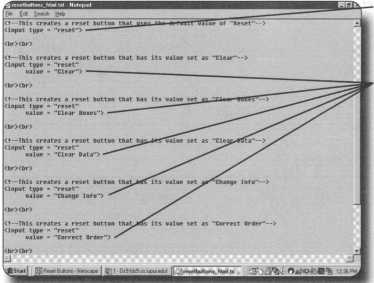

Use the `<input type = "reset">` tag to create a Reset button.

The `value` attribute of the `<input>` tag controls the text in the Reset button. This text should succinctly describe to the users the action that the button performs.

NOTE

The `name` attribute is not normally used with the Reset button. The form will send the name value of the Reset button only when you use the `name` attribute. Like the Submit button, this sends mostly worthless information to the application—the information will generally be `"reset, Reset"`.

Using Active Images

The final type of action button you might use on your forms is the active image. Active images are not actual buttons; however, they function like buttons and are used to submit form information to the server. When the image is clicked, the data from all fields is submitted to the application along with the location of the cursor on the image. The image sends the coordinates of the mouse cursor as x and y values, which are appended to the image `name` attribute. The values are based on the upper-left corner of each image as the point of origin (0,0).

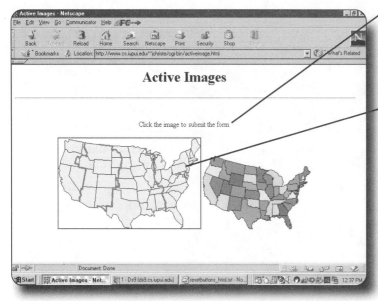

The users need to be told that the active image is a means of submitting the form to the application.

All other input fields (text boxes, radio buttons, menus, and so on) should be positioned before the active image, as their values are sent to the application when the image is clicked.

The text displayed when the cursor moves over the image is the name attribute of the active image. This name attribute is explained shortly.

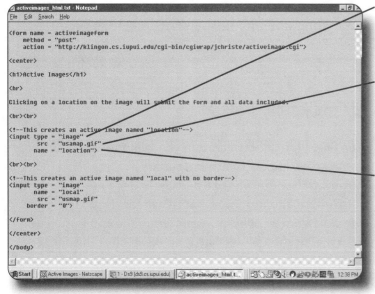

You use the `<input type = "image">` tag to create an active image on your form.

Set the src attribute to the URL of the image on the server, just like a standard HTML image tag.

The name attribute contains the value that is sent to the server with the x and y coordinates appended to it.

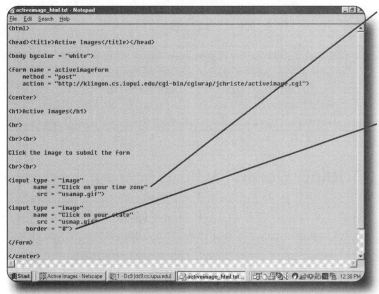

The text in the `name` attribute is displayed when the mouse cursor rolls over the image. This text can instruct the users further.

The `border` attribute controls the border that surrounds the image. Setting the `border` to 0 removes a border from the image.

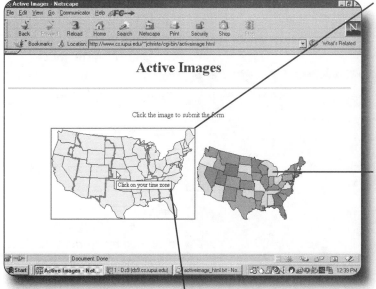

Removing the border gives the form a cleaner look; however, some designers find it useful to have a border in order to let the users know that the image is active (this is the same as an image that is a hot link).

Notice how the image without a border appears to be a standard image on the page, whereas the image with a border stands out like an active image (link).

Notice also that the text that appears with the mouse cursor is more informative than the text displayed in the previous Web page example.

NOTE

The `value` attribute is not used with active images because the mouse cursor location appends the `name` attribute to the x and y coordinates of the clicked location.

Adding Default Values to Your Forms

You have learned how to set default values inside the individual input fields, but default values and their uses have not been explained in detail. This section explains the benefits of using default values and shows you an additional way to add default values to your form.

Why You Use Default Values

Default values are often used to display the most common answers to queries. If the form asks for the country where the users live, the most common reply on your form might be the United States—if so, this is a good value to use as a default.

In my mail program, I have the default `Send to:` value set to `jrchrist@iupui.edu` because the program was designed for students to e-mail me. However, the users can type another e-mail address into the text box and the program will use the new data to send the message.

Another use of default values is to declare the default value for the data source. This can be useful when you collect data that your program requires.

Setting Default Values

The previous sections detailed the attributes you need to use for the individual input fields, so you do not need to be bored with repeat instructions. Instead, consider this additional means of adding default values to your form.

You can include default data in the `<form>` tag of your HTML page.

You accomplish this using the `action` attribute and adding the default data to the end of the application's URL.

The default data includes a question mark (?), the name of the data, an equals sign (=), and then the actual default data.

If you want to include additional default data, you insert an ampersand (&), the name of the second data, an equals sign, and then the value of the second data. This is inserted directly after the first default data value, without any spaces.

```
defaultdata_html.txt - Notepad
File  Edit  Search  Help

<!--This creates a form that calls an application and assigns single data-->
<!--You will need to change the URL to the URL where your CGI application is stored-->
<!--The assigned data is the last section of the URL-->
<Form
 action = "http://klingon.cs.iupui.edu/cgi-bin/cgiwrap/jchriste/classSyllabus.cgi?class=220Web"
 method = "post">

<!--This creates a form that calls an application and assigns multiple data-->
<!--You will need to change the URL to the URL where your CGI application is stored-->
<!--The assigned data is the last section of the URL-->
<Form
 action = "http://klingon.cs.iupui.edu/cgi-bin/cgiwrap/jchriste/
          classSyllabus.cgi?class=220Web&days=TR"
 method = "post">
```

The final step is to set the `method` attribute to `post`. The `method` attribute is explained in detail in the "Using Environment Variables" section of this chapter.

Adding Links to Your Forms

You can use URL links to access your CGI applications and as a means of inputting data to your applications. The benefit to using links in this way is the decreased amount of code that you need to write, both in HTML and Perl.

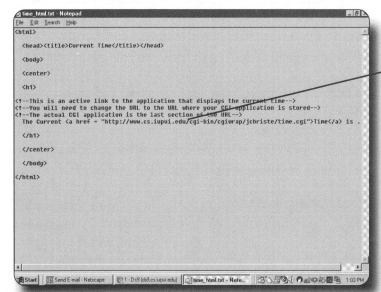

Linking to an Application

You can have a link directly access your application by including the application URL in the `<a href>` tag. The reason you might do this is to run a simple application that does not require any input from users.

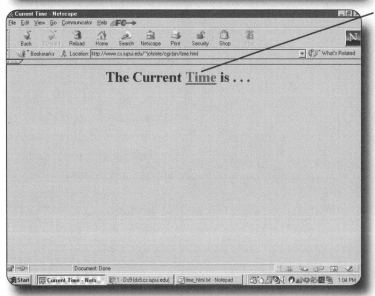

Using a link, you eliminate the need to create a form with input fields and Submit buttons.

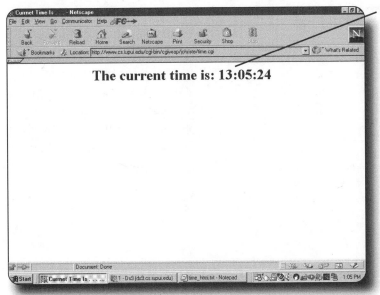

This simple link activates the CGI application and returns the current time from the application's server.

Getting Data from a Link

The other use of a link is to gather data into your application. This process is similar to the second default value process detailed earlier in this chapter. The difference is that you include the data in the `<a href>` tag instead of in the `<form>` tag.

You include the data at the end of the `<a href>` tag.

The default data includes a question mark, the name of the data, an equals sign, and then the value of the actual data.

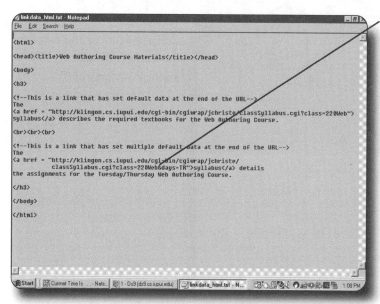

If you want to include additional data, you insert an ampersand, the name of the second data, an equals sign, and then the value of the second data. This is inserted directly after the first data value, without any spaces.

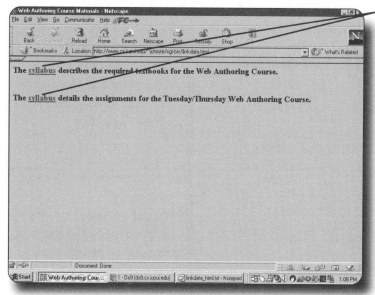

The links do not look that different; however, the data that is added to the end of the `<a href>` tag changes the information received by your application. This results in different outputs being sent back to the users.

Using Environment Variables

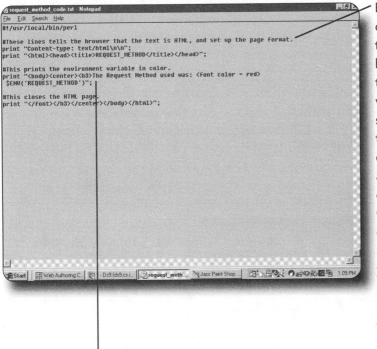

```
#!/usr/local/bin/perl

#These lines tells the browser that the text is HTML, and set up the page format.
print "Content-type: text/html\n\n";
print "<html><head><title>REQUEST_METHOD</title></head>";

#This prints the environment variable in color.
print "<body><center><h3>The Request Method used was: <font color = red>
 $ENV{'REQUEST_METHOD'}";

#This closes the HTML page.
print "</font></h3></center></body></html>";
```

Environment variables comprise a group of data that is set every time the browser sends information to the server. These variables are stored in a specific area called %ENV; this is a hash that is set every time the application is accessed. Hashes are explained in detail in Chapter 8, "Hashes." The environmental variables that are of the greatest value to you are the ones that provide information concerning the data sent to the server.

NOTE

The environmental variables in this section must be UPPERCASE characters. Notice that they all start with $ENV{' and end with '}, and that they are contained in the double quotation marks of the print statement. The statement must also end with a semicolon (;).

Using Post versus Get

Earlier examples mentioned the method attribute of the <form> tag as the means of sending data to the server. In order to fully understand what this attribute does and the differences between the two types, you will look more closely at each of them.

When the users click on the Submit button or activate a CGI application link, the data from the form or link is sent to the server. This data is sent by either the post or get value of the method attribute. Post allows unlimited amounts of data to be sent to the server, therefore, you generally use post on your forms.

Data added to a link is always sent to the server using the get method. If you add data that is contained in the <form> tag to a URL, the added data is sent by the get method, whereas the other data from the form is sent by the post method. A nice feature in CGI is that you can determine which method was used to send the data to the server.

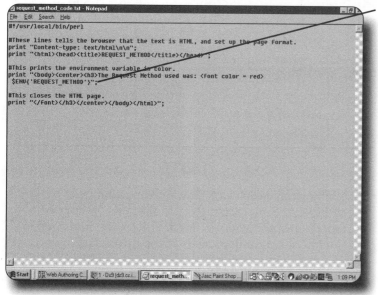

To determine which method was used, you can run a simple application using the REQUEST_METHOD environmental variable.

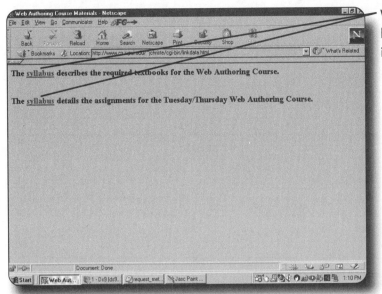

When the users click on the link that contains this code, it generates an HTML page.

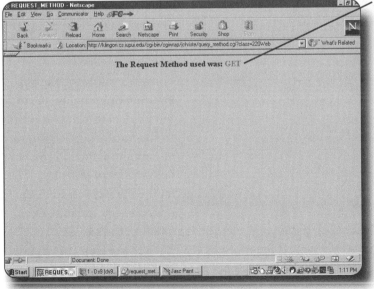

The generated HTML page displays the method used to send the data to the server.

Another useful environment variable, QUERY_STRING, displays the value received by the application from the get method.

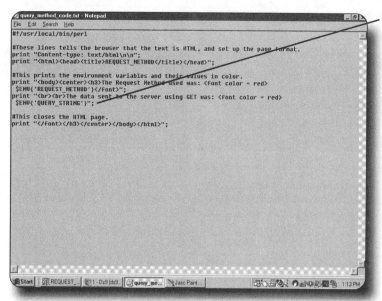

You use this variable in the same manner as the `REQUEST_METHOD` variable, and you generally use both of these variables together.

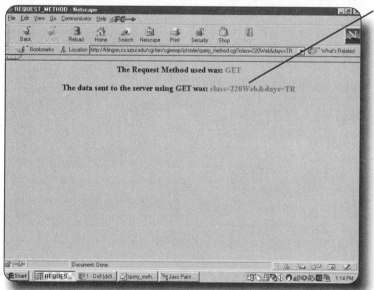

The data added to the URL of the link is displayed in the same way in which you entered it in the HTML code.

The last environment variable you will use with the `post` and `get` methods, `CONTENT_LENGTH`, displays information obtained when the `post` method sends data to the application. Unlike the `get` method, the information received from the `post` method is not stored in an environment variable. Data sent using the `post` method is stored on the server in a location called *Standard Input*. This is the reason that data sent by the `post` method does not have a limit on its size. In order to find the data in Standard Input, you have to know how many bytes are in the data. The `CONTENT_LENGTH` variable displays the size of the data sent in bytes.

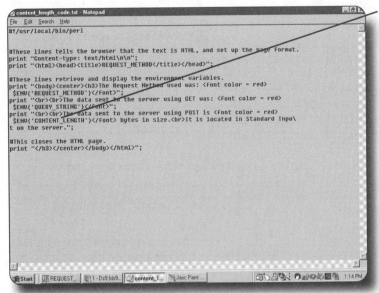

The CONTENT_LENGTH variable is used like the REQUEST_METHOD and the QUERY_STRING and can all be included together in the same application.

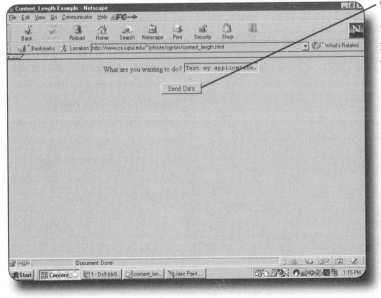

When data is submitted directly from a form, the post method sends the data to the server.

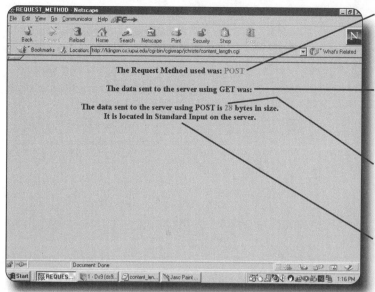

This results in information being displayed for the `post` method.

Note that the `get` data is blank because of the `post` method.

The CONTENT_LENGTH variable displays the size of the data sent in bytes.

It is a good idea to include a reminder of the location of the data sent by the `post` method.

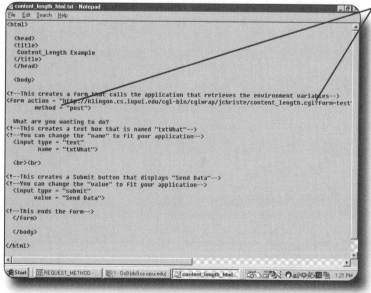

Recall that some data might be sent using both the `post` and `get` methods from the same form. This happens when you use the `post` method to send the form data and include default data in the `action` attribute of the `<form>` tag.

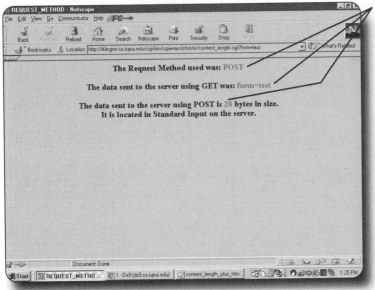

The HTML page generated by the application contains information in all the fields because both post and get are used.

This code can display only the information that is actually sent from the HTML page. Doing this takes more know-how than the code shown and is introduced in Chapter 9, "Conditional Statements."

Determining Browser and Platform Information

You can also use environment variables to determine the browser your users are using to visit your Web page. This information is useful when you want to include design features that are not supported by all browsers, in which case you should base your design around the most common browser or provide alternative pages for specific browsers.

To get browser information, use the HTTP_USER_AGENT variable in the same manner as the other environment variables.

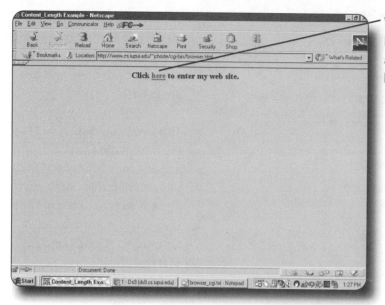

When the users click on this link, the link accesses the application that obtains their browser information.

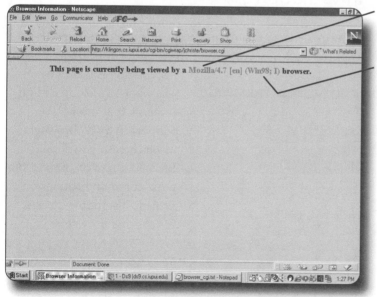

The page that is produced reports the browser type.

It also displays the computer's operating system.

Determining Navigation Information

You can determine what page your users were viewing prior to visiting your Web page using the HTTP_REFERER

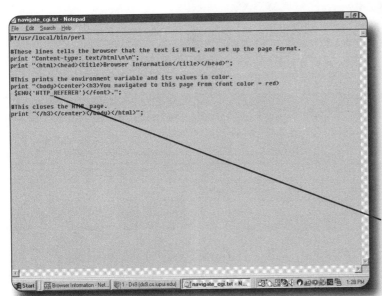

environment variable. This can be useful when you want to locate pages that have links to your page. The problem with this method is that when the users type your name in the URL text field, this variable will show the page they were last on, even if it does not contain a link to your site.

Use the HTTP_REFERER like the other environment variables in this section.

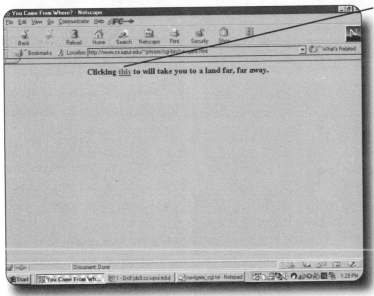

When this link is clicked, the page the users currently are viewing is noted by the application.

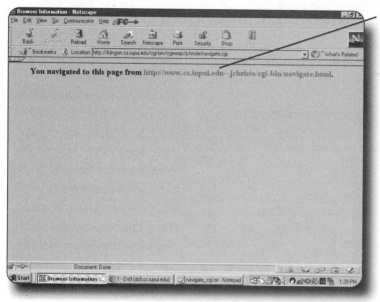

The application displays a page informing the users of the URL from which they came.

Viewing All Environment Variables at Once

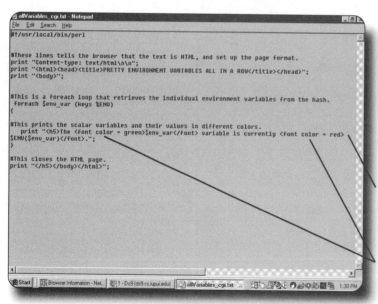

The final process that deals with environment variables enables you to view every environment variable. This process is more involved, code-wise, than the previous processes, but it is a powerful and useful application.

The code that generates this response looks complicated, but it is easy to create.

I added font colors so that the variable names and values can be quickly identified.

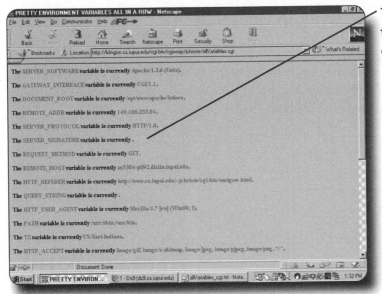

The application locates all the viewable variables and displays them.

NOTE

These examples use links to access the applications; however, you can use the application's URL in the `action` attribute of the `<form>` tag. Doing so enables you to view the variables sent from the `post` method.

Also, these examples use HTML output in order to provide easier viewing of the responses. If you want the information for yourself, you can have the responses e-mailed to you or stored in a file. Using files this way is explained in Chapter 15, "Files and Directories."

Summary

In this chapter, you learned how to get information from your Web page visitors using a variety of methods, including using text input fields, selected choice inputs, action buttons, links, and environment variables. You created some powerful CGI applications and saw their results. You now are ready to discover how to get this data into your CGI application, which, not coincidentally, is the topic of the next chapter.

5

Getting the Data Into Your CGI Application

In the previous chapter, you learned how to solicit information from your users, but this information is useless unless you port it into your application. In this chapter, you'll learn:

- The importance of the data in your application
- How to input the users' data
- How to input data yourself
- Data problems that might arise

The Importance of the Data in Your Application

The data from the form is sent to the server when your users click on the Submit button; however, it needs to get to your application to be of any value. Without porting the data to your application, you have created nothing more than an HTML form.

The Ability to Interact

By inserting the data into your application, you are able to interact with your users. Without this interaction, you have no need for a CGI application. The users are counting on the form they complete to produce some sort of result—this can be as simple as sending a message or as advanced as submitting a purchase order. Whatever the result, your application needs the information from the form in order to process it.

The Means of Communicating with Your Visitors

You know that when you click on a Submit button, you expect a response. This response can be the result of a search request, a confirmation of an order, or a Web page that uses the form input to display a specific page. These are all ways of communicating with your users. The type of communication depends on the outcome that you want to achieve. As simple as this sounds, it is the most important aspect of CGI application design. Without the users, there is no need for a Web page or a CGI application.

Inputting User Data

The data sent to the server by your users can come from a variety of sources. This section looks at the three most common sources of user data: forms, links, and environment variables. There can be other sources of user data; however, these three are the types that you will see in the majority of applications you write or borrow during your adventures as a Web programmer.

To understand these processes, you need to have a basic understanding of how the data is sent to the server. When users click on a link or a Submit button, the server receives the data (name-value pairs) in one continuous stream. In order for your application to use that data, it must be broken into smaller, usable chunks—the term for this is *parsing*. You will find that parsing scripts are commonly used and are an essential part of most Web applications.

Parsing Data from Forms and Links

When you parse data, you take the continuous data that is sent to the server and break it into pieces of information that your application can use.

NOTE

For this example I changed the input field names by removing the prefixes I suggested using in Chapter 4, "Getting the Data from Visitors to Your Web Page." This better exhibits how this particular parsing script works. I include a more complete example, using the original input field names, at the end of this section.

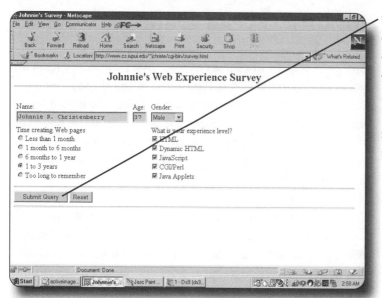

When the users complete the input fields and click on the Submit Query button, the data is sent to the server as a giant piece of information that includes the names and values separated by characters.

The equals sign separates the name from the value.

The name/value pairs are separated by ampersands.

Spaces are separated by plus signs.

As you can see, it is hard for your application to make sense of this data. It is also difficult for you to analyze data in this format. Data analysis is covered in Chapter 10, "Handling Data with Regular Expressions."

When you parse the data that is sent to the server, you break the data into pieces that correspond to the application.

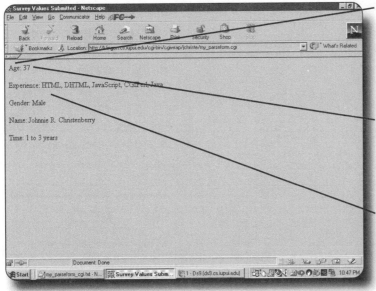

In this application, the `name` attributes are listed first, followed by a colon. In this example the first name is "Age."

The `value` attributes are then listed for each corresponding `name` attribute.

For ease of viewing, the name-value pairs are on separate lines.

The data that was sent from the form is now in a usable format that makes sense.

NOTE

Notice that the data is not in the same order as the input fields on your form. In fact, it's now listed in alphabetical order. As your skill level progresses in this section, you will learn various ways to arrange the data in a manner that best fits your needs. For now, just concentrate on the parsing of the data.

The concept of parsing data might sound difficult; however, it is not as complicated as it sounds. There are numerous parsing scripts available on the Web that you can incorporate into your applications. Often, the parsing script is a subroutine used in your application. You will gain knowledge of subroutines in Chapter 11, "Subroutines." Now, you need to look at a parsing script to understand what it does and how you can use it in your applications.

```
my_parseform_cgi.txt - Notepad
File  Edit  Search  Help

#!/usr/local/bin/perl

if ($ENV{'REQUEST_METHOD'} eq 'GET') {
        @pairs = split(/&/, $ENV{'QUERY_STRING'});
} elsif ($ENV{'REQUEST_METHOD'} eq 'POST') {
        read (STDIN, $in, $ENV{'CONTENT_LENGTH'});
        @pairs = split(/&/, $in);
} else {
        print "Content-type: text/html\n\n";
        print "<P>Use Post or Get";
}

foreach $pair (@pairs) {
        ($name, $value) = split (/=/, $pair);
        $name =~ s/\+/ /g;
        $name =~ s/%(..)/pack("C", hex($1))/ge;
        $value =~ s/\+/ /g;
        $value =~ s/%(..)/pack("C", hex($1))/ge;
        $value =~ s/<!--(.|\n)*-->//g;

        if ($parseform{$name}) {
                $parseform{$name} .= ", $value";
        } else {
                $parseform{$name} = $value;
        }

}

print "Content-type: text/html\n\n";
print "<html><head><title>Survey Values Submitted</title></head><body>";
foreach $name (sort keys($parseform)) {
        print "<h1>$name: $parseform{$name}</h1>";
print "</body></html>";
}
```

Start | my_parseform_cgi.tx... | Survey Values Submitted. | 1 - Ds9 (ds9.cs.iupui.edu) | 3:21 AM

This is the entire parsing script used in the previous example. You are probably looking at it and wondering what functions the lines of code perform. With that in mind, this section breaks the code down and deciphers the confusing elements.

> **NOTE**
>
> This script contains *block conditional statements,* which have not been covered yet. Conditional statements are explained in detail in Chapter 9, "Conditional Statements." For now, just pay attention to what the lines of code are accomplishing in the script.

```
Untitled - Notepad
File  Edit  Search  Help

if ($ENV{'REQUEST_METHOD'} eq 'GET') {

        @pairs = split(/&/, $ENV{'QUERY_STRING'});

} elsif ($ENV{'REQUEST_METHOD'} eq 'POST') {

        read (STDIN, $in, $ENV{'CONTENT_LENGTH'});

        @pairs = split(/&/, $in);

} else {

        print "Content-type: text/html\n\n";

        print "<P>Use Post or Get";

}
```

Start | my_parsefor... | Survey Valu... | 1 - Ds9 (ds9... | Untitled -... | 3:23 AM

The first line determines whether REQUEST_METHOD is set to Get.

The second line names the array you create to hold the name-value pairs from your form. You can choose any name for your array; however, you need to use the same name throughout the script.

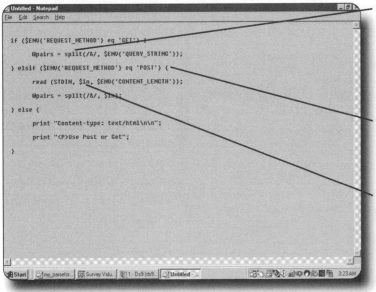

This command splits the data sent by the Get method at every ampersand in the QUERY_STRING environment variable.

The third line determines whether REQUEST_METHOD is set to Post.

The fourth line reads the variable that holds the contents of the unparsed data that was sent to the server, if Post was used. The variable in this example is named $in; however, you can use any name as long as it is used throughout the script.

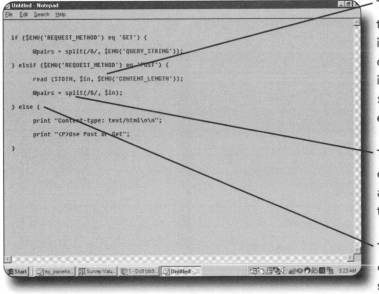

The read function needs to know the data's length in order to input it correctly. This information is gleaned from the $ENV{'CONTENT_LENGTH'} environment variable.

The fifth line splits the data of the $in variable, at every ampersand and assigns it to the @pairs array.

The sixth line is added in case neither Post nor Get sends the data.

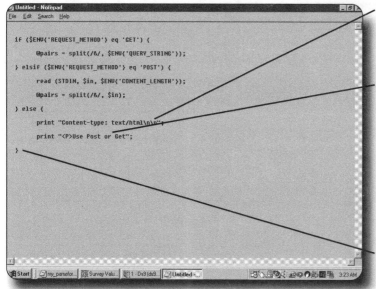

```
if ($ENV{'REQUEST_METHOD'} eq 'GET') {
    @pairs = split(/&/, $ENV{'QUERY_STRING'});
} elsif ($ENV{'REQUEST_METHOD'} eq 'POST') {
    read (STDIN, $in, $ENV{'CONTENT_LENGTH'});
    @pairs = split(/&/, $in);
} else {
    print "Content-type: text/html\n\n";
    print "<P>Use Post or Get";
}
```

The seventh line prepares the browser to accept HTML type input.

The eighth line displays a message to the browser informing the users to use Post or Get to send the data to the server. This message is displayed only when Post or Get were not originally used.

The last line ends the else statement.

You use the first line in this block of code to sort the name-value pairs contained in the @pairs array from the previous block.

```
foreach $pair (@pairs) {
    ($name, $value) = split (/=/, $pair);
    $name =~ s/\+/ /g;
    $name =~ s/%(..)/pack("C", hex($1))/ge;
    $value =~ s/\+/ /g;
    $value =~ s/%(..)/pack("C", hex($1))/ge;
    $value =~s/<!--(.|\n)*-->//g;

    if ($parseform{$name}) {
        $parseform{$name} .= ", $value";
    } else {
        $parseform{$name} = $value;
    }
}
```

The second line creates the variables that hold the data's name and value from the server.

The split function separates the name-value pairs at every equals sign.

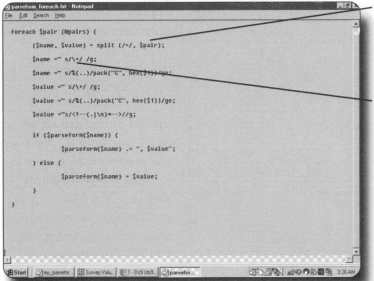

The last function performed in the second line creates the variable used in the `foreach` loop.

These lines substitute and convert ported data into data that is usable and meaningful to your application.

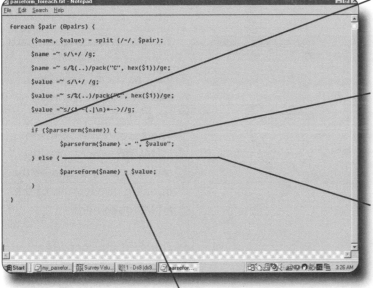

The eighth line determines whether the name $parseform has already been assigned to the hash.

The ninth line adds the value to an existing hash and separates it by a comma if the previous line returns a true value.

The tenth line prepares to execute the next line if the eighth line returns a false value.

The eleventh line stores the name and value in the $parseform hash if the eighth line returns a false value.

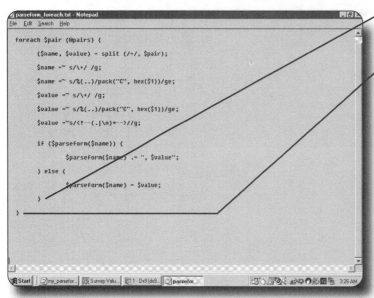

The twelfth line ends the `else` statement.

The thirteenth line ends the `foreach` statement.

The last part of the script might look familiar to you—you used most of it when you created HTML output from your first CGI application. However, I break down each of these lines as I did previously in case you are referencing this section without having read the previous chapters.

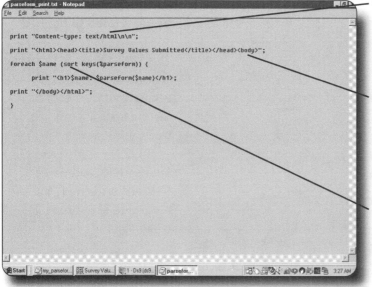

The first line is the standard Content-type line that informs the browser to expect HTML type text.

The second line opens the HTML document, creates the header, and creates the opening `<body>` tag of the HTML document.

The third line contains a `foreach` statement that sorts the `$name` values for every key in the `$parseform` hash.

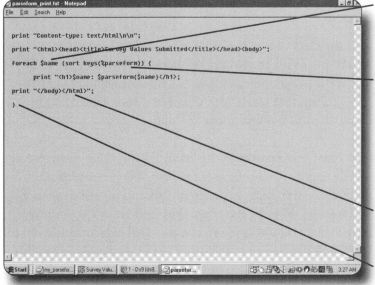

The fourth line prints each $name key followed by a colon.

The last portion of the fourth line prints the value of each $name key in the $parseform hash. Each of these corresponds to the $name keys.

The fifth line closes the body and the HTML document.

The last line ends the foreach statement.

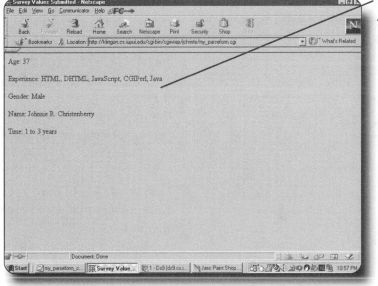

This completes the script that displays the following HTML page.

The Promised Example

At the start of this section, I promised to provide an example using the input field names from Chapter 4. The script is exactly the same as the previous example until the final block that starts with the `print` command; therefore, I only explain the final block of code.

As mentioned earlier in the book, having more control over your application requires more involved code—this does not mean the code is harder, just that there are generally more lines of code and more time and work involved. With that said, you are ready to see the code that enables you to arrange the output in the order you desire and display the text you want. Recall that the input field names in the previous example were displayed in the output page exactly as they appeared in the input tags of the HTML form.

This standard Content-type line tells the browser to expect HTML type text.

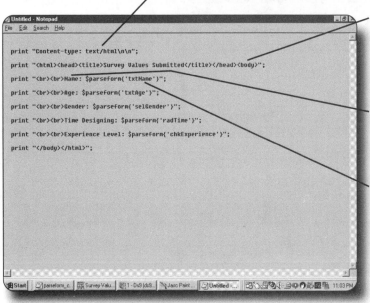

The second line opens the HTML document, creates the header, and opens the body of the HTML page.

The third line prints the text you want to display followed by a colon.

Then the `value` of the `txtName` input field from the `$parseform` hash is displayed.

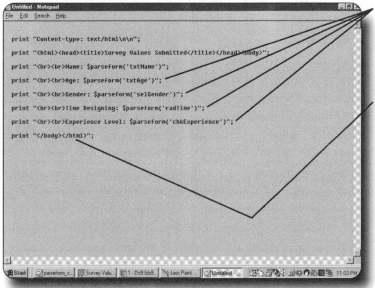

The next four lines repeat this process for each input field `value` you want to display.

The last line closes the body and the HTML document.

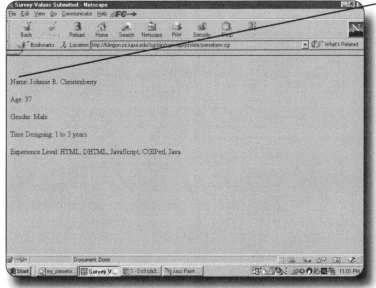

The values displayed by the HTML page are the same as the previous example; however, you control the text that is displayed before the colon and the order in which the variables are displayed.

You should now understand the concept of parsing data and how beneficial it is to your applications. You use this script to get data from forms or links to your application. In Chapter 11, you will discover how to use the parseform.cgi script as a subroutine in your applications. The next type of user data that you input to your application comes from environment variables.

Inputting Data from Environment Variables

The process of inputting data from environment variables looks like a blend of the previous parsing procedure and the environment variables procedures from Chapter 4. The reason it looks like this is because that is exactly what it is. The environment variable procedures from Chapter 4 actually parse the data received from the form: how convenient. In this section, you combine the procedures in a more sensible manner than the environment variable examples did in Chapter 4. The biggest difference between this example and the environment variable example used in Chapter 4 is that, here, the environment variables are assigned to scalar variables.

The environment variable that returns the browser information is assigned to the scalar variable named $browser.

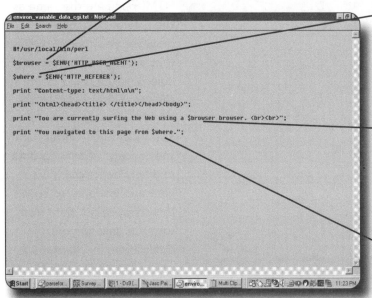

The environment variable that returns the previous URL information is assigned to the scalar variable named $where.

The $browser variable displays the browser information in the text of the print command line, which is output as HTML.

The $where variable displays the previous URL information, which is output as HTML, in the print command line.

NOTE

Remember that Perl uses the equal sign to assign values to variables—the interpretation of the equals sign is best thought of as *gets*. The line of code that starts with $browser says "The $browser variable gets the value $ENV{'HTTP_USER_AGENT'}." If it is easier, you can think of the equals sign as meaning *is assigned the value* instead of *gets*. The important thing to understand is that $browser does not equal the assigned value, because the value can change during the execution of the application.

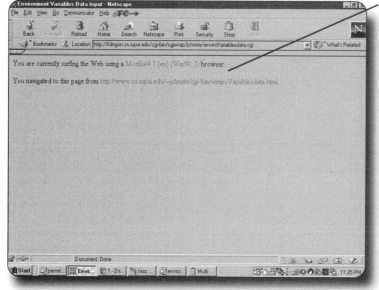

This output is the same as in the example from Chapter 4; however, you do not have to use the complete environment variable name to output the value. You only need to use the variable that has the environment variable value assigned to it.

Now that you understand the primary means of getting visitor data into your application, you need to understand the ways you can manually input data into the application.

Inputting Data Yourself

Your application is not limited to data that is sent to the server from your users: You have the ability to input data directly into your applications using scalars, arrays, and hashes. You gain a better understanding of scalars in Chapter 6, "Scalars," arrays in Chapter 7, "Arrays," and hashes in Chapter 8, "Hashes." For now, focus on the input process and don't worry about all the properties of the individual pieces of data.

Inputting Data from Scalars

There will be times when your application uses the same data all the time every time. You can use scalar variables to include this kind of data in your application. This process is simple; however, it is powerful and useful in many applications.

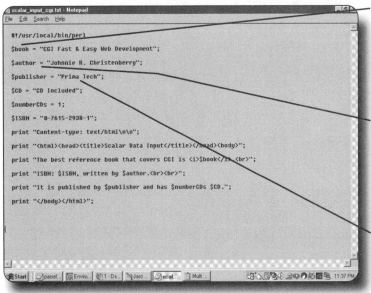

You create your scalar variable by using a dollar sign as the first character and then the name you want to use for the variable.

You assign a value to the variable using an equals sign between the variable name and the value you want to assign to it.

If the value you are assigning is a string, it needs to be enclosed in single or double quotation marks. I generally use double quotation marks to differentiate between string values and the name of an environment variable. This is especially helpful when debugging.

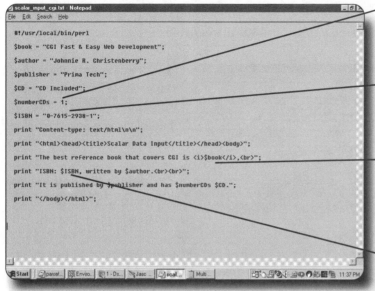

You are not required to enclose numbers within quotation marks.

However, if the number is used as a string, it should be enclosed in quotation marks.

You then include the scalar variables in place of the value as though they are the actual text.

Scalar variables do not have to be used in the same order they are created; this is one of the benefits of using this type of data input.

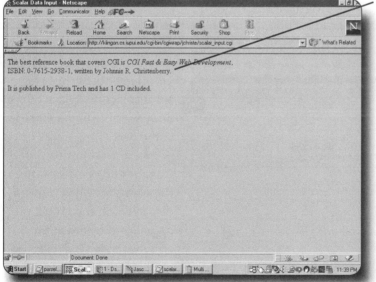

The text looks like it was written without the use of scalar variables, which is just what you want.

You are now ready to look at a slightly more complex method of inputting data.

Inputting Data from Arrays

You might need to include a list of data that you want to be used every time your application executes. You can use an array to accomplish this task. *Arrays* are lists of data contained in the same variable.

You create array variables using the at sign, followed by the name you choose for the variable.

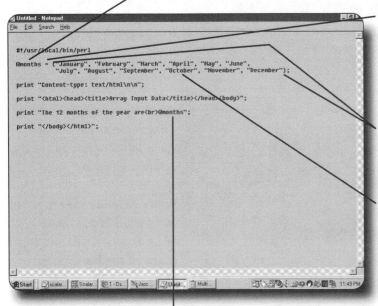

You then assign a value to the variable by including an equals sign between the variable name and the value you want to assign to it.

You enclose the data you are assigning to the array variable in parentheses.

If the elements in the array are strings, you need to enclose them in quotation marks: An exception to this appears in the next example.

You can include the array variable in your text as though it is the actual list.

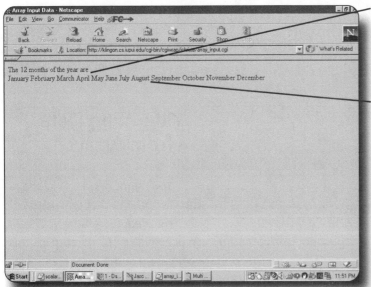

The elements of the array are displayed in place of the array variable name you use in the text.

Commas do not separate the elements when they are displayed on the HTML page like they are in the array variable. They also do not have the quotation marks. Chapter 7 shows you how to manipulate the manner in which array variables are displayed.

The exception to enclosing strings in quotation marks basically saves time and reduces the amount of typing you do when creating the array variable.

You start the array variable with the at sign, the array name, and the equals sign, just like the previous example.

You then use qw before the opening parenthesis. The qw stands for quote word and designates the following text as quoted literals.

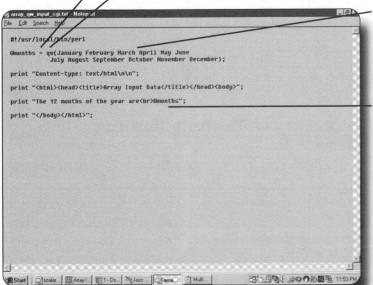

You then list the elements without quotation marks or commas; they are separated only by spaces in the output.

You include the array variable name in your text just like in the previous example.

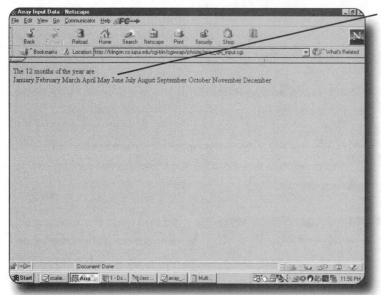

Notice that the HTML page is identical to the HTML page from the previous example. Nothing changed except for the amount of typing involved in creating the array.

Now that you understand how to create an array, you are ready to move on to associative arrays, more commonly referred to as *hashes*.

Inputting Data from Hashes

Hashes differ from arrays in that the order of the elements is important. Recall from Chapter 2 that elements in hashes come in pairs—the first element is the key, and the second element is the value. However, the element pairs can be in any order, and you can access the values using the keys.

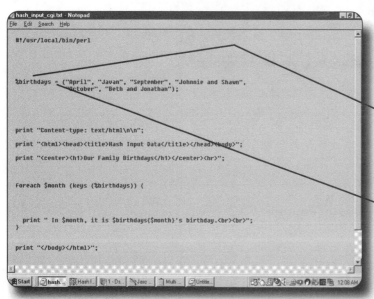

You create a hash variable by using the percent sign followed by the name you want to use for the hash.

As usual, you assign a value to the variable by using an equals sign between the variable name and the value you want to assign to it.

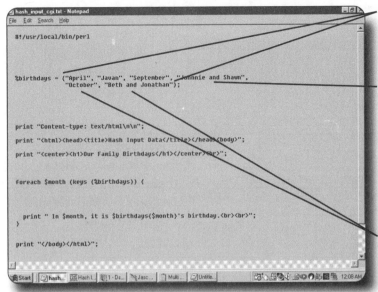

You then enclose the data you are assigning to the hash variable in parentheses.

If the elements in the hash are strings, you need to enclose them in quotation marks. An exception to this rule is when using the qw process outlined in the previous example.

It is extremely important that you list the elements in pairs with the key first and the value second.

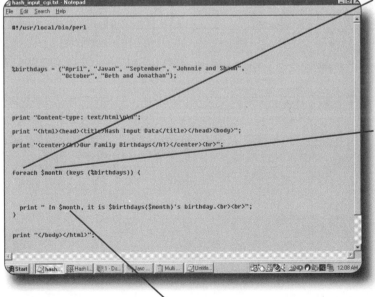

You use a foreach statement to display the hash elements in your HTML page. The foreach statement is explained in detail in Chapter 9.

The $month scalar variable gets the key of each of the element pairs in the %birthdays hash. This step and the next two steps will be clearer once you read Chapter 8; for now, focus on what is occurring and not how it occurs.

You use the $month variable in place of the key elements, in this case for the months.

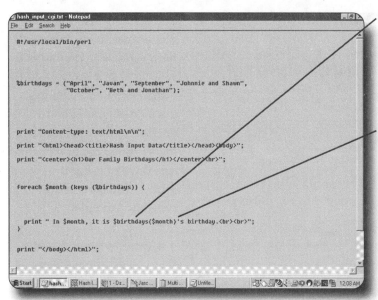

You use `$birthdays{$month}` in place of the `value` of the element pairs, in this case for the family member names.

I got cute and added an apostrophe to the family member's name. Notice that there is not a space between the variable and the apostrophe.

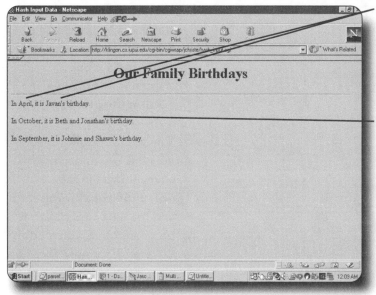

The HTML page generated by the application displays the month with the appropriate family member's name.

The apostrophe looks like it is a part of the name to which it is attached.

You are now empowered with the knowledge to use scalars, arrays, and hashes as a means of inputting data into your applications. The next three chapters explore each of these variables in depth. You learn how to manipulate them to fit individual applications. As simple as the processes for getting data into your application appears, there can still be glitches that wreak havoc on your applications.

Dealing with Potential Problems

Right now you probably feel pretty confident in your ability to get data into your applications. But what if the users type the wrong data into the input fields? Will your application still execute? Will it execute correctly? These are the questions that might keep you up at night worrying about the stability of your applications and your Web site. The hardest part of this dilemma is that you cannot anticipate such problems.

I address the more common problems and their solutions in later chapters. If I explained the solutions at this time you might be more confused because you have not learned the material that enables you to find and correct the problems or create the safety net to catch them before they corrupt your application. The two areas that you need to be aware of involve fixing incorrect input from your users and faulty data that you input. I am mentioning these problems and not their solutions in this section as a preventative maintenance procedure. I hope that by understanding the problems you can avoid them when creating your form and application.

Incorrect Input from Your Users

The problems you might experience from user input generally involve using numbers instead of strings and strings instead of numbers. These problems usually do not corrupt your application—they generally create strange HTML page outputs or text that does not make sense. Users also might enter characters that do not convert correctly and thus produce text that is unintelligible. You are limited in your ability to control what the users input. You can use menus, radio buttons, and check boxes instead of text fields to eliminate some problems. You can also evaluate the data and inform the users that they need to correct their mistakes. More on this later.

Faulty Data that You Input

As funny as this sounds, this is the area you can control but it is also the area in which it is hardest to correct problems. The dilemma in correcting problems in this area is that you will often overlook the solution because your code looked correct when you originally created it, and it still looks correct. The most common problems I have experienced are the simplest to correct but the hardest to locate.

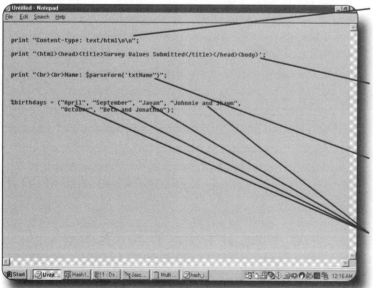

I often forget to include one of the quotation marks around a string.

This example uses a single quotation mark when it needs a double quotation mark.

This example uses a double quotation mark when it needs a single quotation mark.

Be careful also to match the `keys` to the correct `values` in hash variables.

There are numerous other silly errors that are difficult to locate, but I think you get the idea. You will probably find that there are a few that you make more than others, and you will consequentially get good at catching them before they create problems.

Summary

You began this chapter with the ability to solicit data from your users, and you are finishing this chapter knowing how to insert that data into your application. You now understand the process of parsing data and how to adapt it to your applications. You also have the ability to input data directly into your applications and display it as usable information to your users.

Also, you should have enough knowledge about CGI applications to begin asking questions about how things are accomplished. You are ready to immerse yourself into the realm of scalars, arrays, and hashes so that you will be prepared to swim with the sharks (too many years as a SCUBA instructor and too little sleep). If you are ready, take the plunge!

6

Scalars

You were briefly introduced to scalars in Chapter 2, "Writing Your CGI Application," and you used scalars to input data into your application in Chapter 5, "Getting the Data Into Your CGI Application." You will now discover the full potential and uses of scalars in CGI applications. You know that any piece of data—a string or a number, a constant or a variable—can be a scalar, and scalars always start with the dollar sign, which represents the "s" in scalar. You have already used scalars to store information; however, this chapter presents the information again in case you skipped ahead. The rest of this chapter focuses on using scalars in your applications to perform the required tasks. In this chapter, you'll learn:

- Storing scalar information
- Using numbers as scalar variables
- Using strings as scalar variables
- Assigning values to a variable

Storing Scalar Information

There are two basic ways that you store information using scalars. The first is to set the initial value of the scalar, and the second is to store the result of an operation. You have already set the initial value in earlier chapters, but you have not used scalars to handle results of operations.

NOTE

Remember that Perl uses the equals sign to assign values to variables: The real meaning of the equals sign in this context is "gets." If it is easier you can think of the equals sign as meaning "is assigned the value." The important point to understand is that the variable does not equal the assigned value, because the value can change during the execution of the application.

Initial Data

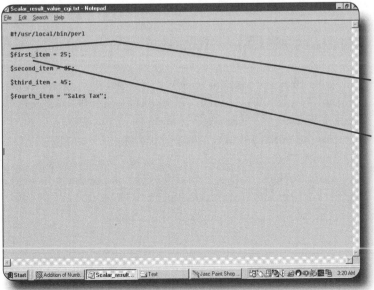

Setting the initial data of a scalar is simple and straightforward.

You start the scalar variable name with a dollar sign.

It is important to note that variable names cannot include spaces; therefore, use the underscore character (_) to separate terms in variable names.

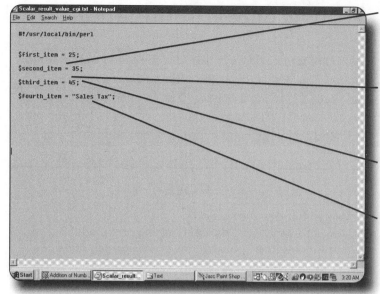

You separate the variable name from the `value` using the equals sign.

The `value` you want to assign to the variable follows the equals sign.

Finally, you end the sentence with a semicolon.

Remember, if you are assigning a string `value` to the variable, you need to enclose the `value` in quotation marks.

The value you assign to a variable can be modified within the application, and you learn how to do this in the upcoming section, "Manipulating Variable Values." But for now, you need to know how to use a scalar to store the result of an operation.

Results of Operations

You will often use a scalar variable to store the results of an operation performed within your application. This might sound challenging; however, it is simply a modification of setting the initial value of the scalar variable you have now mastered. The operations can be performed on strings, numbers, scalars, arrays, or hashes. The examples you see in this section focus on operations involving scalars, because scalars are the topic of this chapter.

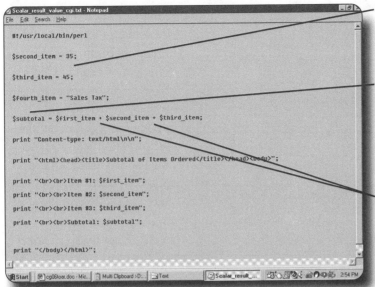

You can use the script from the previous example to start this application.

You create a new scalar variable (`$subtotal`) to hold the result of the operation you want to perform.

In this case, `$subtotal` is adding the previous scalar values together to from a subtotal. The mathematical operations are detailed in the next section, "Using Numbers as Scalar Variables."

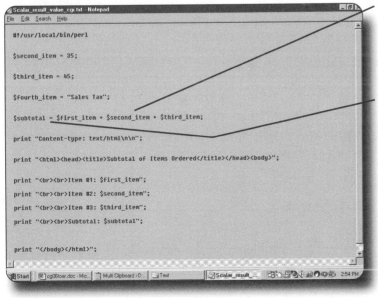

Notice that the original scalar variables are now included in the value of the `$subtotal` variable.

This is because you are assigning the result of the operation to the `$subtotal` variable.

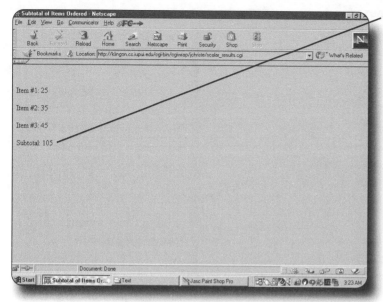

By including the HTML `print` script introduced in earlier chapters, you can display the results in an HTML page by creating a form or link to the application. I often use the test.html file. You can find that file on the CD that accompanies this book in the Chapter 3 examples.

You are now ready to learn the basic concepts for using mathematical operations.

Using Numbers as Scalar Variables

Numbers might be less confusing to use since you are already familiar with mathematical operations. With this in mind, you will likely find this section easy to understand and will be using the concepts in a short amount of time. Perl uses the basic mathematical symbols from everyday math; these are called the *mathematical operators*. You use mathematical operators on *operands*, which are the scalar variables on which you perform the operations.

Addition

You perform addition here just as you do using a standard calculator. You saw the addition of scalar variables in the previous section when you created and stored the result of an operation in a scalar variable.

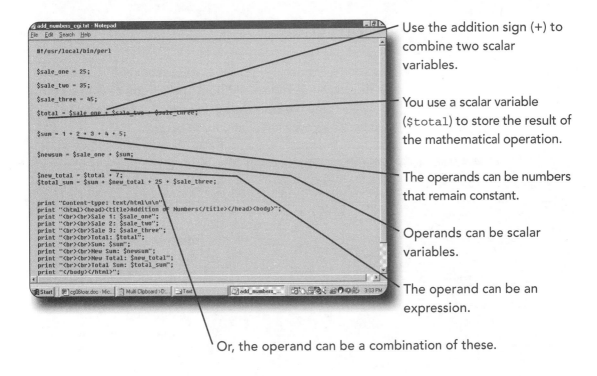

Use the addition sign (+) to combine two scalar variables.

You use a scalar variable ($total) to store the result of the mathematical operation.

The operands can be numbers that remain constant.

Operands can be scalar variables.

The operand can be an expression.

Or, the operand can be a combination of these.

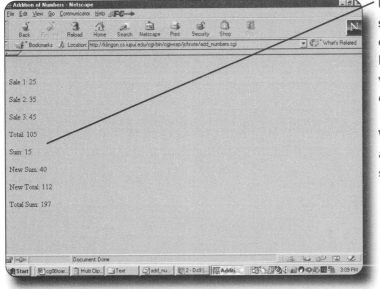

Using the HTML print script as before, you can output the results as an HTML page that shows the values of the mathematical operations.

With addition mastered, you are ready to start using subtraction.

Subtraction

As you have probably realized, you accomplish subtraction in the same manner as addition. The difference is that you now combine the operands using positive and negative values (see your elementary math books).

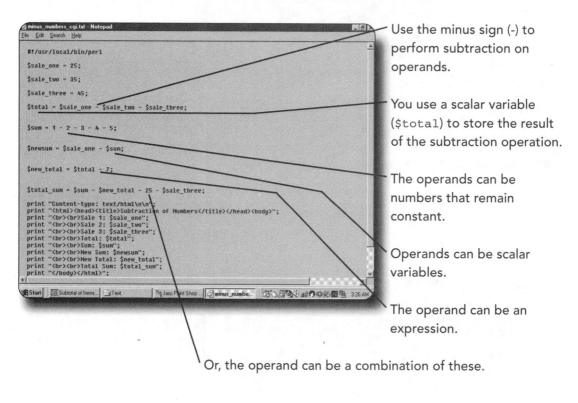

```
minus_numbers_cgi.txt - Notepad
File  Edit  Search  Help

#!/usr/local/bin/perl

$sale_one = 25;

$sale_two = 35;

$sale_three = 45;

$total = $sale_one - $sale_two - $sale_three;


$sum = 1 - 2 - 3 - 4 - 5;

$newsum = $sale_one - $sum;

$new_total = $total - 7;

$total_sum = $sum - $new_total - 25 - $sale_three;

print "Content-type: text/html\n\n";
print "<html><head><title>Subtraction of Numbers</title></head><body>";
print "<br><br>Sale 1: $sale_one";
print "<br><br>Sale 2: $sale_two";
print "<br><br>Sale 3: $sale_three";
print "<br><br>Total: $total";
print "<br><br>Sum: $sum";
print "<br><br>New Sum: $newsum";
print "<br><br>New Total: $new_total";
print "<br><br>Total Sum: $total_sum";
print "</body></html>";
```

Use the minus sign (-) to perform subtraction on operands.

You use a scalar variable ($total) to store the result of the subtraction operation.

The operands can be numbers that remain constant.

Operands can be scalar variables.

The operand can be an expression.

Or, the operand can be a combination of these.

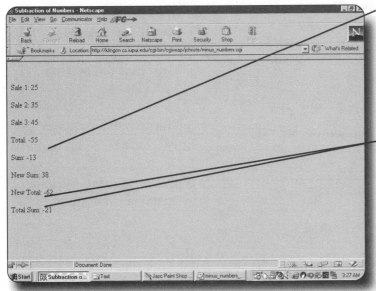

Using the HTML `print` script as before, you can output the results as an HTML page that shows the values of the mathematical operations.

Notice that the values are displayed a little differently from the previous example. The results are now displayed as negative values when the operation results in a negative value.

You can now use the basic concepts of addition and subtraction to perform the operations of multiplication and division.

Multiplication

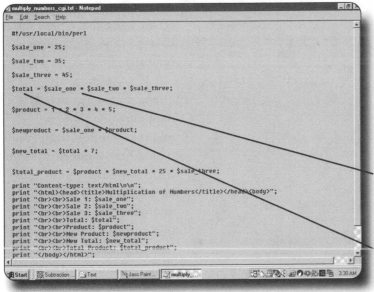

Multiplication is basically multiple addition operations that are performed by the computer, calculator, or human. Thus, the process of using this mathematical operation is like addition and subtraction.

Use the asterisk symbol (*) to perform multiplication on operands.

You use a scalar variable ($total) to store the result of the multiplication operation.

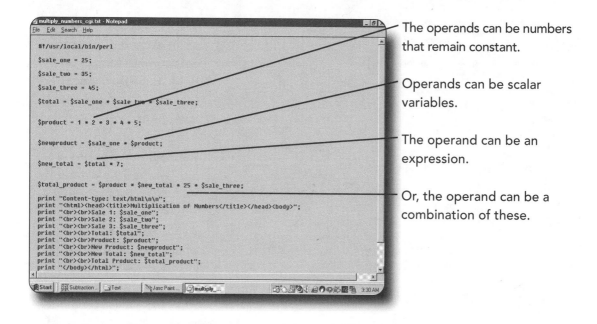

The operands can be numbers that remain constant.

Operands can be scalar variables.

The operand can be an expression.

Or, the operand can be a combination of these.

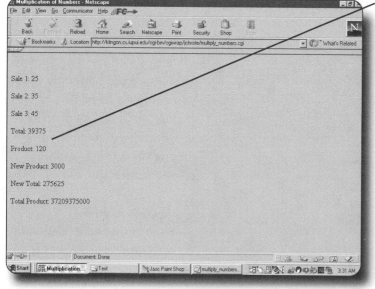

Using the HTML `print` script as before, you can output the results as an HTML page that shows the values of the mathematical operations.

There is an extension of multiplication that you might remember from your high school algebra class; it deals with exponents. Luckily, Perl has a mathematical operator for this purpose. Now that you have a grasp on multiplication of numbers, it is time to learn how to use exponential notation in your applications.

Raising to an Exponential Power

You should be familiar with exponential notation in mathematical operations; however, there is a good chance that it has been a while since your last math class, so this section looks at the process in detail.

NOTE

Remember, raising a number to an exponential power means multiplying that number by itself the number of times of the exponent. (2^5 equals $2 \times 2 \times 2 \times 2 \times 2$, not 2×5.)

You can enter the number you want to raise to an exponential power and multiply it by itself the number of times of the exponent: This works for small exponential values.

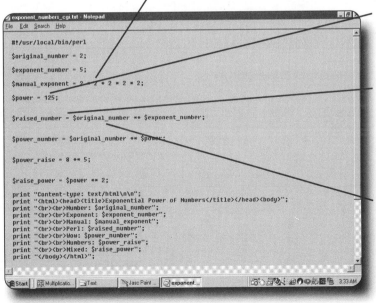

However, manually inputting the value when it's raised to a large power is not feasible.

To use the exponential operation, you type the scalar variable name used to store the result, followed by the equals sign.

You then type the operand of the number you are raising to a power.

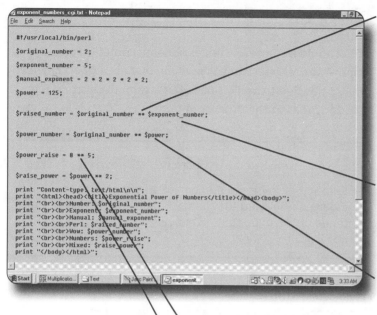

The operator for raising a number to an exponential power is two asterisks (**). The asterisks cannot have a space between them—placing a space between the asterisks causes problems in the execution of the application.

The double asterisks are followed by the power to which you are raising the initial operand.

You can use scalar variables as exponential power operands.

Number constants can also be used as operands.

Or, you can use a combination of both number constants and scalar variables as operands.

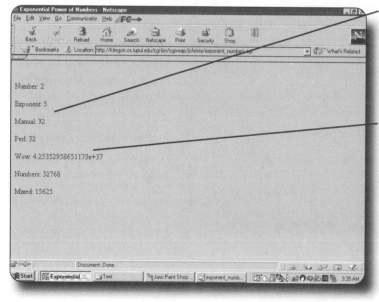

Using the HTML `print` script as before, you can output the results as an HTML page that shows the values of the mathematical operations.

Notice that Perl automatically converts the results to scientific notation when the number becomes too large to display normally. This is a helpful feature of Perl that keeps the application from producing errors. In some languages, the programmer has to write code to convert the value to scientific notation to prevent an error.

> **NOTE**
>
> Perl follows the common mathematical order of operations when computing mathematical operations. In the upcoming section "Using Multiple Operators," you learn how to force Perl to follow your order of operations instead of the normal order.

You are now ready to move on to division, the final mathematical operation that you learn in this section.

Division

Division is the reverse of multiplication. Thus, the process of using this mathematical operation is like addition and subtraction.

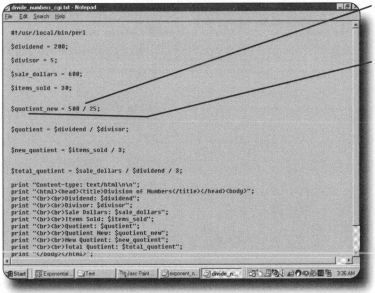

```perl
#!/usr/local/bin/perl

$dividend = 200;

$divisor = 5;

$sale_dollars = 600;

$items_sold = 30;

$quotient_new = 500 / 25;

$quotient = $dividend / $divisor;

$new_quotient = $items_sold / 3;

$total_quotient = $sale_dollars / $dividend / 3;

print "Content-type: text/html\n\n";
print "<html><head><title>Division of Numbers</title></head><body>";
print "<br><br>Dividend: $dividend";
print "<br><br>Divisor: $divisor";
print "<br><br>Sale Dollars: $sale_dollars";
print "<br><br>Items Sold: $items_sold";
print "<br><br>Quotient: $quotient";
print "<br><br>Quotient New: $quotient_new";
print "<br><br>New Quotient: $new_quotient";
print "<br><br>Total Quotient: $total_quotient";
print "</body></html>";
```

Use the forward slash (/) to perform division on operands.

You use a scalar variable ($quotient_new) to store the result of the division operation.

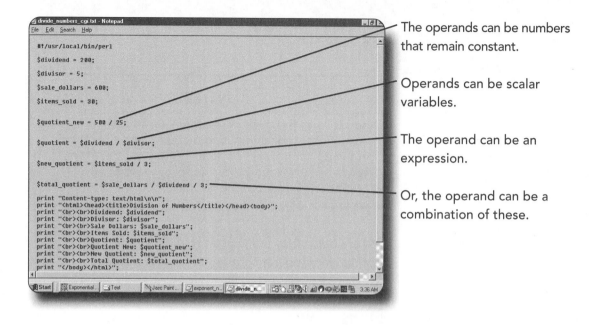

The operands can be numbers that remain constant.

Operands can be scalar variables.

The operand can be an expression.

Or, the operand can be a combination of these.

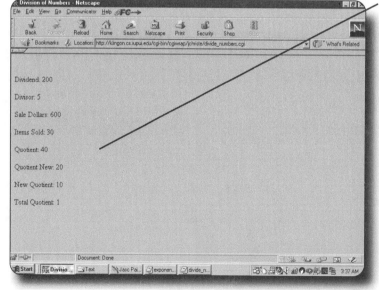

Using the HTML `print` script as before, you can output the results as an HTML page that shows the values of the mathematical operations.

There is the possibility that you will have a remainder from your division operation. Luckily, Perl has a mathematical operator for this purpose as well. Now that you have a grasp on division, it is time to learn how to get the remainder of a division operation.

Remainders from Division

In division operations, there is the possibility that the quotient is not an exact number and that it contains a remainder. Perl has created a function that deals with this situation; it is called the *modulus* operator.

CAUTION

The modulus operator does not return the answer to the division operation. The modulus operator returns only the remainder value of the division operation. If you want to return the answer of the division operation, you need to include the division operator, (/), in a line of code also. The following example includes both operators in order to show the result of the division as well as the remainder. Note that the division operator still displays the result as a decimal number—this decimal is the basis of the remainder displayed by the modulus operator.

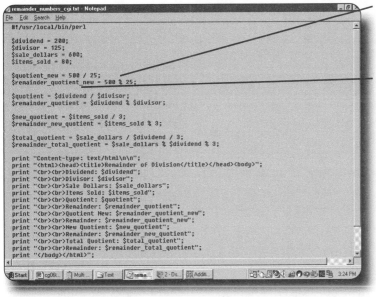

Use the percent sign to display the remainder of the division operation.

You use a scalar variable ($remainder_quotient_new) to store the result of the modulus operator.

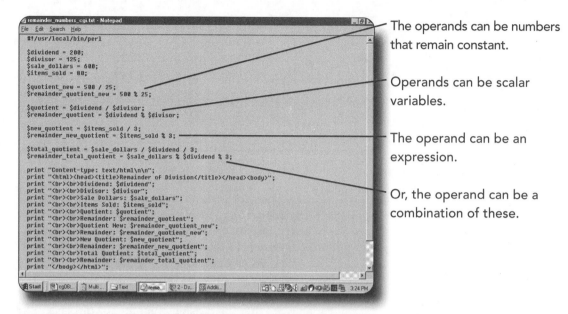

The operands can be numbers that remain constant.

Operands can be scalar variables.

The operand can be an expression.

Or, the operand can be a combination of these.

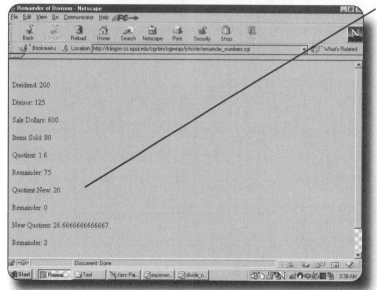

Using the HTML `print` script as before, you can output the results as an HTML page that shows the values of the mathematical operations.

Now that you know how to perform the various mathematical operations, it is time to learn how to force Perl to follow your order of operations instead of the common mathematical order of operations.

Using Multiple Operators

The standard mathematical order of operations follows a simple format. Parentheses are operated on first, followed by exponents, which are followed by multiplication, division, addition, and finally subtraction. These operations are always completed from left to right based upon the previous stipulations.

TIP

The following common mnemonic device used by schoolteachers might be helpful for remembering this order: Please Excuse My Dear Aunt Sally. The first letter of each word is the first letter of the mathematical operations in the correct order. (Parentheses, Exponents, Multiplication, Division, Addition, and Subtraction.)

The first operation, use of parentheses, is the secret to forcing Perl to follow your order of operations. You can use parentheses to make Perl perform the operations in the manner that fits your application.

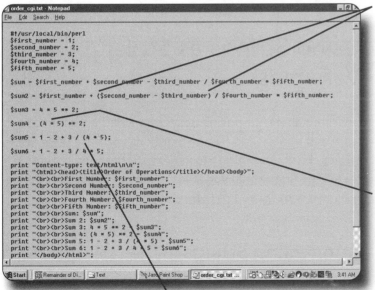

```
#!/usr/local/bin/perl
$first_number = 1;
$second_number = 2;
$third_number = 3;
$fourth_number = 4;
$fifth_number = 5;

$sum = $first_number + $second_number - $third_number / $fourth_number * $fifth_number;

$sum2 = $first_number + ($second_number - $third_number) / $fourth_number * $fifth_number;

$sum3 = 4 * 5 ** 2;

$sum4 = (4 * 5) ** 2;

$sum5 = 1 - 2 + 3 / (4 * 5);

$sum6 = 1 - 2 + 3 / 4 * 5;

print "Content-type: text/html\n\n";
print "<html><head><title>Order of Operations</title></head><body>";
print "<br><br>First Number: $first_number";
print "<br><br>Second Number: $second_number";
print "<br><br>Third Number: $third_number";
print "<br><br>Fourth Number: $fourth_number";
print "<br><br>Fifth Number: $fifth_number";
print "<br><br>Sum: $sum";
print "<br><br>Sum 2: $sum2";
print "<br><br>Sum 3: 4 * 5 ** 2 = $sum3";
print "<br><br>Sum 4: (4 * 5) ** 2 = $sum4";
print "<br><br>Sum 5: 1 - 2 + 3 / (4 * 5) = $sum5";
print "<br><br>Sum 6: 1 - 2 + 3 / 4 * 5 = $sum6";
print "</body></html>";
```

Notice that the variables and constants in this example are arranged in the same order: The difference in the mathematical operation is because of the parentheses. Using the parentheses changes the order of the operations.

By enclosing the numbers in parentheses, you force Perl to perform the multiplication before raising the number to an exponential power.

If you place the parentheses at the end of the mathematical expression, that part of the calculation is operated on first, even though the division is to the left of the parentheses.

You need to be careful when using parentheses because it is easy to become confused and produce an unintended result.

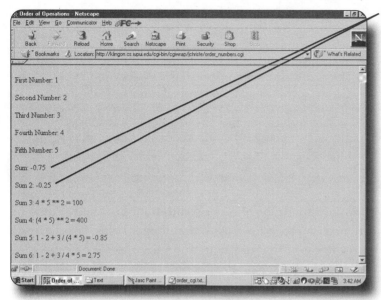

Notice that the result of $sum is different than the result of $sum2, even though they are in the same order.

You have enough knowledge about numbers as scalar variables; now you need to learn about using strings as scalar variables.

Using Strings as Scalar Variables

Unlike numbers, strings do not have myriad operations to learn and understand. The two options you have when using strings are concatenating (connecting) them and repeating them. The first option you learn is concatenation, which is the most widely used of the two options.

Connecting Strings

The correct terminology for connecting strings is *concatenation*. This is one of those words that you can use at parties to make yourself sound like a programmer or a computer nerd. As technical as it sounds, it is nothing more than joining two or more words, phrases, or expressions together. It is extremely useful when you want to display the contents of the form in a readable format.

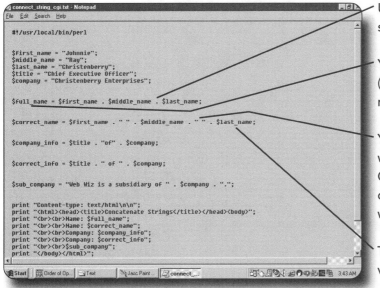

Use the period to combine string scalar variables.

You use a scalar variable ($full_name) to store the result of the concatenation.

You have to include spaces within quotation marks. Otherwise, the concatenation joins the words into a single string.

The strings can be scalar variables.

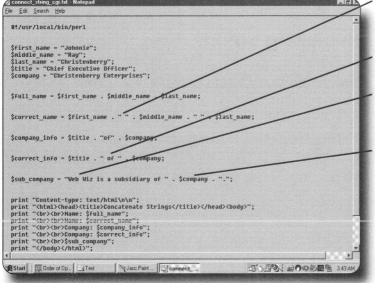

A string can contain an individual character.

A string can contain a term.

An expression or complete sentence can be a string.

Or, the operand can be a combination of these.

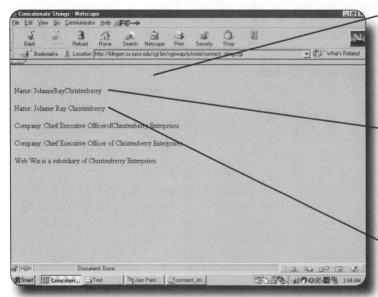

Using the HTML `print` script as before, you can output the results as an HTML page that shows the concatenated values.

Note how the strings are joined into a single string. This happens because no spaces were included in the variable `value`.

By including spaces within quotation marks in the variable `value`, you ensure that the text includes spaces and is readable.

This small but important step is often overlooked by beginning programmers and results in output that is confusing if it is even readable. Now that you know how to concatenate strings, you need to know how to repeat a string in your application.

Repeating Strings

Repeating a string is not an operation you use often; however, I include it here to make this a well-rounded reference tool for your Web development endeavors. This is a handy tool if you are creating a Mad Lib application, or an application that uses data to create a song, refrain, or cute statement.

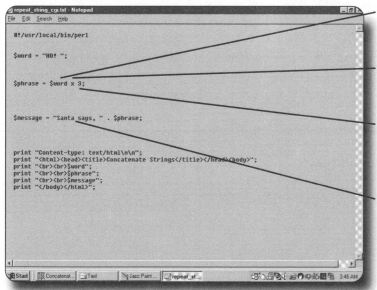

To repeat a string, you use a string or a variable name.

You follow the string or variable with a lowercase x.

This is followed by the number of times you want to repeat the string.

You can combine this syntax with string concatenation to produce a cute message.

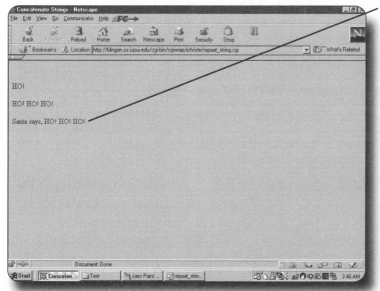

You can use this operation for shortcuts when typing repeated words, such as in this cute Christmas message.

You are now ready to look at ways to manipulate variable values.

Assigning Values to a Variable

There will be instances when you want to assign or change values in a variable. You learn several methods that enable you to do just that in this section.

Manipulating Variable Values

You have a few options that enable you to manipulate a variable's value. These include using the binary assignment operator, incrementing, and decrementing.

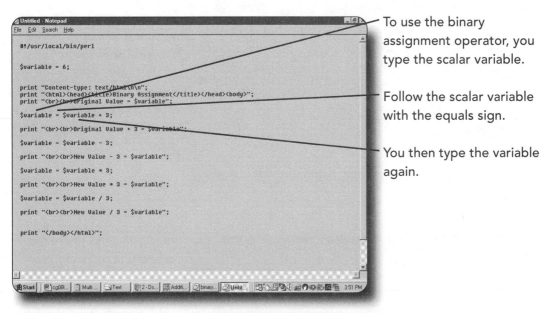

To use the binary assignment operator, you type the scalar variable.

Follow the scalar variable with the equals sign.

You then type the variable again.

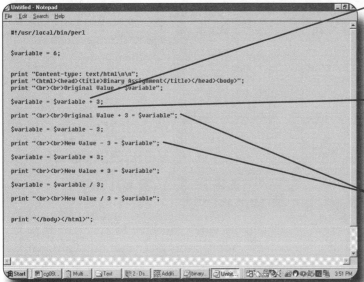

You follow this second variable with the mathematical operator you want to use.

The final step is to type the number you want to assign to the mathematical operation.

You can output the changing values by inserting a `print` statement between the binary assignments.

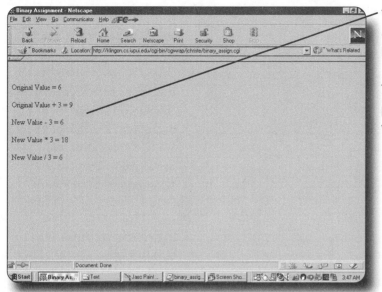

This HTML output shows the changes that result from the binary assignment operation.

The following shortcut provides the same results with less typing on your part.

The shortcut consists of typing the variable name.

You follow this with the mathematical operator you are using.

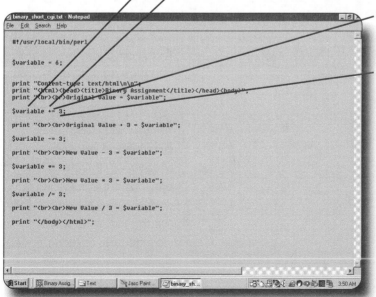

The equals sign follows the operator, without a space.

The final step is to type the value you will use with the operator.

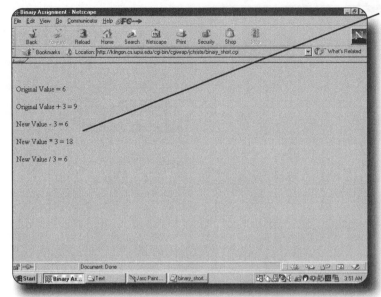

You can see that the results are identical to the longer version.

The next options you explore enable you to increment or decrement a variable. You will find this extremely beneficial in Chapter 9, "Conditional Statements."

Incrementing Variables

Incrementing basically involves adding 1 to the value of a variable. There are two ways that you can type this into your application: Both ways produce the same result.

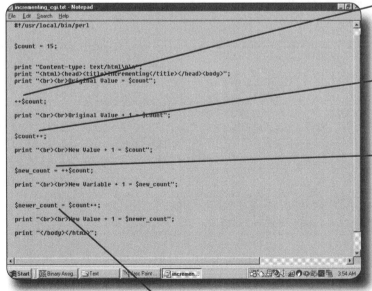

The first way to increment is to type two plus signs directly before the variable.

The second way is to type two plus signs directly after the variable.

You can also assign the incremented variable to another variable using the previous procedures. If you want the new assignment to use the value after it is incremented, include the plus signs before the variable.

If you want the new assignment to use the value before it is incremented, include the plus signs after the variable.

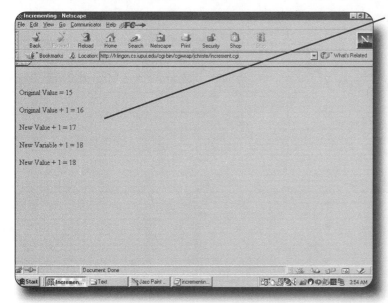

The results show the difference between using the autoincrement operator before and after the variable.

Now you can explore the process of decrementing a variable.

Decrementing Variables

You have probably realized that decrementing is the opposite of incrementing. The rules are the same and you need only change the plus signs to minus signs (--).

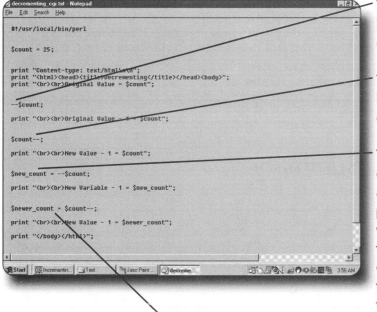

The first way to decrement is to type two minus signs directly before the variable.

The second way to decrement is to type two minus signs directly after the variable.

You can also assign the decremented variable to another variable using the previous procedures. If you want the new assignment to use the value after it is decremented, include the minus signs before the variable.

If you want the new assignment to use the value before it is decremented, include the minus signs after the variable.

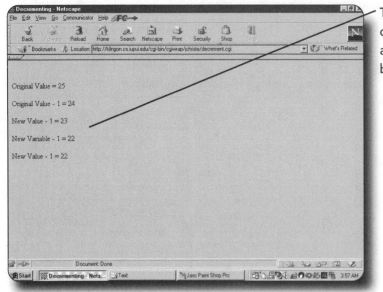

The results show the difference between using the autodecrement operator before and after the variable.

NOTE

The autoincrement operator works on numbers and strings only when they contain numbers and letters only. The autodecrement operator will not work on numbers and strings; the autodecrement operator only works on numbers.

Summary

In this chapter, you gained the knowledge necessary to use scalar variables in varying degrees in your applications. You know how to store values, how to manipulate numbers and strings, how to store and manipulate variable values, and how to increment and decrement variables. These skills will be useful as you explore arrays and hashes in the next chapters, and they will be priceless when you begin the in-depth look at conditional statements in Chapter 9. Well, it's now time to learn about arrays.

7

Arrays

Now that you understand scalar variables and their uses, you need to gain a better understanding of arrays. You know that a scalar is any piece of data, and in Chapter 2, "Writing Your CGI Application," you learned that arrays are groups of scalars and can be thought of as lists of data. You also know that scalars can be groups of constants or variables, and arrays can be numbers or strings. Remember that all arrays begin with the at sign, and the @ shape represents the "a" in array. After a review of basic array information, it is time to look at what you will learn in this chapter. In this chapter, you'll learn how to:

- Split a scalar into an array
- Determine and store the length of an array
- Modify an array
- Manipulate an array

Splitting a Scalar Into an Array

In Chapter 6, "Scalars," you learned how to create an array variable from a list of data; however, you were not told how the data is referenced. The elements in the array are numbered automatically, starting with 0. This means that the reference number will be less than the number of elements.

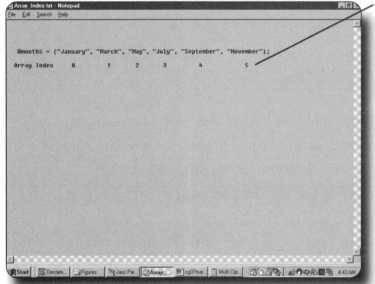

For example, if you have six elements in your array, they are numbered from 0 to 5.

This can be confusing and often causes problems in your applications if you forget this basic concept. The reference number is usually called the *array index*. Your application uses the array index when you use, modify, and manipulate arrays.

Reasons for Splitting a Scalar

You are probably wondering when or why you would need to split a scalar. This is a good question. Remember how the server receives the data from your form?

The server receives data in a single, continuous line that shows all the `names` and `values` separated by equals signs, ampersands, and plus signs.

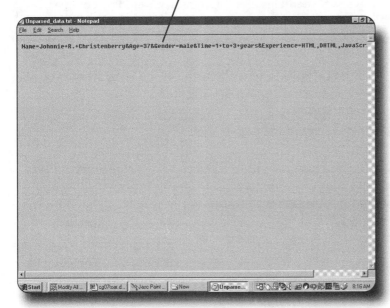

The data is not useful to your application in this state. Also, the process of parsing a form's data results in a single scalar variable with the `values` separated by commas. Splitting a scalar into an array enables you to convert the `values` of the scalar variable into an array that has an array index.

The Process of Splitting a Scalar

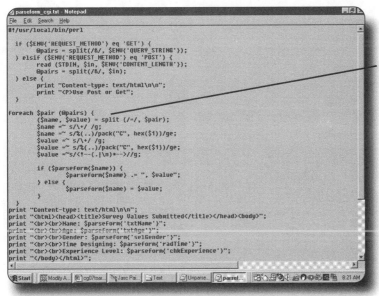

The process of splitting a scalar into an array is simple.

You have already seen this process in the parseform.cgi script created in Chapter 5, "Getting the Data Into Your CGI Application."

Now, you can see what actually occurred when you used the `split` function in that script.

NOTE

This splitting process works only when the scalar variable contains a list of items separated by commas, such as menu selections or check boxes from your form.

The first step is to type the name of the array where you want to store the scalar variable items.

Next, you type the equals sign.

Then you type the `split` command with an open parenthesis.

This is followed by the expression, usually a comma, which separates the scalar `values`. The comma is enclosed in forward slashes (/ , /).

Finally, you type a comma, a space, the scalar variable `name` that you want to split, the closing parenthesis, and the semicolon that ends the statement.

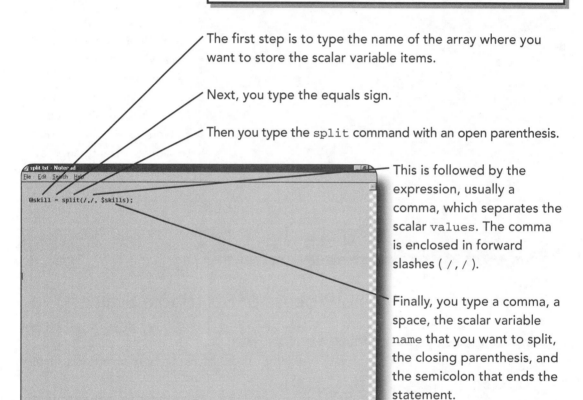

NOTE

Since the primary delimiter used with server data is a plus sign, Perl uses the regular expression `/\s+/` to separate the string into pieces automatically if you do not include a specific expression.

This explains the process of splitting a scalar variable, which you use in your parsing scripts and other applications. The next section shows you how to determine the number of elements in a particular array.

Determining the Length of an Array

You might find it useful to know how many elements are in an array when data has been entered into it. You generally use one of two ways to get this information—either using a scalar variable or using the index number. Both methods are discussed next.

Using a Scalar Variable

The way you can determine the length of an array is to store the array in a scalar variable. This is a simple process and involves a single line of code.

```
store_array_length_scalar_cgi.txt - Notepad
File  Edit  Search  Help
#!/usr/local/bin/perl
require "subparseform.lib";
&Parse_Form;

$skills = $parseform{'chkExperience'};


@skill = split (/,/, $skills);


$length = @skill;


print "Content-type: text/html\n\n";
print "<html><head><title>Storing an Array Length in a Scalar Variable</title></head><body>";

print "<h3>You selected <font color = red>$length</font> skills for your experience level.";
print "</h3><br><br>";
print "<h3>Your Web skills include the following skills:</h3>";

print "<ol type = 1>";

foreach $item (@skill)  {
  print "<li><font color = green>$item</font>";
}

print "</ol>";

print "</body></html>";
```

The first thing you do to parse the data into usable terms is use a form-parsing subroutine, which is discussed fully in Chapter 11, "Subroutines." Don't worry about what the subroutine is accomplishing at this point. Focus on the code that follows.

You then split the scalar using the code from the previous section.

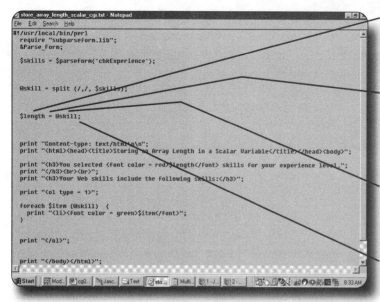

You include a scalar variable name in which you want to store the length of the array.

You use the equals sign to assign the number of array elements to the scalar variable you just created.

You then type the name of the array whose length you want to determine.

Finally, you type a semicolon to end the statement.

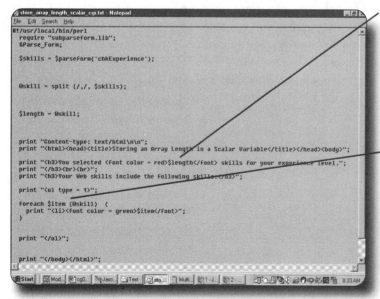

You include the scalar name that contains the array length in the text of the print command.

NOTE

The foreach lines are discussed in Chapter 9, "Conditional Statements." The important thing to note at this point is that the scalar $item refers to the items selected from the @skill array. These are the choices made on the form by the users.

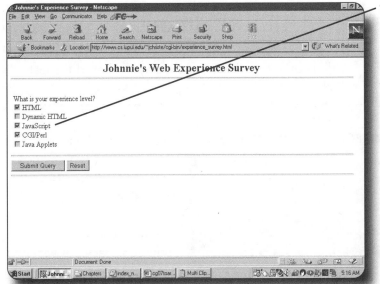

The form, experience_survey_html.txt located on the CD in the examples from this chapter that calls the store_array_length.cgi application, has three of the five choices selected.

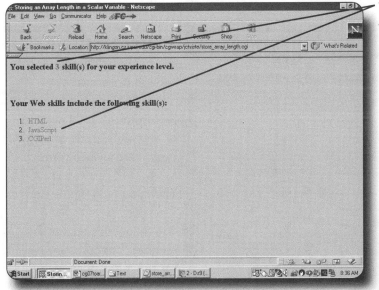

The page generated by the application displays the number of elements and displays the selections in a list.

Using the Index Number

You can also use the index number to determine the length of an array. There are a couple of different ways to achieve this. The first way returns the index number of the last element in the array; the second way returns the total number of elements in the array.

CAUTION

Remember that the index numbers of an array start with 0 not 1; therefore, if the index number of the last item is 4, the array contains five elements.

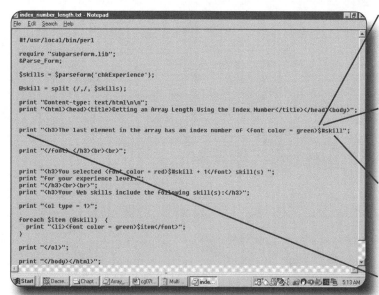

To determine the index number of the last element in an array, you use the dollar sign.

You then type a pound sign without a space between the characters.

The name of the variable, without the at sign, follows. Again, there are no spaces between the characters.

You type this information in the print statement as though it were text.

To return the total number of elements in the array, you type the previous term.

Then you type a plus sign.

You follow this with the number 1 to compensate for the index number beginning with 0.

You also include this code within the print statement as though it were text.

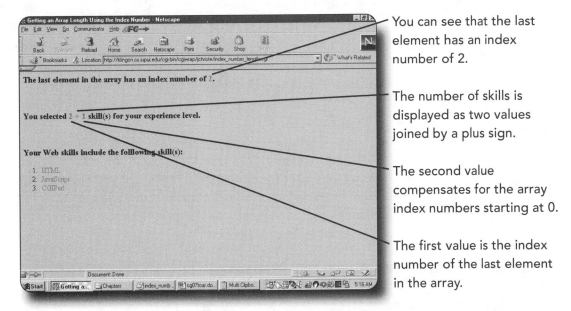

You can see that the last element has an index number of 2.

The number of skills is displayed as two values joined by a plus sign.

The second value compensates for the array index numbers starting at 0.

The first value is the index number of the last element in the array.

Now that you know how to determine the length (or number of elements) of an array, you need to know how to retrieve data from an array.

Retrieving Array Data

When you retrieve data from an array, you have two basic choices: You can retrieve a specific item or you can retrieve multiple items. You use the index numbers of the array to accomplish this, and you learn how to do both in this section.

CAUTION

Remember that the index numbers of an array start with 0, therefore, there is always one more element than the number value. If the last index number is 3, there are four elements in the array.

Retrieving a Specific Item

There will be times when you want to get a specific piece of data from an array. You can retrieve any piece of data from the array. The following examples walk you through the options.

The first thing you do is type the name of the array from which you want to get the data. Note that you use a dollar sign instead of an at sign. This is because you are retrieving an individual piece of data (which is scalar), not the list of data.

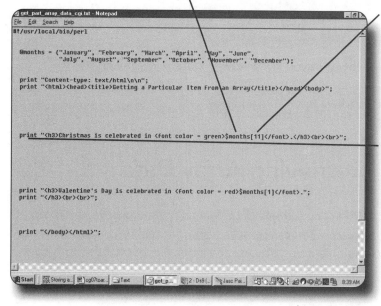

You then type the index number of the data you want to retrieve, enclosed in brackets ([ ]). There cannot be a space between the name and the bracket.

You include this code within a print statement as though it were text.

```
get_part_array_data_cgi.txt - Notepad
File  Edit  Search  Help

#!/usr/local/bin/perl

@months = ("January", "February", "March", "April", "May", "June",
    "July", "August", "September", "October", "November", "December");

print "Content-type: text/html\n\n";
print "<html><head><title>Getting a Particular Item From an Array</title></head><body>";


print "<h3>Christmas is celebrated in <font color = green>$months[11]</font>.</h3><br><br>";


print "<h3>Valentine's Day is celebrated in <font color = red>$months[1]</font>.";
print "</h3><br><br>";


print "</body></html>";
```

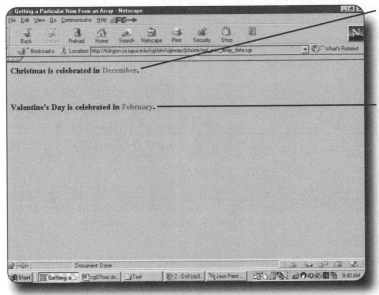

The HTML page displays the month that corresponds to the index number of the element from the array.

Notice that the elements do not have to be used in their numbered sequence. February is before December in the array, but you can retrieve them in any order you want.

You can also assign a particular piece of data from an array to a scalar variable.

To do this, you include the scalar variable name you are going to use to assign the data.

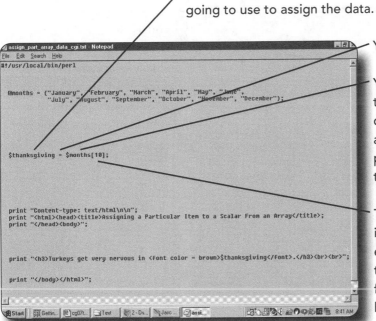

You then type an equals sign.

You then type the name of the array (starting with a dollar sign—remember you are retrieving an individual piece of data) from which the data will come.

This code is followed by the index number of the element you are assigning to the scalar variable. Don't forget to enclose it in brackets.

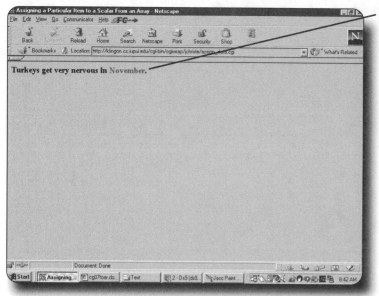

You can see that the correct month was assigned from the array.

Another option you have is to assign the elements to scalar variables starting with the first element.

You accomplish this by typing the scalar variable name enclosed in parentheses.

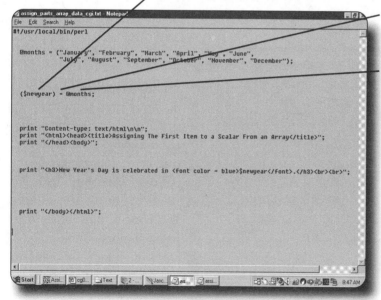

You then type the equals sign.

Finally, you type the array name, starting with an at sign. Be sure to end the statement with a semicolon.

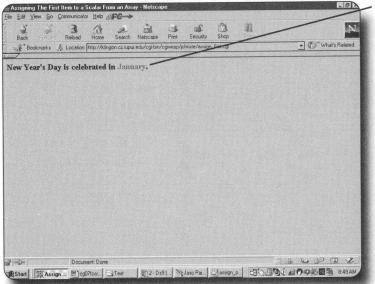

You can see that the correct month was assigned from the array.

You can repeat this for as many of the elements as you want to assign; however, the elements are always assigned in consecutive order.

You type the same beginning as before to assign the first element to a scalar variable.

Then you use a comma to separate the scalar variable names.

Next, you type the second scalar variable name where you want the second element to be assigned.

You repeat the two previous steps for each scalar variable that will hold the sequential array elements.

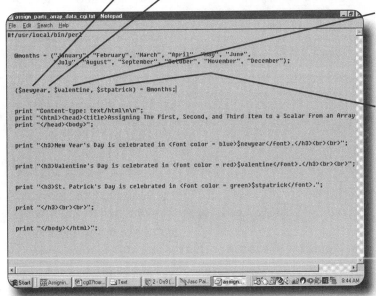

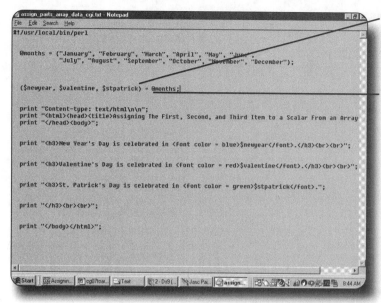

Remember to end the scalar variable list with a closing parenthesis.

As usual, you type the equals sign and the array name, which starts with an at sign. Be sure to end the statement with a semicolon.

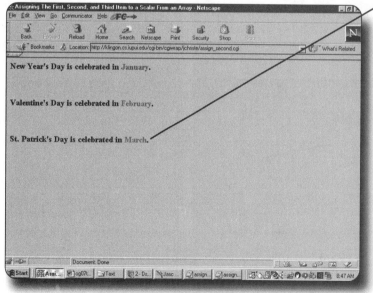

You can see that the correct months were assigned.

Having mastered retrieving specific items, you are ready to learn how to retrieve multiple items from an array.

Retrieving Multiple Items

There might be times when you want to retrieve more than one item from an array, and these items might not be sequentially listed. For this reason, you need to know how to retrieve multiple elements from an array.

You need to create an array that contains the values you will be retrieving. Because the array's index numbers start with 0, you might want to include a bogus value as the first element. The use of a bogus value will eliminate problems that occur when using a counter variable to retrieve the elements from the array.

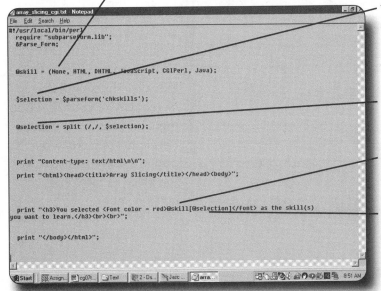

You then create a scalar variable and assign the parsed data from your form's check boxes.

Then, you split the scalar variable into an array.

To use the retrieved data, you type the original array name.

You follow this by the name of the array you created to hold the split scalar data. This starts with the at sign because you are retrieving a list of data.

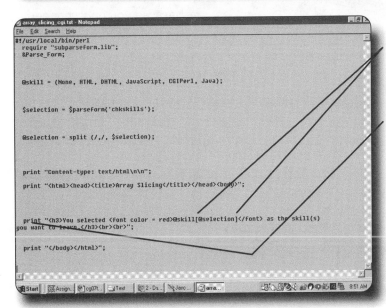

The second array name needs to be enclosed in brackets.

You include the two previous steps in the print statement as though they were text.

The entire HTML code for this example, array_slicing_html.txt, is located on the CD in the examples for this chapter.

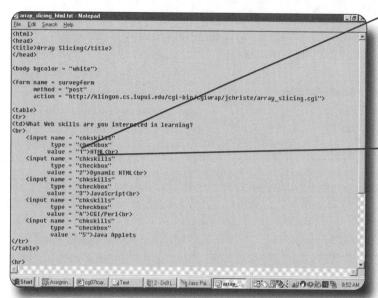

Notice that the values of the check boxes have changed from the previous examples. They are now numerical values starting with 1 and ending with 5.

These numbers match the index numbers of the array elements that correspond to the labels used in the form. Recall that you created a bogus first element to take the place of the 0 starting index number.

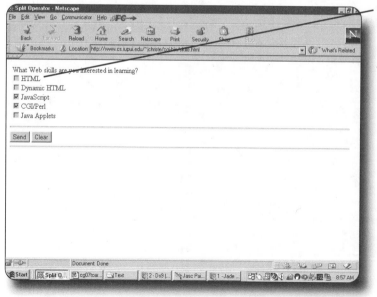

The form looks the same as in the previous examples because you only changed the values.

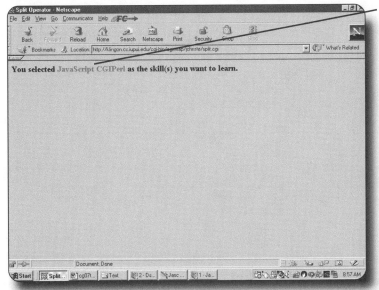

The HTML page generated by the application displays the selections the users choose embedded in the text.

You also have the option of displaying any of the elements from the array on the generated HTML page.

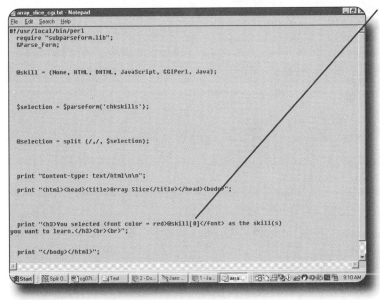

To accomplish this, you replace the name of the second array from the previous example with the index number of the element you want to display.

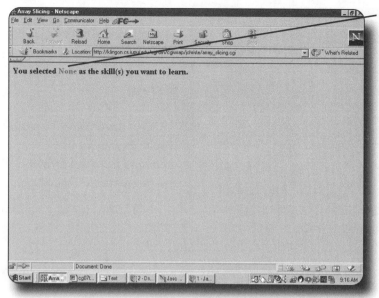

Notice that you can display an element from the array that was not one of the selections available on the form.

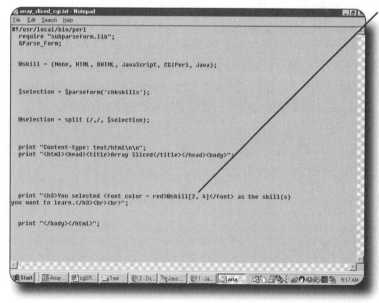

To display multiple elements using this option, type the index numbers of the elements you want to display separated by commas.

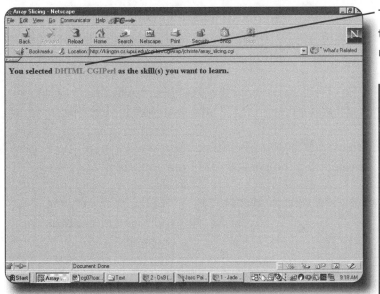

This displays the elements that correspond to the index numbers of the array.

With data retrieval under your belt, it is time to move forward and learn how to modify an array.

Modifying an Array

You are probably asking yourself why you would need to modify an array when the elements are assigned by you or by the users' choices. There are numerous reasons to modify an array, and they will become clear as you progress through the following examples. Recall that you modified scalar variables in the previous chapter; now you learn how to modify arrays.

Modifying the Entire Array

In earlier examples, you saw the `foreach` loop used to assist in the display of array elements. The `foreach` loop is explained in detail in Chapter 9. When this operation is performed, the array is modified permanently. Knowing this enables you to use the `foreach` loop to make modifications to the entire array.

The complete code for this example, modify_all_array_cgi.txt, can be found on the CD in the examples for this chapter.

To modify all elements using the `foreach` loop, you begin by splitting the parsed data from your form.

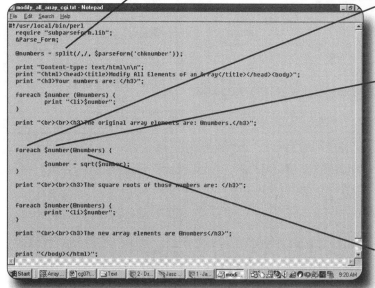

To actually modify the data, you type the **foreach** command.

You then type the `name` of the scalar, starting with a dollar sign because you are retrieving individual data (scalars). You can use any name for the scalar. I used `$number` because it made logical sense.

This is followed by the array name, starting with an at sign because you are referencing the entire list of elements.

The array `name` needs to be enclosed in parentheses.

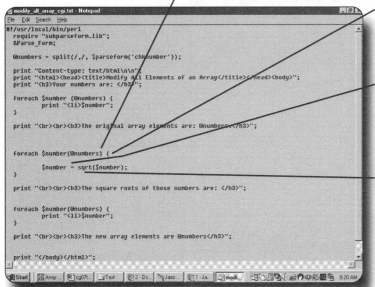

To start the loop, you need to use the open brace character (**{**).

Next, you type the scalar `name`, starting with the dollar sign. Be sure to include the equals sign next.

You follow this with the operator you are using to change the array elements.

You enclose the scalar `name`, starting with the dollar sign in parentheses.

You then type a semicolon to end the statement.

Finally, you type the closing brace character (**}**) to end the loop.

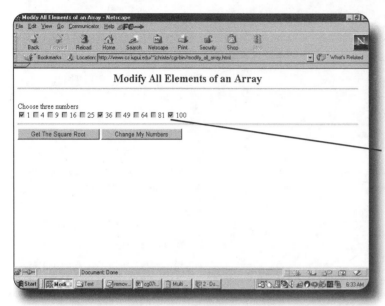

The complete code for this example, modify_all_array_html.txt, can be found on the CD in the examples for this chapter.

The users make their selections and submit the form here.

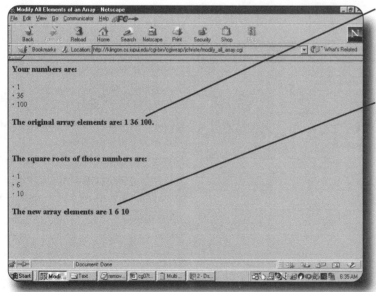

The original array elements created by the user's selection are displayed once the form is submitted.

The modified array elements are also displayed.

Basically, you have retrieved each of the elements from the array, modified each of them, and assigned the new elements back to the original array. Pretty simple, huh? Now you need to know how to add elements to an array.

Adding Elements to an Array

You have two options when adding elements to an array: You can either add the elements to the beginning of the array, or you can add the elements to the end of the array. This section discusses both methods.

The HTML code for the following examples is located on the CD in the examples from this chapter.

Adding Elements to the Beginning of an Array

Luckily, there is a Perl function designed specifically to add elements to the beginning of an array. This example uses the add_begin_array_html.txt example on the CD.

First, type **unshift**. It is the Perl operator that performs the "add to beginning" function.

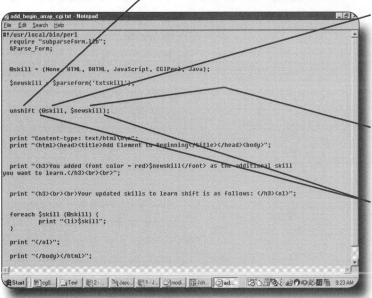

You follow this operator with the name of the array to which you are adding the new element, followed by a comma.

You then include the name of the scalar variable that contains the new element.

Both the array name and the scalar name need to be enclosed in the same set of parentheses.

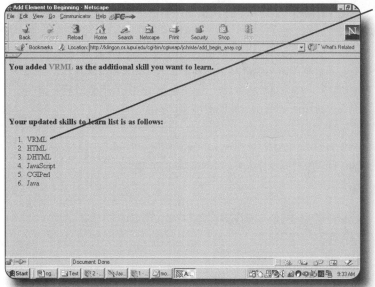

The array now contains the new skill as the first element in the array.

You can also assign the new element to the existing array. This example uses the add_begin_array2_html.txt example on the CD.

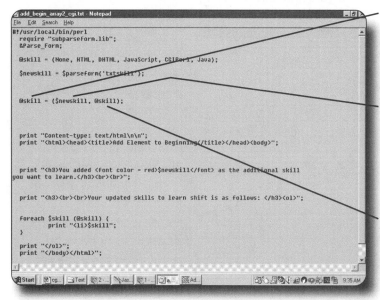

To assign a new element to an existing array, type the array name, followed by an equals sign.

Then, you type the element you are adding—the element can be scalar constant, a variable, or an array—followed by a comma.

You then type the array name again. Be sure to enclose the new element and the array name in parentheses and to end with a semicolon.

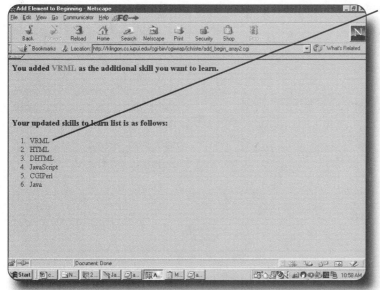

This option results in the same response as the previous example.

The process of adding an element to the end of an array is similar.

Adding Elements to the End of an Array

You can use a predefined Perl operator to add an element to the end of an array. This example uses the add_end_array_html.txt example on the CD.

You first type **push**, the Perl operator that performs the "add to end" function.

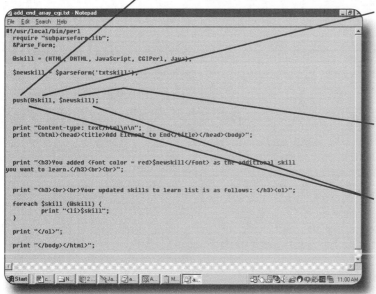

You follow this operator with the name of the array to which you are adding the new element, followed by a comma.

You then type the name of the scalar variable that contains the new element.

Both the array name and the scalar name need to be enclosed in the same set of parentheses.

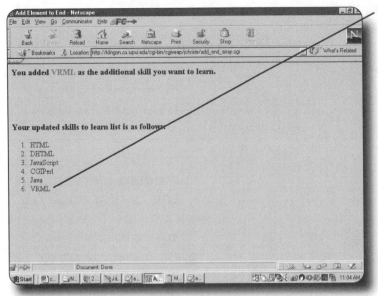

The array now contains the new skill as the last element in the array.

You can also assign the new element to an existing array. This example uses the add_end_array2_html.txt example on the CD.

To assign a new element to an existing array, type the array name followed by an equals sign.

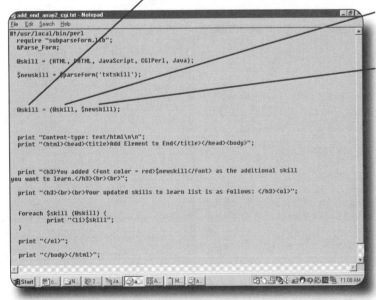

You then type the array name again followed by a comma.

Then, you type the element you are adding—the element can be a scalar constant, a variable, or an array. Be sure to enclose the array name and the new element in parentheses, and to end with a semicolon.

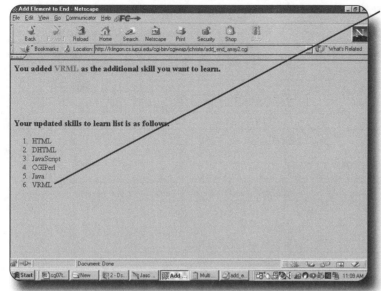

This option results in the same response as the previous example.

Removing Array Elements

There might be times when you want to remove elements from an array. Just like when you add elements to an array, Perl has predefined operators for this function.

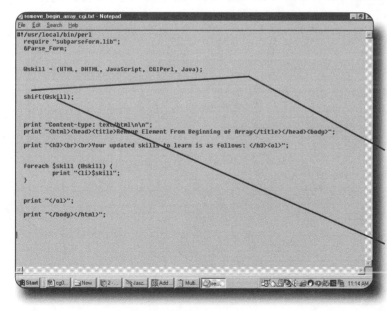

Removing the First Element

If you want to remove the first element of an array, you use the `shift` operator.

You first include the `shift` operator, which performs the "remove first element" function.

You then type the `name` of the array from which you want to remove the element.

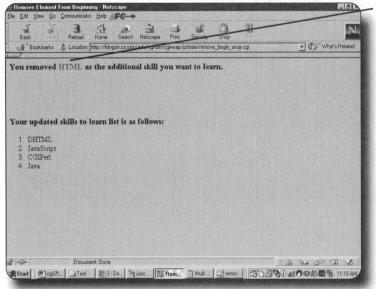

This process removes the first element from the list, as shown by the generated HTML page. Notice that the individual element is not listed in the "removed" sentence.

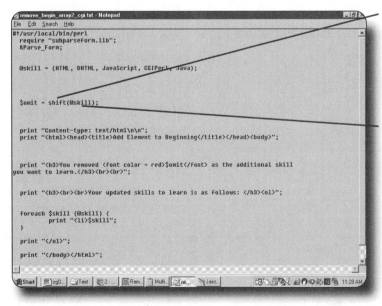

Another option is to assign the removed element to a scalar variable. This enables you to show the elements that have been removed.

The final step is to type the name of the array that you are modifying, enclosed in parentheses.

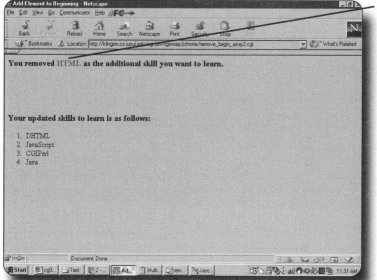

This response looks like the previous example because they perform the same function. However, because you assigned the removed element to a scalar variable, you can display it on the HTML page.

Removing the Last Element

Removing the last element is similar to removing the first element, except you use a different operator.

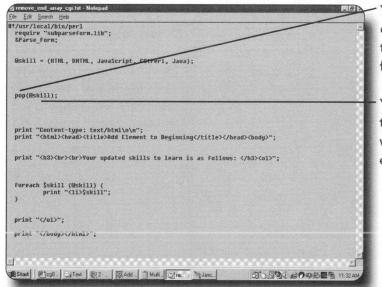

You first include the pop operator, which performs the "remove last element" function.

You then type the name of the array from which you want to remove the element.

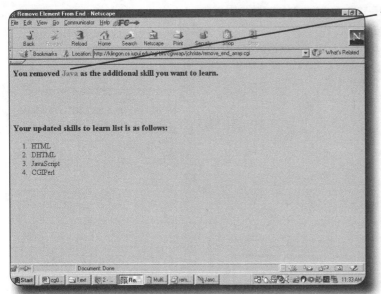

This process removes the last element from the list, as shown by the generated HTML page. Notice that the individual element is not listed in the "removed" sentence.

Another option is to assign the removed element to a scalar variable. This again enables you to show the elements that have been removed.

To assign the removed element to a scalar variable, you type the name of the scalar that holds the element, followed by the equals sign.

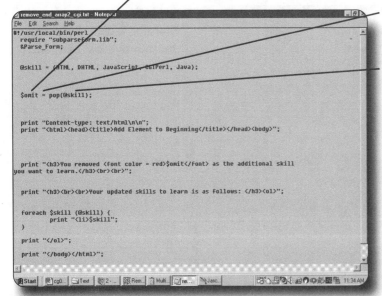

You then type the pop operator.

The final step is to type the name of the array that you are modifying, enclosed in parentheses.

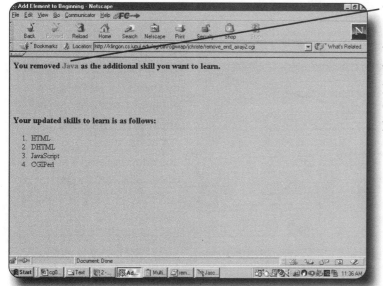

This response looks like the previous example because they perform the same function. However, because you assigned the removed element to a scalar variable, you can display it on the HTML page.

Replacing Array Elements

Perl also has predefined operators that enable you to replace individual elements of an array. This can be performed on a single element or on multiple elements.

Replacing a Single Element

Replacing a single element in an array is a simple, yet powerful, process.

To replace a single element, you type the `name` of the array you are modifying.

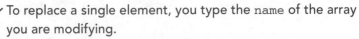

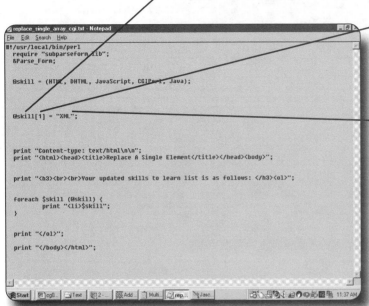

This is followed immediately by the index number of the element you want to replace, enclosed in brackets.

You then type an equals sign, followed by the scalar variable, or scalar constant, to be inserted into the array. Remember, if you are using a quoted literal it must be enclosed in quotation marks.

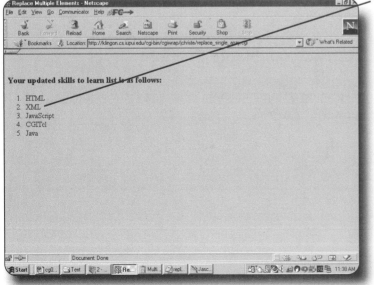

This removes the original element with the index number you used and replaces it with the new element.

Replacing Multiple Elements

Replacing multiple elements in an array is a slightly more involved process than replacing a single element.

To replace multiple elements, you type the name of the array you are modifying.

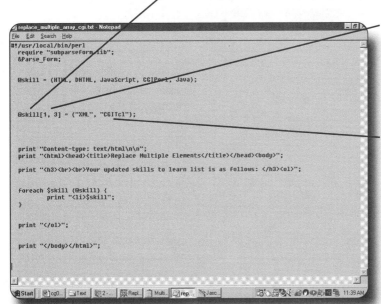

This is followed immediately by the index numbers of the elements to be replaced, enclosed in brackets, and separated by commas.

You then type an equals sign, followed by the new values for the scalar variables, or scalar constants, to be inserted into the array enclosed in parentheses. Remember, if you are using a quoted literal it must be enclosed in quotation marks.

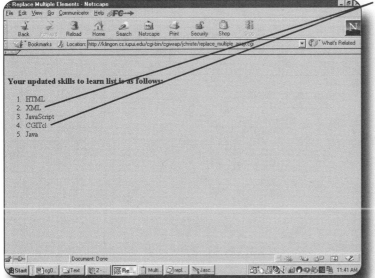

This process removes the original elements with the index numbers you used and replaces them with the new elements.

Reversing the Order of Elements

Perl enables you to reverse the order of the elements of an array using a predefined operator. This process also changes the index numbers of the elements because their order in the array has changed. The best method for doing this is by assigning the reversed array to a new array.

First, you type the new array name to which you will be assigning the reversed array, followed by the equals sign.

To reverse the order of the elements in an array, you include the reverse operator.

This operator is followed by the name of the array whose order you want to reverse, enclosed in parentheses.

This process reverses the order of the elements of the array.

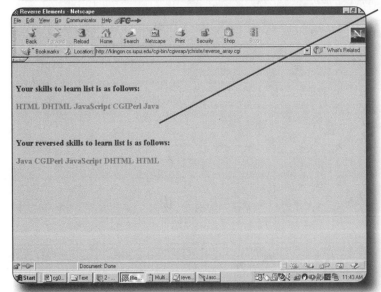

Manipulating Arrays

Another feature you might find useful in Perl is the capability to use predefined operators to manipulate arrays. The methods you use include combining arrays and sorting arrays.

Combining Arrays

The ability to combine the elements of two arrays can be powerful, depending on how you use it in your applications. As complicated as it might sound, it is actually a simple process.

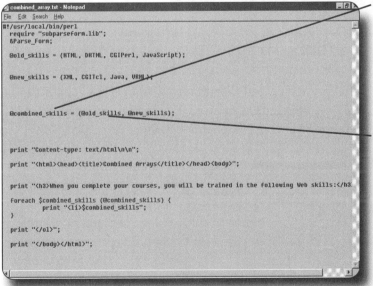

To begin combining two arrays, you need to type the name of the new variable that you will use to store the new array, followed by the equals sign.

You then type the name of the first array, a comma, and then the name of the second array. This text should be enclosed in parentheses.

TIP

If you want the elements of the second array to be listed at the beginning of the new array, simply reverse the order of the original arrays in the parentheses.

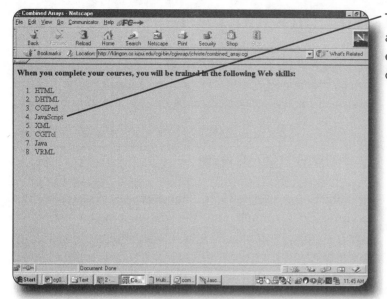

The result is a larger array that contains the elements from both of the original arrays.

Sorting Arrays

The final manipulating feature you learn is the capability to sort the elements in an array. This feature enables you to arrange elements in alphabetical order.

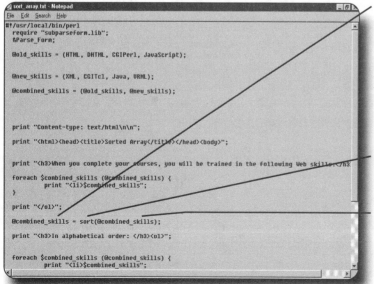

The best way to sort elements in alphabetical order is to assign the rearranged array back to itself. So, you need to type the array name followed by the equals sign.

You then include the sort operator.

This operator is followed by the array name, enclosed in parentheses.

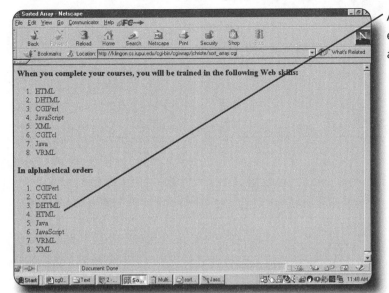

As you can see, the elements are now listed in alphabetical order.

Summary

In this chapter, you learned how to split a scalar into an array, how to determine the length of an array, and how to retrieve data from an array. You were also introduced to various forms of modifying and manipulating arrays. Now that you have mastered arrays, you need to understand a more advanced form of an array, the *hash*, which is covered in the next chapter.

8

Hashes

Hashes, known also as associative arrays, consist of associated elements that are arranged in pairs. These pairs appear in a specific order, starting with the key and then the value. The order of the key and value is important; however, the order of the pairs does not matter.

The pair order is of little importance because the hash uses the key to reference the value instead of using an index number, as in an array. Each pair's key is taken from the `name` attribute of the input tag from the form where the data has been received, whereas the value of the hash is derived from the `value` attribute of the same input tag. Remember that all hashes begin with the percent sign (%), and the % shape represents the linked pairs in a hash. In this chapter, you'll learn about:

- Checking for the existence of a key
- Retrieving hash values using keys
- Retrieving all hash values and keys
- Retrieving specific keys and values
- Removing key-value pairs

NOTE

Many of the examples in this chapter use conditional statements (if/else, foreach, while, etc.) that you are not introduced to until Chapter 9, "Conditional Statements." Don't worry about understanding the conditional statements; instead, focus on the operation at hand. You will probably realize what the conditional statements are doing if you take the time to read through them; however, it is not necessary for you to do so.

Checking for the Existence of a Key

You might want to check a hash to determine whether a particular key exists before you attempt to use the key in your application.

Why Checking Is Important

Checking for a key prior to using it in your application not only saves time, it enables you to double-check that you are using the correct spelling. For example, in the applications in Chapter 7, "Arrays," you saw that some of the array names differed only by an "s"; this can also happen with a key. Forms often have to address input fields that are named Address1 and Address2. You can see that this similarity can lead to complications and make it easier to use the wrong name for the key.

How to Check for a Key

Checking for a key requires that you use an operator that makes logical sense, as you noticed about the operators in Chapter 7.

You need to include the exists operator—it searches for the existence of a hash key.

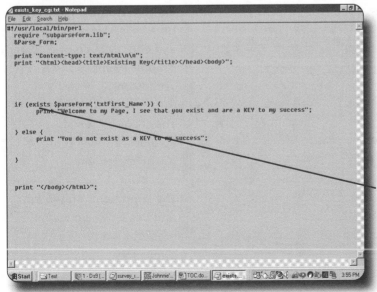

```
exists_key_cgi.txt - Notepad
File  Edit  Search  Help
#!/usr/local/bin/perl
require "subparseform.lib";
&Parse_Form;

print "Content-type: text/html\n\n";
print "<html><head><title>Existing Key</title></head><body>";


if (exists $parseform{'txtFirst_Name'}) {
     print "Welcome to my Page, I see that you exist and are a KEY to my success";

} else {
     print "You do not exist as a KEY to my success";

}


print "</body></html>";
```

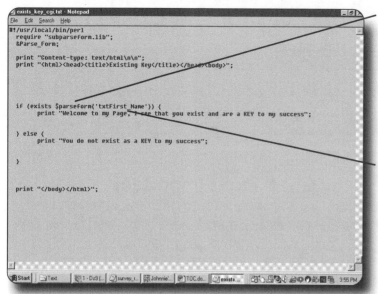

Next, type the name of the hash that you want to check. Start the hash name with the dollar sign because you are looking for an individual piece of data (scalar) from the hash.

You then type the name of the key, enclosed in single quotation marks (' '), which in turn need to be enclosed in curly brackets ({ }).

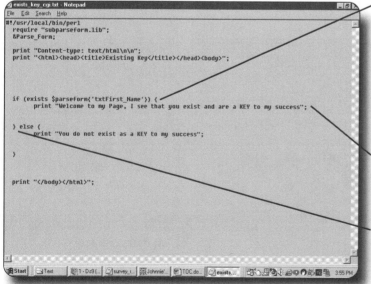

Because this is part of a conditional statement, the entire statement needs to be enclosed in parentheses, and ends with an open curly bracket ({) instead of a semicolon.

The required semicolon appears at the end of the print statement.

The conditional statement requires a closing curly bracket (}) after the semicolon.

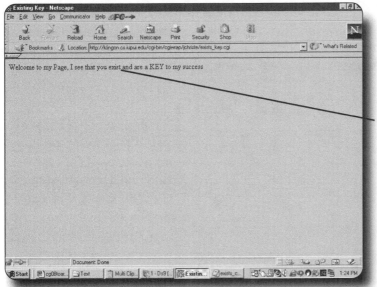

The complete code for this example, exists_key_html.txt, can be found on the CD in the examples for this chapter.

This example shows that the key exists; the application produces an HTML page that verifies its existence.

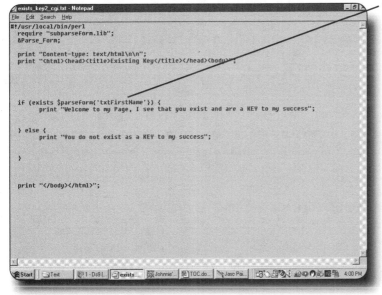

This example shows the key misspell in the application.

The complete code for this example, exists_key2_html.txt, can be found on the CD in the examples for this chapter.

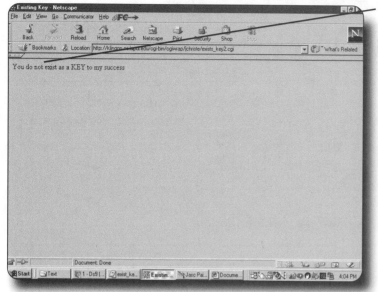

Now, the HTML page notes that the key does not exist.

The dual response is not a part of the `exists` operator, but a function of the conditional statement. It was used here so you can see how the `exists` operator functions.

Retrieving Hash Values Using Keys

Now that you know how to check for the existence of a key, you can learn how to retrieve the `values` of a hash using the key. You can either retrieve a single `value` or multiple `values`.

Retrieving a Single Value

As mentioned earlier, each pair of elements in the hash is linked to each other by the key and value, so they are often referred to as *key-value pairs*. Knowing this, you can use the key to retrieve its value. This enables you to use the value in your application.

Start by typing the `name` of the scalar variable that you will use to store the retrieved `value`. This is followed by an equals sign.

Next, you type the `name` of the hash from which you are retrieving the `value`, again starting with the dollar sign. Remember, you are retrieving an individual piece of data.

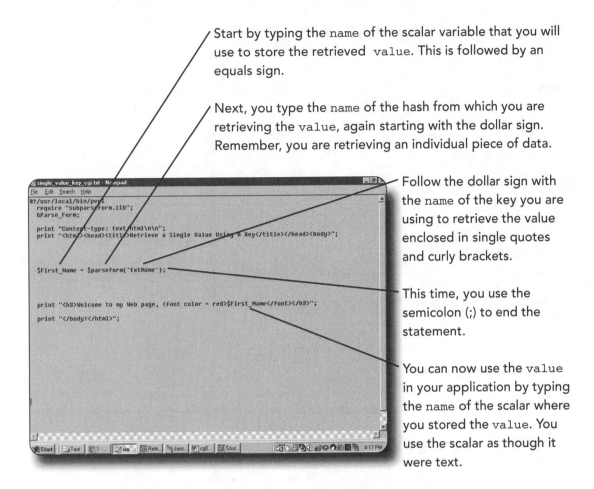

Follow the dollar sign with the `name` of the key you are using to retrieve the value enclosed in single quotes and curly brackets.

This time, you use the semicolon (;) to end the statement.

You can now use the `value` in your application by typing the `name` of the scalar where you stored the `value`. You use the scalar as though it were text.

The complete code for this example, survey_single_value_html.txt, can be found on the CD in the examples for this chapter.

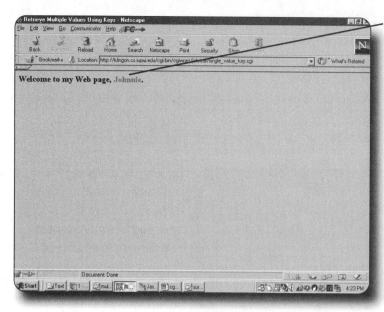

This enables you to personalize your Web page. You have probably seen this done on Web pages and wondered how they inserted your name on the page. Sometimes, when you revisit a site, it welcomes you personally without you having provided any data. In Chapter 12, "Retaining Visitor Data," you'll see how Web pages do this, and you can incorporate such tricks into your Web page. Cool, huh?

Retrieving Multiple Values

Rarely do you retrieve just a single piece of data from a form. Therefore, you need to know how to retrieve multiple values using keys. When you retrieve values from a hash using the names of keys, you are *slicing* the hash. More useful terminology that you can use at parties!

To retrieve multiple values using keys, you type the name of the array in which you will store the values. Notice that it is an array, not a scalar, so it starts with the at sign. This is because you are storing multiple pieces of data. The at sign is followed by an equals sign.

You then type the name of the array from which you will get the `values`, starting with the at sign. Again, this is an array because you are dealing with multiple pieces of data.

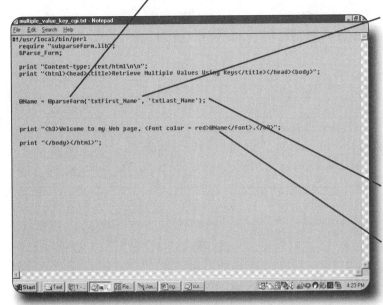

You follow this with the names of the keys whose values you want to retrieve. These names are separated by commas, individually enclosed in single quotes, and the entire set is enclosed in curly brackets.

You end the statement using a semicolon.

You can use the array as though it were text, just like you did with the scalar in the previous example. If the array is included within the quotation marks of the `print` statement, the `values` are separated by spaces when printed.

The complete code for this example, survey_multiple_ values_html.txt, can be found on the CD in the examples for this chapter.

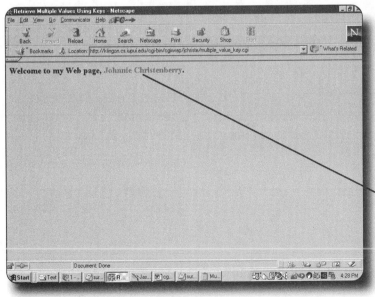

Notice that the `values` printed from the array are separated by spaces.

Retrieving All the Hash Data

There are times when you will want to retrieve all the values or all the keys of a hash. Perl has predefined operators that you can use for both of these functions.

Finding All Hash Values

To begin, you type the name of the array that you use to store the values. This name starts with the at sign because you are storing multiple pieces of data. You follow this with an equals sign.

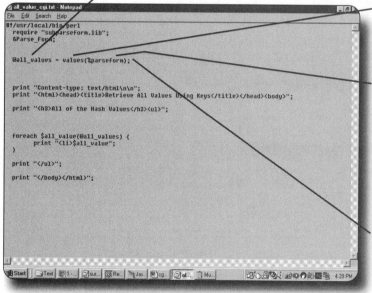

Next, type the operator that retrieves all the values from a hash.

Next, you type the name of the hash from which you are retrieving data. This is a hash that contains key-value pairs, so it starts with a percent sign. It needs to be enclosed in parentheses.

End the statement with the semicolon.

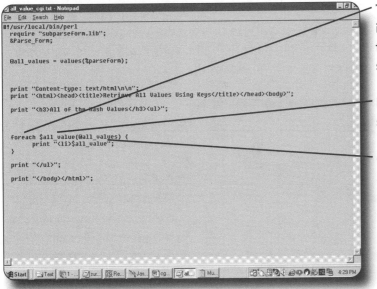

To display the `values`, include the scalar name and the array name in a `foreach` statement.

Remember that you use the scalar with the dollar sign.

Conversely, you use the array with the at sign for multiple pieces of data.

The complete code for this example, survey_all_value_html.txt, can be found on the CD in the examples for this chapter.

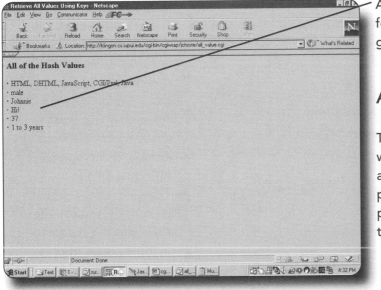

All the `values` from the form are listed on the generated page.

All Hash Keys

There might come a time when you need to retrieve all the keys from a hash. This process is similar to the process used to retrieve all the values.

To retrieve all the keys of a hash, you type the `name` of the array that you will use to store the keys. Because this name holds multiple pieces of data, start it with the at sign. You follow this with an equals sign.

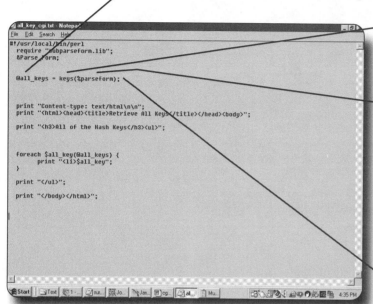

You then type the `keys` operator—it retrieves all the keys from a hash.

Follow this operator with the `name` of the hash that contains the key-value pairs. Because it holds multiple pieces of data, start it with the percent sign. You enclose the hash `name` in parentheses.

End the statement with the semicolon.

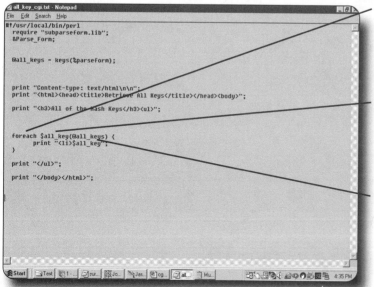

To display the keys, you include the scalar `name` and the array `name` in a `foreach` statement.

Remember that you use the singular form in the scalar with the dollar sign for individual data.

Conversely, you use the array with the at sign for multiple pieces of data.

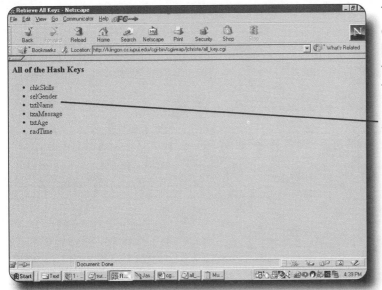

The complete code for this example, survey_all_key_html.txt, can be found on the CD in the examples for this chapter.

All the `keys` from the form are listed on the generated page.

Retrieving Specific Keys and Values

You can use one of two ways to retrieve the keys and values of a hash together. Luckily, Perl has predefined operators for both of these functions. Isn't Perl great?

Retrieving the First Key and Value

To retrieve the first key and value of a hash, you use the `each` operator.

Type the scalars that hold the key and the value from the hash. These scalars start with dollar signs because you are using them to store individual pieces of data. You separate the scalars with commas and enclose them in parentheses.

Follow the scalars with an equals sign.

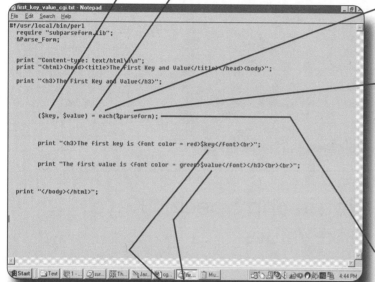

You then type the operator that retrieves the key and value from the hash.

You type the name of the hash from which you want to retrieve the key and value. This name starts with a percent sign as it contains multiple pieces of data. The hash name is enclosed in parentheses.

End the statement with a semicolon.

Use the scalars you created in the print statement as though they were text.

The complete code for this example, survey_firstl_key_html.txt, can be found on the CD in the examples for this chapter.

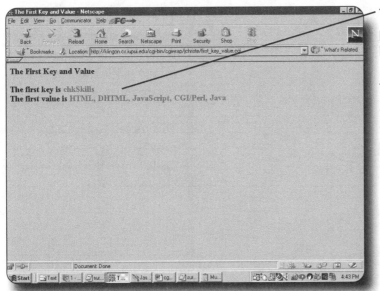

This generates an HTML page that displays the first key and value.

To retrieve additional keys and values in sequential order, repeat the previous steps for each additional key and value you want to display.

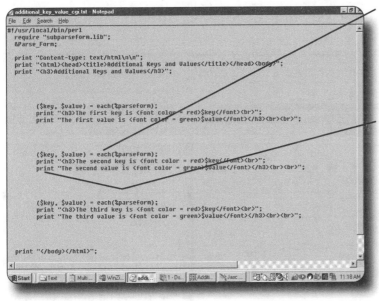

Each sequential key and value you want to retrieve needs its own operator to access the hash and retrieve the data.

Each sequential key and value also needs its own print statement.

You can repeat these steps as many times as you want.

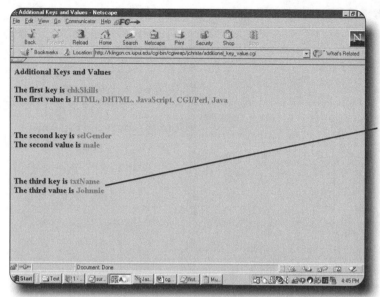

The complete code for this example, survey_add_key_value_html.txt, can be found on the CD in the examples for this chapter.

This page displays all requested keys and values from the hash in sequential order.

Retrieving Each Key and Value

To retrieve each key and value of a hash, you use the each operator with a while conditional statement.

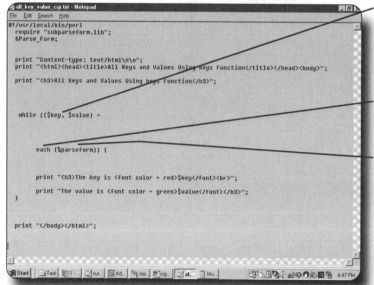

This example is contained in a while conditional statement, so you start by typing this statement.

You then include the each operator.

Follow this operator with the hash name that contains the key-value pairs you want to retrieve. Be sure to start the hash name with the percent sign and to enclose it in parentheses.

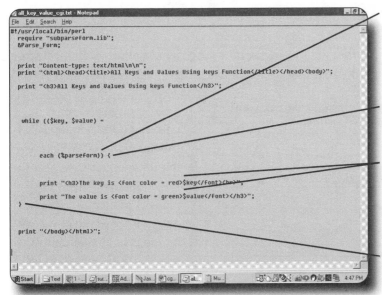

Then you type the closing parenthesis, which matches the open parenthesis in the `while` statement.

Then type an open curly bracket to end this line.

You then type the `print` statements including the scalars in place of text for the key and value.

Finish with the closing curly bracket.

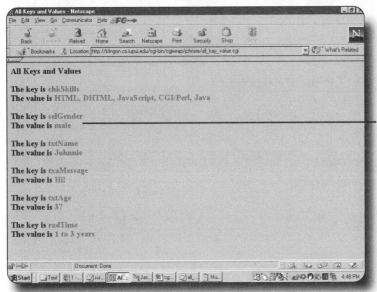

The complete code for this example, survey_all_key_value_html.txt, can be found on the CD in the examples for this chapter.

This code generates an HTML page that displays the keys and their values.

Retrieving Key-Value Pairs with the Keys Function

The second way to retrieve the keys and values of a hash is to use the `keys` function. The benefit of the `keys` function is that you do not need to know the name of the keys in the hash you are accessing. This is nice when you are not the person who created the form.

This operation is contained within a `foreach` loop.

Begin the operation by typing the scalar `name` that will store the `keys` from the hash.

Then you type an open parenthesis and the `name` of the function that will retrieve the data. In this case, use the `keys` function. This is the name of the function and must be typed exactly like it is; you cannot change this name or the application will not execute correctly.

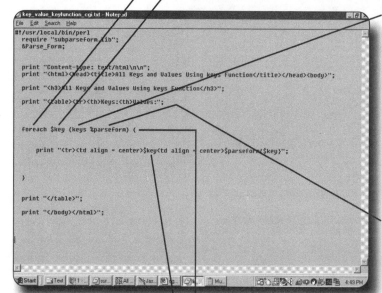

```
#!/usr/local/bin/perl
  require "subparseform.lib";
  &Parse_Form;

  print "Content-type: text/html\n\n";
  print "<html><head><title>All Keys and Values Using keys Function</title></head><body>";

  print "<h3>All Keys and Values Using keys Function</h3>";

  print "<table><tr><th>Keys:<th>Values:";

  foreach $key (keys %parseform) {

      print "<tr><td align = center>$key<td align = center>$parseform{$key}";

  }

  print "</table>";

  print "</body></html>";
```

You then type the `name` of the hash from which you want to retrieve the keys and values. Because it contains multiple pieces of data, use the percent sign to begin the hash `name`.

You type the closing parenthesis followed by the open curly bracket.

You then type the scalar `name` you created to hold the `keys` from the hash in the `print` statement as though it were text.

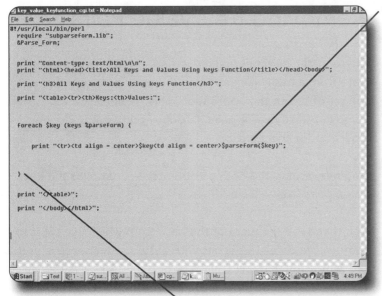

The term you use in the `print` statement to display the `values` is a little more involved. Type the `name` of the hash, starting with the percent sign, and follow it directly with the `name` of the scalar that is storing the `keys` from the hash—the scalar `name` needs to be enclosed in curly brackets. This code uses the key to retrieve the value and prints it. This line ends with a semicolon.

You need to type the closing curly bracket to end the `foreach` loop.

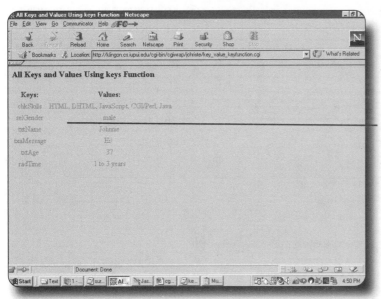

The complete code for this example, survey_key_value_ keyfunction_html.txt, can be found on the CD in the examples for this chapter.

This code generates an HTML page that displays all the keys and their corresponding values.

Removing Key-Value Pairs

There might be times when you find it necessary to remove data from a hash, such as when the data is outdated or no longer of use to the application. This requires you to remove the key-value pairs. Luckily, Perl has a predefined operator for this function.

Begin by typing the `delete` operator—it removes the key-value pairs from a hash.

You then type the `name` of the hash from which you want to remove the data. This starts with a dollar sign because you are removing an individual piece of data. (A key-value pair is considered an individual piece of data.)

Follow this with the `name` of the key that will remove the key-value pair. This needs to be enclosed in curly brackets, and if it is a string it needs to be enclosed in single quotes.

End this line with a semicolon.

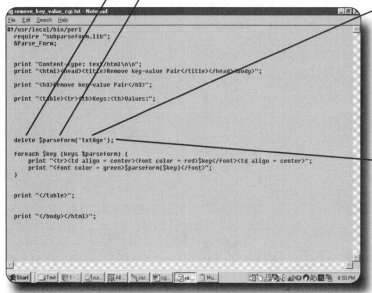

```perl
#!/usr/local/bin/perl
require "subparseform.lib";
&Parse_Form;

print "Content-type: text/html\n\n";
print "<html><head><title>Remove key-value Pair</title></head><body>";

print "<h3>Remove key-value Pair</h3>";

print "<table><tr><th>Keys:<th>Values:";



delete $parseform{'txtAge'};

foreach $key (keys %parseform) {
    print "<tr><td align = center><font color = red>$key</font><td align = center>";
    print "<font color = green>$parseform{$key}</font>";
}

print "</table>";

print "</body></html>";
```

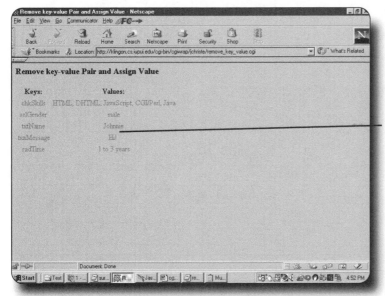

The complete code for this example, survey_remove_key_value_html.txt, can be found on the CD in the examples for this chapter.

The key-value pair is now gone, as is apparent from the generated HTML page.

Another option of this function is to remove multiple key-value pairs. The process is similar, but there are some small differences that cause major changes.

Start the process with the `delete` operator.

You then type the `name` of the hash from which you want to remove the data. This name starts with the at sign because you are removing multiple pieces of data.

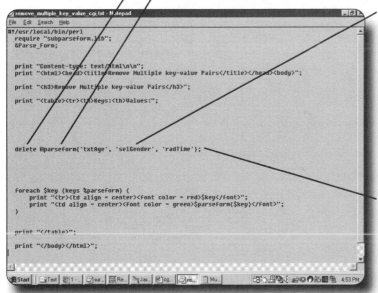

Follow this with the `names` of the `keys` that you want to use to remove the key-value pair. Separate the `keys` with commas. They need to be enclosed in curly brackets, and if they are strings they need to be enclosed in single quotes.

End this line with a semicolon.

The complete code for this example, survey_remove_multi_key_value_html.txt, can be found on the CD in the examples for this chapter.

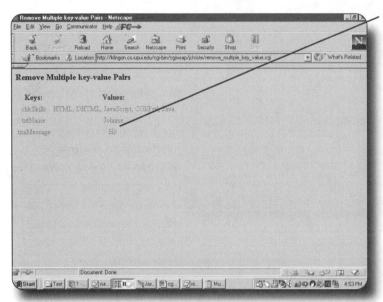

The key-value pairs are now gone, as is apparent from the generated HTML page.

You can assign the removed value to a scalar variable if you want to save it for future reference, or as a backup in case you remove the wrong data.

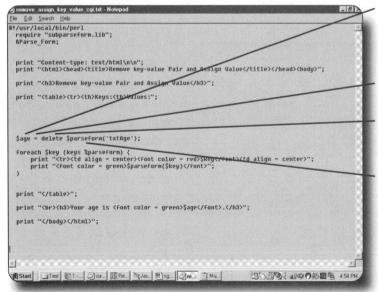

To do this, type the name of the scalar that you want to assign the value.

You then type an equals sign.

Follow this with the delete operator.

You then type the name of the hash from which you want to remove the data. This name starts with a dollar sign because you are removing an individual piece of data.

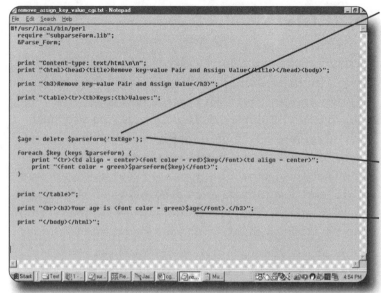

Follow this with the name of the key that you want to use to remove the key-value pair. This needs to be enclosed in curly brackets, and if it is a string it needs to be enclosed in single quotes.

End this line with a semicolon.

You can use the new scalar to display the removed information. Why you would do this in your application is beyond me; however, I display it here to show that it was assigned.

The complete code for this example, survey_remove_assign_key_value_html.txt, can be found on the CD in the examples for this chapter.

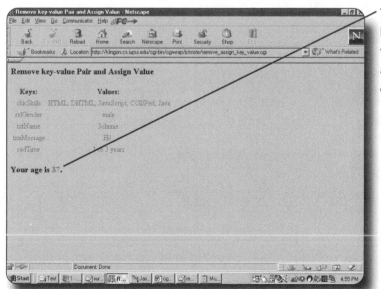

The key-value pair has been removed, and the value has been assigned to a scalar variable that displays the value.

Summary

In this chapter, you gained the knowledge you need to understand and use hashes. You now know the importance of keys, how to check for a key, and how to retrieve individual and multiple values using keys. You also know how to retrieve all the hash values and keys as well as how to retrieve the key-value pairs using the `keys` function. And finally, you know how to remove key-value pairs from a hash and how to store a removed key-value pair value in a scalar variable. Throughout the examples in this chapter and the previous chapter, you were introduced to various conditional statements that you were told to overlook. Well, now it is time to explain them in detail so that you will better understand them and be able to use them in your applications.

9

Conditional Statements

Many of the examples in the previous chapters used conditional statements as a means to achieve the full extent of their functions. You were usually asked to ignore the conditional statements and to concentrate on the function that was the focus of that chapter or section. If you took the time to look through the conditional statements, you were probably able to make some sense as to what they were doing. If not, that is fine. By the time you finish this chapter, you will be able to look at conditional statements and understand exactly what they are accomplishing and how they are accomplishing it. You will also be able to create your own conditional statements to use in your applications. In this chapter, you will learn about:

- Making comparisons
- Creating your conditional statement
- Using statement blocks
- Using nested conditional statements

The concept underlying a *conditional statement* is simple: it checks for a specific condition and, based upon the value returned (true or false) and the code in the conditional statement, a certain action is taken or not taken. Sounds easy enough, huh? One example involves the decision to eat breakfast in the morning—if you are hungry, you eat breakfast; if you are not hungry, you do not eat breakfast. That is a simple conditional statement. Some of the conditional statements you learn in this chapter are this basic, whereas some of them are complex and involve many steps.

Comparing Values

Value comparison is a basic form of a conditional statement; however, it is often the basis for the rest of an advanced conditional statement. You can compare numbers and strings, and evaluate them without comparison. This section details the differences and how you use them.

Number Comparison

Number comparison is used in many applications. Numbers can be compared to determine whether they are equal or whether one number is larger or smaller than another. A number comparison returns a `true` or `false`.

In this example, the value of a scalar variable (`$Age`) is checked against a constant value.

You can determine whether the two numbers are equal.

You can determine whether the two numbers are not equal.

You can determine whether one number is greater than another.

You can determine whether one number is greater than or equal to another.

You can determine whether one number is less than another.

Or, you can determine whether one number is less than or equal to another.

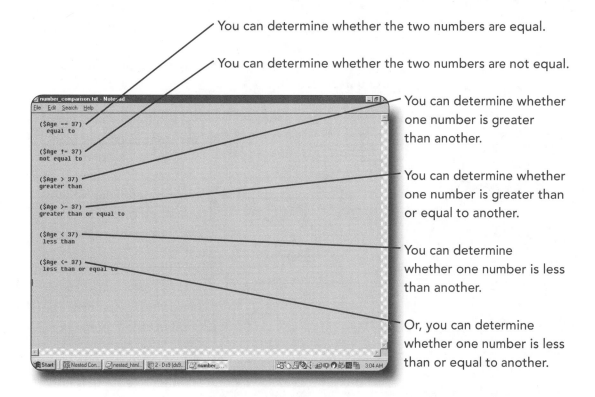

String Comparison

Strings are not compared in exactly the same way as numbers. When you compare numbers, you are usually determining which of the two is bigger. When you compare strings, you generally want to know whether they are the same. String comparisons return a `true` or `false`.

In this example, the value of a scalar variable ($First_Name) is checked against a constant value. Recall that all strings must be enclosed in quotation marks.

You can determine whether the two strings are equal using eq.

You can determine whether the two strings are not equal using ne.

You can determine whether one string is greater than another string using gt.

You can determine whether one string is greater than or equal to another string using ge.

You can determine whether one string is less than another string using lt.

Or, you can determine whether one string is less than or equal to another string using le.

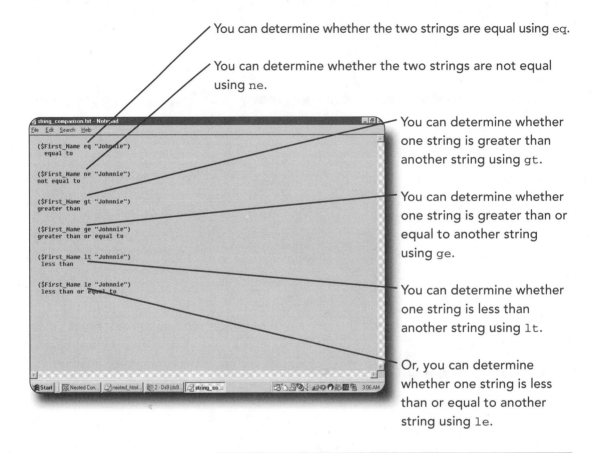

CAUTION

String comparisons are case sensitive; therefore, "Johnnie" is not equal to "johnnie". Also, if you use string operators with numbers, Perl treats the numbers as strings. This can drastically change the condition's return value because the ASCII values are used for the comparison. For example, 37 gt 137 returns true because the ASCII value for 3 is greater than the ASCII value for 1. If you were comparing them as numbers, the return value would be false. This can create havoc in your application.

Evaluating without Comparisons

Using comparison operators is probably the simplest way for you to create a condition, and it is definitely the most common. But, any statement can be used as a condition. Luckily, Perl uses a simple set of rules for determining whether a statement is `true` or `false`. Any statement that is evaluated as 0, an empty string (`" "`), or is undefined, has a return value of `false`; otherwise, it has a return value of `true`. This enables you to determine whether the users have left any of the input fields blank. You have probably experienced this when completing some forms on the Web. Note that any operations that are contained in your condition are executed whether the condition is evaluated as `true` or `false`. This is important to note when you are using the autoincrement function (++).

Checking Multiple Comparisons

You have the ability to evaluate multiple conditions at the same time. Okay, they are not evaluated at the same *exact* time; one is evaluated before the other, but they are evaluated together. There are a couple of options you can use for multiple comparisons. The first requires that both conditions be true; the second requires that only one of the conditions be true. Both options are detailed for you next.

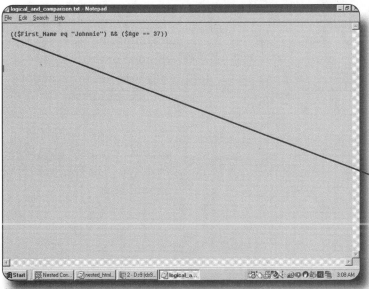

First try the option that requires all the conditions to be true. You type an open parenthesis to begin the set of conditions you are evaluating.

You then type the first condition you are evaluating enclosed in its own set of parentheses.

The logical and operator (&&) follows the first condition.

You type the next condition you want to evaluate enclosed in its own parentheses.

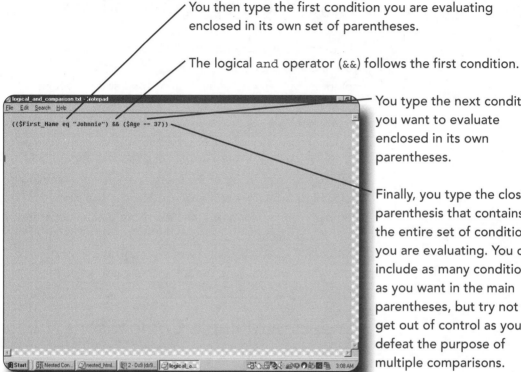

Finally, you type the closing parenthesis that contains the entire set of conditions you are evaluating. You can include as many conditions as you want in the main parentheses, but try not to get out of control as you can defeat the purpose of multiple comparisons.

To use the option that requires only one of the conditions be true, you type an open parenthesis to begin the set of conditions you are evaluating.

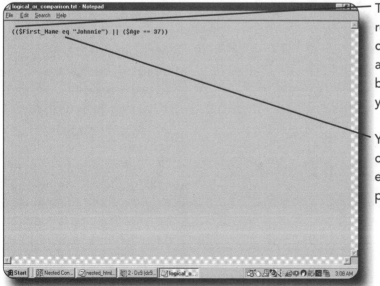

You then type the first condition you are evaluating enclosed in its own set of parentheses.

The logical `or` operator (| |) follows the first condition. You type this operator by using the Shift key and the backslash (\) key on your keyboard for each vertical line in the operator (twice).

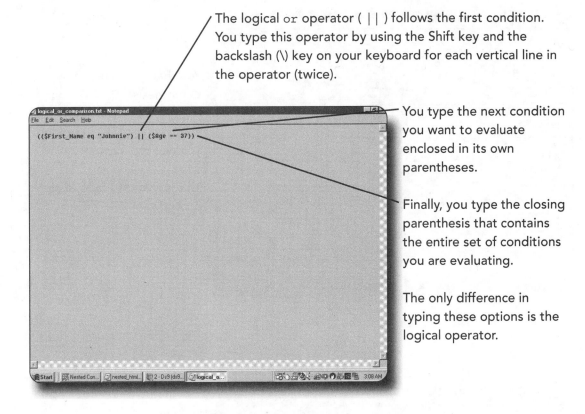

You type the next condition you want to evaluate enclosed in its own parentheses.

Finally, you type the closing parenthesis that contains the entire set of conditions you are evaluating.

The only difference in typing these options is the logical operator.

Creating Your Conditional Statement

If you have ever listened to a rock station on the radio, you might recall a familiar `if` statement as recorded by Pink Floyd: "If you don't eat your meat, you can't have any pudding; how can you have any pudding if you don't eat your meat?" This statement includes everything needed for a conditional statement: It has an `if`, a condition (you don't eat your meat), and an action that is taken if the condition has a return value of `true` (you can't have any pudding). Perl uses the `if` statement in much the same way.

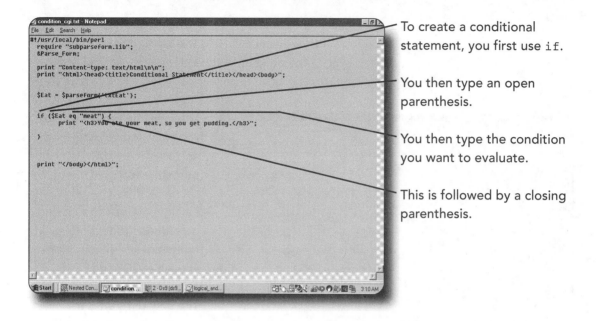

To create a conditional statement, you first use `if`.

You then type an open parenthesis.

You then type the condition you want to evaluate.

This is followed by a closing parenthesis.

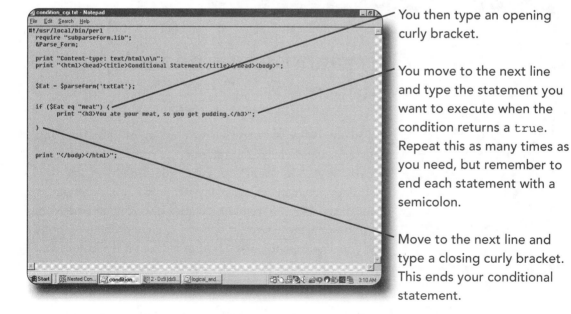

You then type an opening curly bracket.

You move to the next line and type the statement you want to execute when the condition returns a `true`. Repeat this as many times as you need, but remember to end each statement with a semicolon.

Move to the next line and type a closing curly bracket. This ends your conditional statement.

The complete code for this example, condition_html.txt, can be found on the CD in the examples for this chapter.

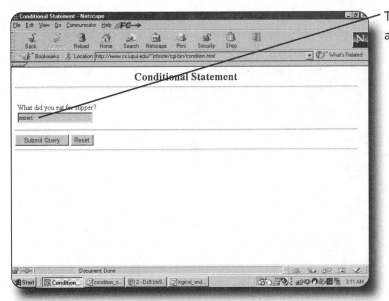

The users complete the form and submit it.

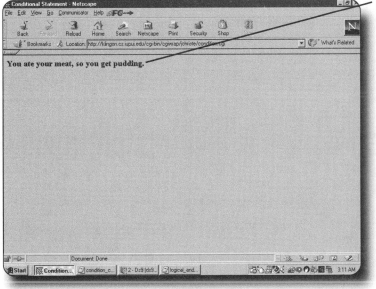

Because the condition returns a true, the print statement is executed and displayed.

Remember, Perl is case sensitive. Therefore, the manner in which the text is entered in the input field is important. This problem can be removed by using the lc or uc operator.

The complete code of the HTML form for this example, condition2_html.txt, can be found on the CD in the examples for this chapter.

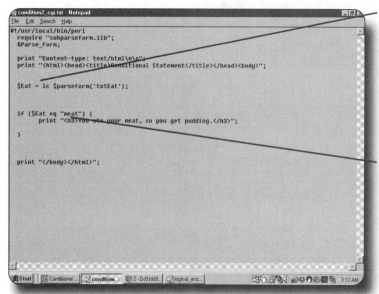

To use the `lc` operator, which is the operator that converts the case of the string to lowercase, you will insert `lc` after the equals sign of your assignment to the `$Eat` scalar.

You need to be sure to have the comparison value written in lowercase in order to match the scalar value.

The complete code of the HTML form for this example, condition3_html.txt, can be found on the CD in the examples for this chapter.

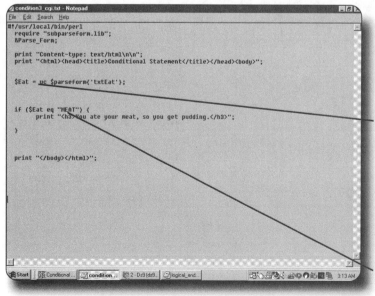

To use the `uc` operator, which is the operator that converts the case of the string to uppercase, you will insert `uc` after the equals sign of your assignment to the `$Eat` scalar.

You need to be sure to have the comparison value written in uppercase in order to match the scalar value.

Using either of these two operators eliminates the problems associated with users typing the word with a case different from the comparison value you check in the application.

You can make the application execute a statement when the condition has a `false` return value also.

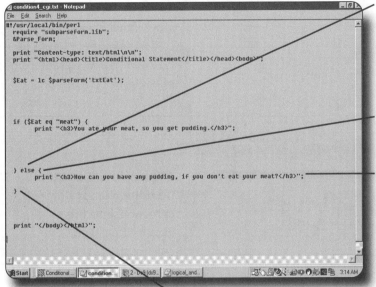

To execute a statement when the condition has a `false` return value, type **else** on the same line as the closing curly bracket.

You then type an open curly bracket on this same line.

Move to the next line and type the statement you want to execute when the return value is `false`. Remember to end the statement with a semicolon.

Move to the next line and type a closing curly bracket.

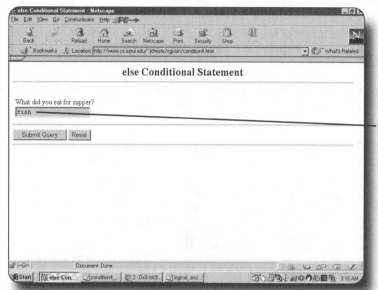

The complete code of the HTML form for this example, condition4_html.txt, can be found on the CD in the examples for this chapter.

If the users type anything in the input field other than meat, in all lowercase, all uppercase, or a mixture of both, the else statement is executed.

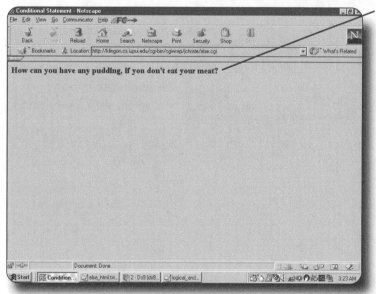

This displays the text from the else statement in response to the incorrect answer.

Conditional statements have many uses that range from simple procedures, like in the previous examples, to extensive procedures that check for multiple conditions and produce multiple HTML pages based upon the data retrieved from the users. The type of conditional statement you use is dependent on your application. In the following sections, you learn how to use myriad types of statement blocks. With this knowledge, you can determine the best conditional statement to use in your applications. Remember that you use conditional statements any time you want to evaluate the data you retrieve from your users and respond in certain ways.

Using Conditional Statement Blocks

The previous examples consisted of conditional statement blocks. They are often referred to by the type of statement you use to preface the condition: The first example is called an `if` statement, or `if` block; the second example is called an `if/else` statement or block. This makes sense because they are the words used in the block. You will see many types in this section. Notice that they have many functions and uses. I try to explain them in as much detail as possible without boring you to death.

The if/unless Statement

The basic `if/else` statement was detailed in the previous section, so I move to the more advanced `if/else` statement. Perl enables you to evaluate additional conditions when the `if` condition has a `false` value before it executes the `else` statement.

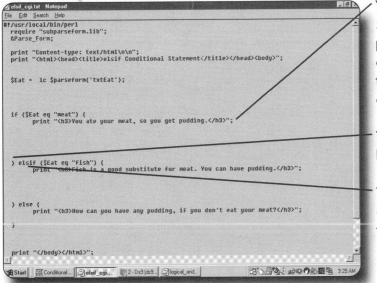

You begin by creating the `if/else` statement from the previous section. Insert the `elsif` statement between the `if` statement and the `else` statement.

To start, type a closing curly bracket.

This is followed by the term `elsif`. Notice the spelling: there is only one "e".

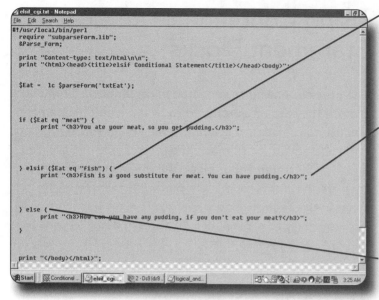

You type the condition you want evaluated in parentheses and end the line with an opening curly bracket.

Move to the next line and type the statement you want to execute when this condition returns a `true`, and end this line with a semicolon.

If both of these conditions return `false` values, the `else` statement executes.

The complete code for the form in this example, elsif_html.txt, can be found on the CD in the examples for this chapter.

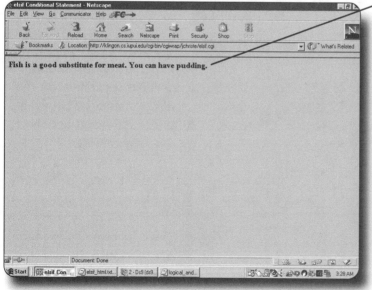

Now if the users type either `meat` or `fish`, they will get to have pudding, as seen by the displayed text.

There might be times when it is more useful to know when a condition is `false`, instead of when it is `true`. Again, Perl has a predefined function that makes this a simple task to achieve.

To execute a statement when the return value is `false`, you first type the predefined construct called `unless`.

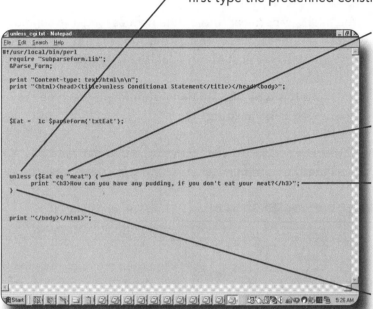

This construct is followed by the condition you want to evaluate, which you enclose in parentheses.

You end this line with an opening curly bracket.

Move to the next line and type the statement you want to execute when the condition is `false`. This line ends with a semicolon.

Move to the next line and type a closing curly bracket.

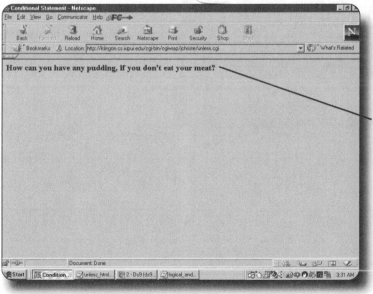

The complete code for the form in this example, unless_html.txt, can be found on the CD in the examples for this chapter.

Now the application executes the statement only when the condition is `false`.

The while/until Statement

You might want to execute a statement as long as a condition is true and remains true. This usually requires a statement that allows the evaluated condition to be changed.

To create this type of conditional statement, you type the predefined Perl construct.

This construct is followed by the condition that is to be evaluated to determine whether the statement is executed.

This line ends with the opening curly bracket.

You then move to the next line and type the statements to be executed when the condition is true. These lines end with semicolons.

Move to the next line and type the closing curly bracket.

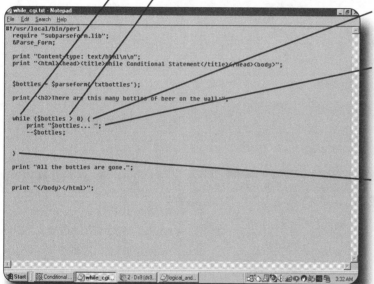

```
#!/usr/local/bin/perl
    require "subparseform.lib";
    &Parse_Form;

    print "Content-type: text/html\n\n";
    print "<html><head><title>while Conditional Statement</title></head><body>";

    $bottles = $parseform{'txtbottles'};

    print "<h3>There are this many bottles of beer on the wall";

    while ($bottles > 0) {
        print "$bottles... ";
        --$bottles;

    }

    print "All the bottles are gone.";

    print "</body></html>";
```

The complete code for the form in this example, while_html.txt, can be found on the CD in the examples for this chapter.

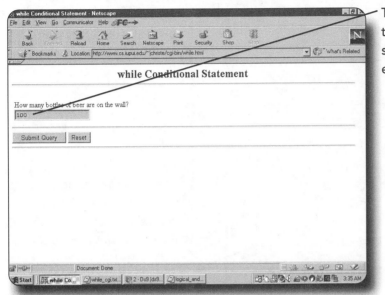

The users enter data into the form. When it is submitted, the application evaluates the condition.

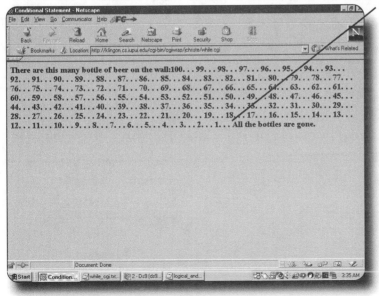

The HTML page displays the result of the while loop. Notice that it continues until the condition is false.

Perl also enables you to execute a statement as long as a condition is false and remains false. This is similar to the while loop; however, now the condition is reversed.

To create this type of conditional statement, you type the predefined Perl construct called `until`.

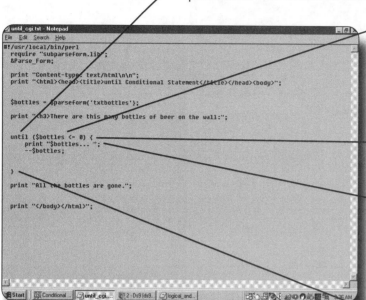

This construct is followed by the condition that is to be evaluated to determine whether the statement is executed.

This line ends with the opening curly bracket.

You then move to the next line and type the statements to be executed when the condition is `false`. These lines end with semicolons.

Move to the next line and type the closing curly bracket.

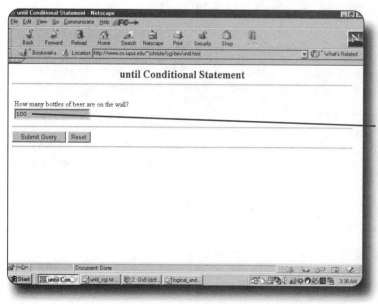

The complete code for the form in this example, until_html.txt, can be found on the CD in the examples for this chapter.

The users enter data into the form. When it is submitted, the application evaluates the condition.

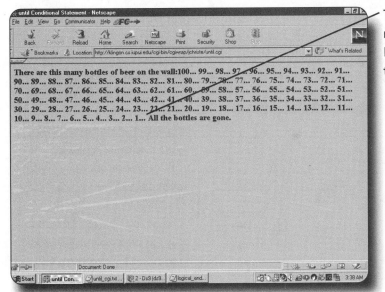

The HTML page displays the result of the `until` loop. Notice that it continues until the condition is `true`.

The do { } while/until Statement

A drawback to using the `while` statement is that when the condition is `false` from the start, the statements in the block never execute. There is a way to get around this: You can use a `do` statement. With a `do` statement, the block statements execute once before the condition is checked. You need to be careful with this statement, as it can create problems. For example, you could have an application that sends a reminder to users who are delinquent on their account payments. You want to see if the user is delinquent before displaying the message to avoid upsetting the users who are current in their account payments. In this case, you would not want to place the delinquent message in a `do` statement.

To execute the block statement at least once, you start by typing the do construct.

This construct is followed by an opening curly bracket.

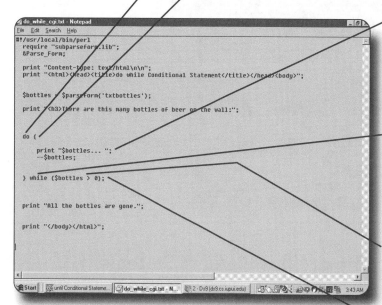

Move to the next line and type the statements that you want executed at least once. These lines end with semicolons.

Move to the next line and type a closing curly bracket followed by the term while, which evaluates when the condition is true.

You then type the condition that you want evaluated, enclosed in parentheses.

You end this line with a semicolon.

The complete code for the form in this example, do_while_html.txt, can be found on the CD in the examples for this chapter.

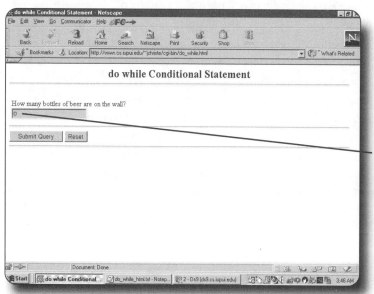

Now when the users input data, the statement executes once before it checks the return value.

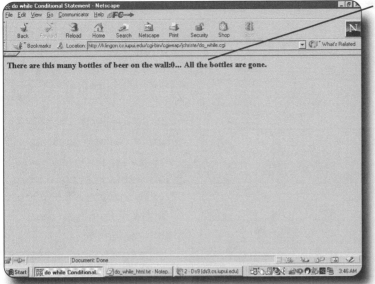

Even though the condition is `false`, the statement in the block executes once before it checks the value of the condition.

You can also make the `do` statement execute once before evaluating the condition, and then have it execute when the return value is `false`.

To execute the block statement at least once, you start by typing the construct.

This construct is followed by an opening curly bracket.

Move to the next line and type the statements that you want executed at least once. The lines end with semicolons.

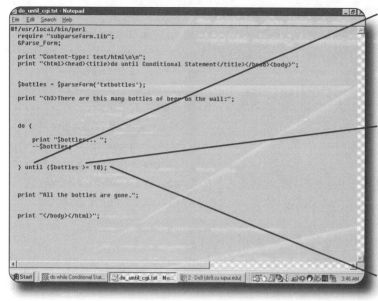

Move to the next line and type a closing curly bracket followed by the term `until`, which evaluates when the condition is `false`.

You then type the condition that you want evaluated, enclosed in parentheses. Notice that I changed the conditional value from 0 to 10: this helped with the demonstration.

You end this line with a semicolon.

The complete code for the form in this example, do_until_html.txt, can be found on the CD in the examples for this chapter.

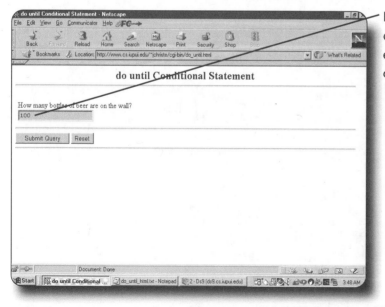

Now when the users input data, the statement executes once before it checks the return value.

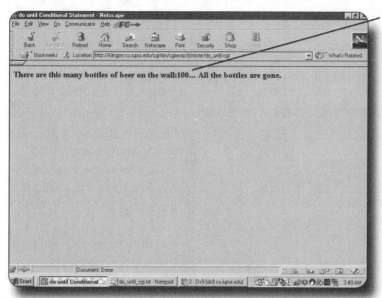

Even though the condition is `true`, the statement in the block is executed because it executes once before it checks the value of the condition.

The for Statement

You now know how to execute statements in a block after evaluating the condition as well as before evaluating the condition. You also know how to execute the block statements while a condition is true or until a condition is true. These are all useful and powerful tools. However, there are a couple of other conditional statements that are also powerful. One of these is having the capability to execute block statements a specific number of times. This involves using a counter variable, which keeps track of the number of times the block statements have been executed.

To start, you type the construct name. In this case, a `for` loop.

You then type an open parenthesis, followed by the `name` of the scalar you are going to use as your counter.

You type an equals sign and the scalar that holds the user's input to assign the value of the scalar to the counter. Follow this with a semicolon.

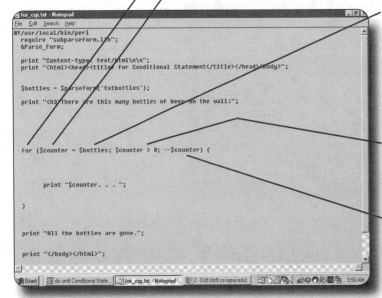

You then type the condition that will be evaluated, followed by a semicolon.

Then you use the autodecrement function (the `--`) for the counter and close the parentheses.

You end this line with an opening curly bracket.

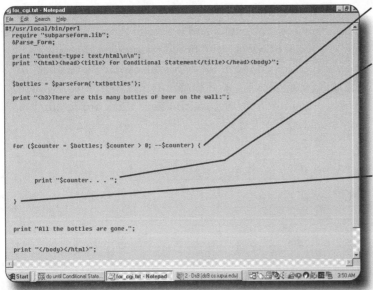

Move to the next line and type the statement that you want executed when the condition is `true`. This line ends with a semicolon.

Move to the next line and end the loop with a closing curly bracket.

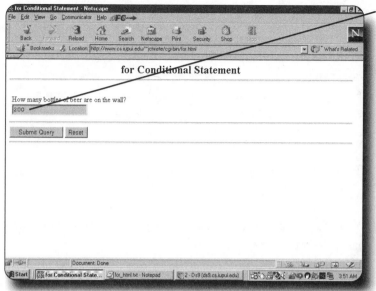

Now when the users submit data from the form, the application uses the value of the text box input field to set the counter's starting value and uses it to count down until the condition is false, at which time the execution ceases.

The complete code for the form in this example, for_html.txt, can be found on the CD in the examples for this chapter.

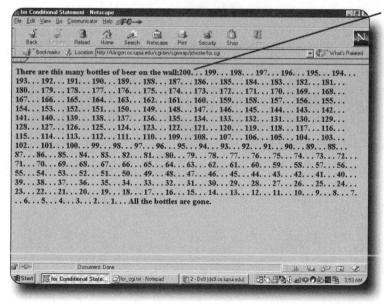

The generated page does not look much different from the previous pages, but you know the behind-the-scenes difference.

The foreach Statement

In the previous chapters, you saw how the `foreach` constructor was used to retrieve elements from an array. Now you are going to learn how it did so and how you can use it in your applications. The example included here was used in the previous chapter to retrieve all the keys of a hash.

To use a block repeatedly to retrieve each item in an array, you use the `foreach` constructor.

You then type the scalar name that you created to hold the keys from the array.

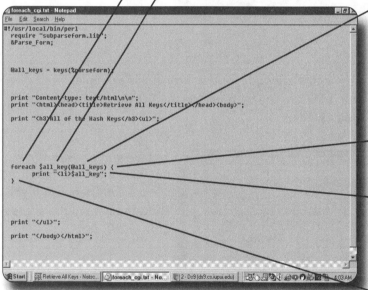

This scalar name is followed by the name of the array that is storing the parsed data from the form. Enclose the array name in parentheses.

End this line with an opening curly bracket.

Move to the next line and type the statement you want to print. Be sure to end the line with a semicolon.

You then move to the next line and type the closing curly bracket.

The complete code for the form in this example, survey_foreach_html.txt, can be found on the CD in the examples for this chapter.

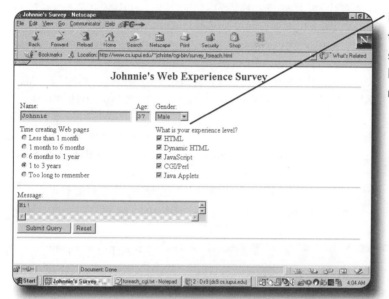

Now when the users submit the form, it executes the statement in the `foreach` loop. This makes a little more sense now, doesn't it?

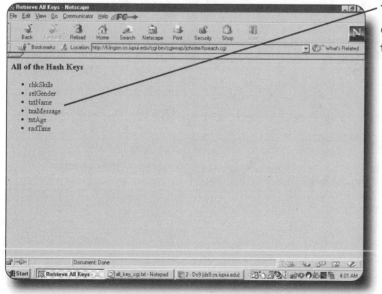

The executed statement displays all the keys from the hash in a list.

Nested Conditional Statements

The final aspect of conditional statements you need to understand is using nested conditional statements. Basically, a nested conditional statement is a conditional statement within another conditional statement. For example, you can modify the code from the `while` conditional statement you just created to determine whether the users typed a decimal number for their input.

To begin, you create the first conditional statement: You are going to use the `while` code created earlier in this section.

Now you insert an `if` conditional statement inside the `while` statement by typing the constructor.

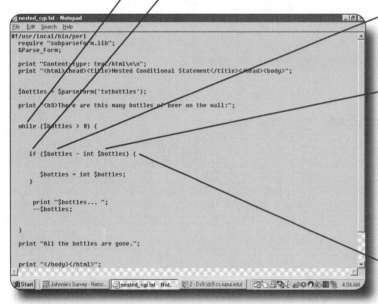

Then you type an open parenthesis and the scalar followed by a minus sign.

Now add the integer operator, the scalar, and a closing parenthesis. This line subtracts the integer portion of `$bottles` from `$bottles` to check if the users entered a decimal number.

End this line with an opening curly bracket.

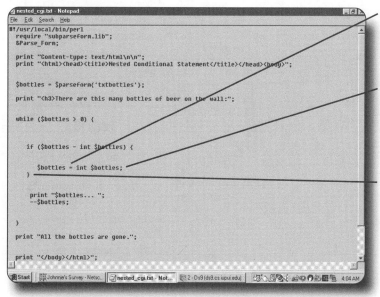

Move to the next line and type the scalar followed by an equals sign.

You then type the integer operator and the scalar again. End the line with a semicolon.

Move to the next line and type the closing curly bracket.

The complete code for the form in this example, nested_html.txt, can be found on the CD in the examples for this chapter.

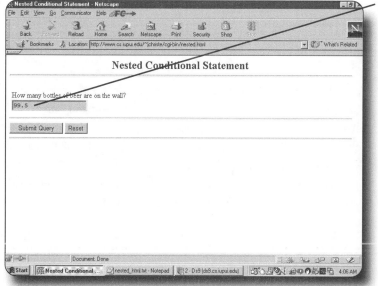

If the users input a decimal number, the application subtracts the integer from the value and stores it in the scalar.

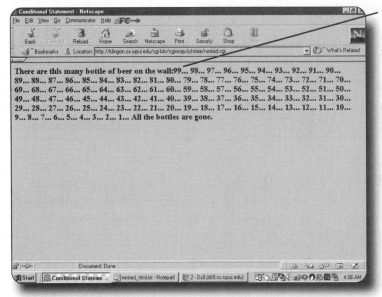

This produces a clean output and eliminates complications from computations involving decimals.

NOTE

The most difficult part of using nested conditional statements is making certain that every opening curly bracket has a closing curly bracket. I have seen more programs execute incorrectly because a single curly bracket was missing. This is always one of the first items I check when I have a problem.

Summary

In this chapter, you finally learned how to use the conditional statements you have been seeing in previous chapters. You now know how to compare numbers and strings, evaluate without comparisons, and evaluate while checking multiple comparisons. You possess the skills and knowledge to create and modify various statement blocks, and you can use nested conditional statements. With these skills mastered, you are ready to look at data analysis.

P A R T I I I

Advanced Data

10

Handling Data with Regular Expressions

Regular expressions are powerful tools for processing text-based information. Therefore, they are perfect tools for creating your CGI applications as well. Regular expressions can be a bit daunting at first, but with practice, you will be able to use them with confidence. Take the extra time to learn the fundamentals of using regular expressions; you'll be glad you did. In this chapter, you'll learn:

- Reasons to use regular expressions
- How to match text patterns with regular expressions
- How to use the match operator in Perl
- How to make substitutions with regular expressions
- How to use the `split` function

Using Regular Expressions

Regular expressions are a mainstay of programming and text processing in the UNIX world. In fact, regular expressions are a fundamental part of scripting engines such as awk, sed, and Perl. Many other applications, such as vi and Emacs, as well as Web search engines, provide regular expressions as a power-user option for searching and manipulating text.

A *regular expression* is a way to describe a set of characters or text strings without having to specify every possible string or character in the set. In other words, a regular expression describes a pattern of characters that you can match to many different strings.

Regular expression tools, like Perl, provide a standard syntax for describing these patterns. This syntax is a miniature programming language of its own. Regular expressions are optimized for matching patterns of text with this syntax, so the matching operation is fast.

I am an advocate of the adage "the right tool for the right job." When you work with lots of text, there is no better tool than regular expressions. They were designed for working with text from the ground up and they are good at it. In fact, I can't think of a reason not to use regular expressions when dealing with large amounts of text.

Regular expressions are efficient. Because they were designed to work with text, they do it quickly. Every operation in a regular expression is optimized to process text quickly and efficiently. Regular expressions are also efficient in terms of your code. They generally are short and succinct. You don't have to write gobs of code to parse a line from your Web log with regular expressions. This makes your code more readable and more maintainable.

Regular expressions are ubiquitous. You can translate your knowledge of regular expressions in one context into another context immediately. If you learn to use regular expressions in Perl, for instance, you can take that skill to ColdFusion or Emacs and be just as productive. Learning how to use regular expressions makes you a more versatile programmer.

Matching Text Patterns

Regular expressions are all about patterns. When you write a regular expression, you are defining a pattern of characters to find in the midst of your target text. Characters come in many categories: alphabetic, numeric, punctuation, capitalized, and so on. Regular expressions enable you to match individual or groups of characters based upon their category or their literal representation. You also can create your own categories called *character classes*. You can match zero, one, more than one, or a range of instances of a character, class, or group by using modifiers.

Single Character Patterns

The simplest pattern is a single character. For instance, if you are looking for a capital A in a line of text, you use the match operator (m//, or just //) with a single character: m/A/. You can also use square brackets ([ ]) to create a character class, which matches one in a set of characters.

This example contains a Web form that asks a multiple choice question. The answer is a single letter (A, B, C, or D), which is submitted to a Perl script for form decoding. The script uses a regular expression to determine what the user answered and to return an appropriate response.

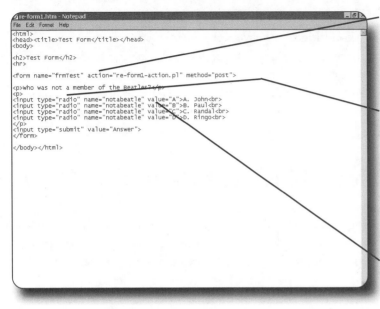

Set the form `action` attribute to the Perl script that performs the form decoding.

The question has four possible choices, but you want the users to select only one. Therefore, you use a radio button with the same field name for each response to limit the user's selection.

Make sure you give each radio button response a different value.

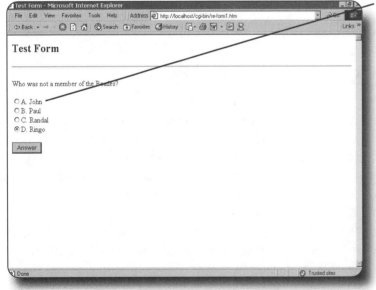

The radio buttons enable the users to select only one of the four responses.

The form-decoding script has the standard CGI variable parsing code you saw in Chapter 5, "Getting the Data Into Your CGI Application." This code is necessary to retrieve, or decode, the values of the fields from the form so you can access them in your script.

The $_ variable is called the *default pattern match space* variable in Perl. If you don't specify where the regular expression should look for the text, it looks at this variable.

Reassign the value of $parseform{notabeatle} to the default pattern match space variable, $_.

Use a character class pattern as the regular expression. This class consists of the literal characters A, B, and D. The match operator returns a true value when one of these characters is present in $_.

If the match operator returned true, it found an incorrect answer in the user's response. Here, you print a message that informs the users of the result and what the actual answer is.

```perl
#!/usr/bin/perl -w
my ($in, @pairs, $pair, $name, $value, %parseform);

if ($ENV{REQUEST_METHOD} eq "POST") {
    read(STDIN, $in, $ENV{CONTENT_LENGTH});
    @pairs = split(/&/, $in);
} elsif ($ENV{REQUEST_METHOD} eq "GET") {
    @pairs = split(/&/, $ENV{QUERY_STRING});
}

foreach $pair (@pairs) {

    ($name,$value) = split(/=/, $pair);
    $value =~ tr/+/ /;
    $value =~ s/%([a-fA-F0-9][a-fA-F0-9])/pack("C", hex($1))/eg;
    if (defined($parseform{$name})) {
        $parseform{$name} .= ",$value";
    } else {
        $parseform{$name} = $value;
    }
}

print "Content-type: text/html\n\n";

print "<html><head><title>Test Form Results</title></head>\n";
print "<body>\n";

print "<h2>Test Form Results</h2>\n";

$_ = $parseform{notabeatle};

if (m/[ABD]/) {
    print "Incorrect!  The correct answer is C, Randal.<br>";
} else {
    print "Correct!  Randal was not a Beatle.<br>";
}

print "</body></html>";
```

If the match operator returned a false value, the user answered correctly.

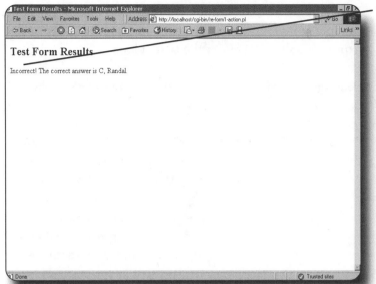

Wow! And I thought this would be an easy one. Always inform the users of the result of an action they have taken, as well as a corrective action to take if applicable.

Using Perl Shortcut Classes

Perl has created some shortcuts to assist you in script writing. This section presents the shortcut and then shows the long version of the function. You'll see an example of using these shortcut classes later in this chapter.

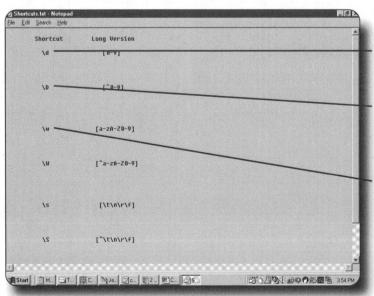

The first shortcut matches any digit.

The second shortcut matches any character that is not a digit.

The third shortcut matches any uppercase or lowercase letter, digit, or the underscore character.

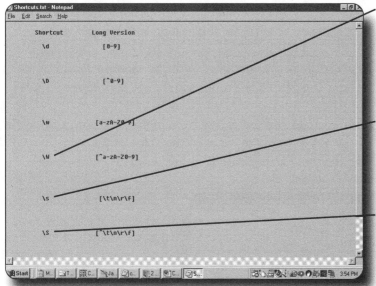

The fourth shortcut matches a character that is not an uppercase or lowercase letter, digit, or the underscore character.

The fifth shortcut matches any space, tab newline, return, or formfeed character.

The sixth shortcut matches any character that is not a space, tab newline, return, or formfeed character.

Group Patterns

Single character matches are fine, but you'll find yourself wanting to match larger and larger patterns as you find more uses for regular expressions. Regular expressions can have grouped characters to match in the target text to help in these situations. You group a set of characters or classes by enclosing them in a set of parentheses. You can group any number of times in a regular expression; you can even nest sets of grouping parentheses inside one another.

The regular expression remembers the groups in order and you can access them as variables $1, $2, $3…$n, up to the number of groups in the expression.

In this example, you create a character class with a list of characters, including a range operator that specifies a range of characters. You also modify this class to match one or more characters of the class. Finally, you ask the regular expression to remember the group of characters that it matches. You can use this remembered match later in the script. You extract the

Netscape browser compatibility level from the CGI variable, `HTTP_USER_AGENT`, and display it on a Web page.

First, display the unadulterated CGI variable on the HTML page. This provides a reference for the subsequent display.

You can use your default pattern match space trick from the previous example to reassign the value of the `HTTP_USER_AGENT` string.

```
group-match.pl - Notepad
File  Edit  Format  Help
#!/usr/bin/perl

print "Content-type: text/html\n\n";

print "<html><head><title>CGI Variables</title></head>\n";
print "<body>\n";

print "<h2>Group Matching</h2>\n";
print "$ENV{HTTP_USER_AGENT}<br>";

$_ = $ENV{HTTP_USER_AGENT};

if (/Mozilla\/([0-9.]+)/) {
    print "This browser is version $1 Netscape compatible<br>\n";
}
print "</body></html>";
```

This part of the regular expression is a simple character match of the string "Mozilla". Because you are using the forward slash as the delimiter for the match operator, you need to escape the forward slash that you want to match in the text with a backslash.

This is the group match, beginning with the parenthesis. The 0-9 indicates a range of all the numeric characters from 0 to 9. The period is a literal period. So the character class here is any one of 0, 1, 2, 3, 4, 5, 6, 7, 8, 9, or . (period).

The plus sign following the class tells Perl to match one or more of any characters in the class. So a string such as "3.4.5" will match, as will "4.61". The ending parenthesis closes the group match.

NOTE

You can alter the way a class or single character is matched by following the character or class by a plus to match one or more of the character or class or an asterisk to match zero or more of character or class. Be careful with the asterisk; the zero match might match text patterns you are not expecting.

NOTE

The remembered match variables $1, $2, and so on, are valid only until another regular expression with group matches is used. If you need to use these values later, it is best to save them to other variables. That way, you don't overwrite them on your next regular expression.

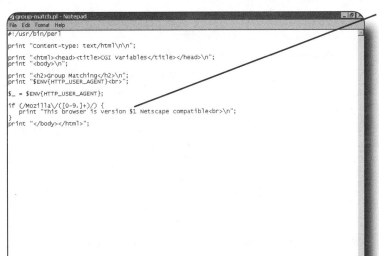

This is the first and only group match result from the last regular expression. It contains the characters matched, without the parentheses. You can use it just like any other variable in Perl. Display the result of your match in the browser with a `print` statement.

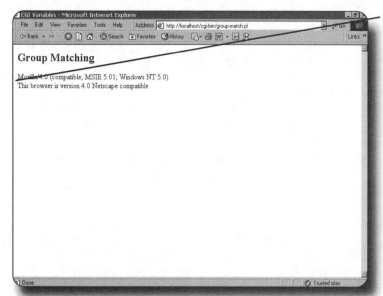

The browser compatibility version is a rough estimate of about how closely the current browser will support Netscape Navigator features.

You can also use groups in the substitution function to replace particular parts of a target or swap chunks of text. You see how this works later in this chapter.

Anchor Patterns

You can anchor a pattern to find to one end of a line with the anchor operators. The caret (^) anchors the pattern to the beginning of a line and the dollar sign operator ($_) anchors a pattern to the end of a line. You need to be careful about these operators when you are matching text with embedded newline characters. By default, the anchor operators match the end or beginning of the entire text string, not the logical lines denoted by embedded newline characters.

If you want the anchor operators to match around embedded newline characters, you need to specify the /m switch at the end of the match operator.

In this example, you search a log file of form submissions for the entries that included a non-empty QUERY_STRING CGI variable. You'll learn how to create this log file using regular expressions later in the chapter. The log file is arranged so the QUERY_STRING entry appears at the end of a line; if the QUERY_STRING is empty, there is a bare comma at the end of the line.

The log file consists of a date and time stamp, the IP address of the browser, the HTTP_USER_AGENT string from the browser, the script requested, and the QUERY_STRING submitted. The values are comma-delimited.

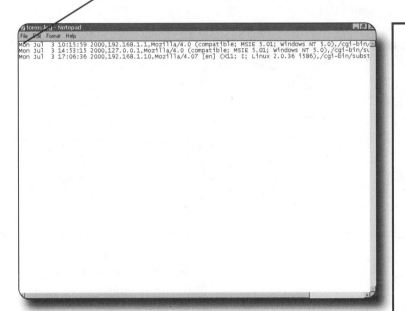

NOTE

When writing regular expressions to parse text, it is important to know what to expect. It is difficult to write a regular expression unless you know what you are looking for. Always get a sample of the text you will be processing before you write your code. Look at the patterns in the text and, in particular, at the exceptions to the patterns.

Open the log file and assign a file handle of LOG. This file path is different for your server, so change it accordingly.

Using the `while` statement, read in a line at a time from the LOG. Note that the `$_` (default pattern match space variable) contains the line just read in from the file. Chop off the last newline character with the `chop` function; this uses the `$_` variable as the target. This makes the match easier later.

The `$` in the regular expression anchors the match to the end of line. The character class is a special one. Because the caret is inside the square brackets, its meaning is different. In this situation, the caret is a *negation* operator. The regular expression matches any character at the end of the line that is *not* a comma (thus the QUERY_STRING is not empty).

```perl
#!/usr/bin/perl -w

print "Content-type: text/html\n\n";

print "<html><head><title>Checking the Form Submission Log</title></head>\n";
print "<body>\n";

print "<h2>Checking the Form Submission Log</h2>\n";

open (LOG, "/inetpub/wwwroot/cgi-bin/forms.log") || die "can't open forms.log: $!\n";
print "The following log entries included a QUERY_STRING<br><br>\n";

while (<LOG>) {
    chop;
    if (/[^,]$/) {
        print "$_<br>\n";
    }
}
close LOG;

print "</body></html>";
```

Now, print the line that matched (contained in `$_`) to the browser window with a break tag.

Don't forget to close the file handle of the open log file!

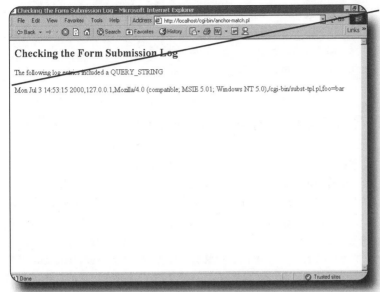

It looks like there was only one line in the log file that had a QUERY_STRING entered.

Precedence

You will find that a lot of the text you deal with has repeating patterns. Sometimes this is good, sometimes not. When the match operator begins its matching operation with the regular expression, it will stop at the first successfully matched pattern that it finds; this behavior is called precedence. What this means for you, the developer, is that you have to know ahead of time what you need to match.

If you find that your regular expression is matching unintended text, you might need to refine it. Alternatively, you might need to chop up the text you are processing and do the matches against smaller pieces of the text.

Using the Matching Operator

The matching operator (m//) is your primary tool when applying your regular expressions. You have in fact already been using the operator in several examples. In Perl, the operator is so ubiquitous that you can abbreviate the already short operator by omitting the preceding "m".

It is the matching operator that does all the work of your regular expression. The expression itself merely contains the instructions to the regular expression engine in the matching operator. The engine does the actual parsing and matching based upon the instructions you give it in the regular expression.

Choosing a Different Target

By default, the matching operator applies the regular expression to the default pattern match space variable, $_. But this is often inconvenient. In the previous examples, you had to reassign the variable value you wanted to match to $_. Actually, you can instruct the matching operator to use a different target for the pattern match operation. You can use the binding operator (=~) to bind a different variable to the matching operator.

In this example, you extract the operating system information from the HTTP_USER_AGENT strings in the form submission log file. You use a more elaborate regular expression and bind it to a variable other than the default pattern match space.

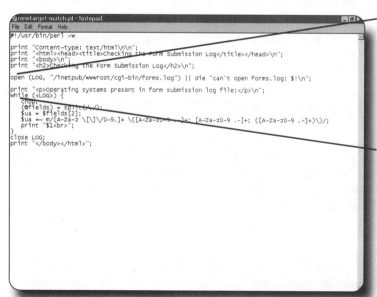

```
newtarget-match.pl - Notepad
File Edit Format Help
#!/usr/bin/perl -w

print "Content-type: text/html\n\n";
print "<html><head><title>Checking the Form Submission Log</title></head>\n";
print "<body>\n";
print "<h2>Checking the Form Submission Log</h2>\n";

open (LOG, "/inetpub/wwwroot/cgi-bin/forms.log") || die "can't open forms.log: $!\n";

print "<p>Operating systems present in form submission log file:</p>\n";
while (<LOG>) {
    chop;
    (@fields) = split(/,/);
    $ua = $fields[2];
    $ua =~ m/[A-Za-z \[\]\/0-9.]+ \(([A-Za-z0-9 .-]+; [A-Za-z0-9 .-]+)\)/;
    print "$1<br>";
}
close LOG;
print "</body></html>";
```

Open the log file and assign it the file handle LOG. Don't forget: Your path is likely different on your server, so you need to change it accordingly.

Read in a line at a time from the file and chop the trailing newline character. This should be a familiar process from the previous example.

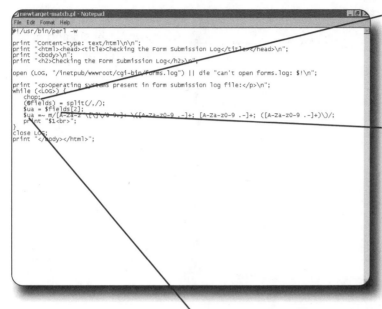

Use the `split` command to divide the line into pieces as defined by the comma character. Save the results in an array called `@fields`.

You are interested only in the third field on the line, the `HTTP_USER_AGENT` field. You can access this field by using the array notation with the array index set to 2. Remember that arrays in Perl are zero-based, so the third element is 2, not 3.

You can instruct the matching operator to use the `$ua` variable as the target by using the binding operator, `=~`.

The regular expression uses several character classes interspersed with literals and one grouping. For instance, the first character class matches one or more of the following: any letter, upper- or lowercase, from A to Z, a space, any number from 0 to 9, [,], ., or /. Note that this will match `"Mozilla/4.0"` or `"Mozilla/4.61 [en]"` in the target.

The group around the last character class holds the client browser's string value in the `$1` variable. This might not be an adequate character class for matching all possible operating system strings, but it is sufficient for the data in the sample forms.log file.

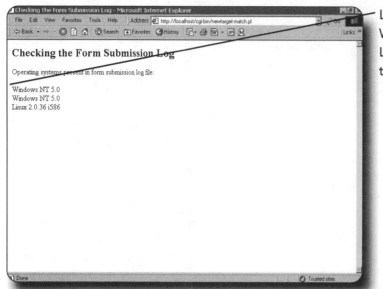

Looks like you have two Windows NT hosts and one Linux host represented in the log file.

Ignoring String Case

By default, the matching operator uses a case-sensitive match operation. That is, A is not equal to a, by default. You can force the matching operator to ignore case in the target string by using the /i switch. By using this switch, you can avoid limiting the references in your character classes to one case or the other.

In this example, you repeat the previous regular expression, but you reduce the size of the regular expression by eliminating references to the uppercase letters in the character classes.

Open the log file and set the file handle to LOG, as in the previous examples. Change the path of the log file.

Read in the log file one line at a time, and chop the trailing newline character with `chop`.

Split the line on the commas, as in the previous examples, and then assign the value of the third element to the variable $ua.

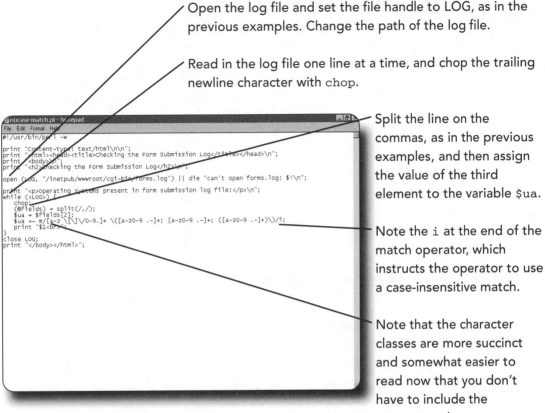

```
nocase-match.pl - Notepad
File  Edit  Format  Help
#!/usr/bin/perl -w

print "Content-type: text/html\n\n";
print "<html><head><title>Checking the Form Submission Log</title></head>\n";
print "<body>\n";
print "<h2>Checking the Form Submission Log</h2>\n";

open (LOG, "/inetpub/wwwroot/cgi-bin/forms.log") || die "can't open forms.log: $!\n";

print "<p>operating systems present in form submission log file:</p>\n";
while (<LOG>) {
    chop;
    (@fields) = split(/,/);
    $ua = $fields[2];
    $ua =~ m/[a-z \[\]\/0-9.]+ \([a-z0-9 .-]+; [a-z0-9 .-]+; ([a-z0-9 .-]+)\)/i;
    print "$1<br>";
}
close LOG;
print "</body></html>";
```

Note the `i` at the end of the match operator, which instructs the operator to use a case-insensitive match.

Note that the character classes are more succinct and somewhat easier to read now that you don't have to include the uppercase character range.

The results of this example should be identical to the results of the previous example. The changes used in this example simply make the code more readable. More readable code means code that is easier to maintain.

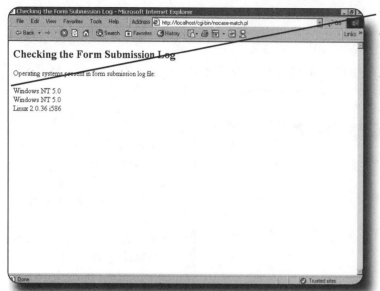

This output is identical to the output of the previous example, as expected. Although clean code is important for readability and maintainability, don't sacrifice function for form.

Using Different Delimiters

The matching operator is versatile. The forward slash delimiters of the operator are the default, but you can change them to whatever you want. It is not unlikely that you will be parsing text that contains many forward-slash characters. You can escape the forward slashes in your regular expression, but there is a better way.

Change the delimiters to something that does not appear in the text you are trying to match. Other punctuation marks are popular, such as the exclamation point, the vertical bar, or the tilde, but you can use whatever works best in that particular situation.

In this example, you use exclamation points to extract the operating system strings from the form submission log. The logic of the script is identical and the output should be identical as well.

The operation of this script is identical to the previous examples. Open the log file, read in a line at a time, chop the trailing newline, and assign $ua the value of the HTTP_USER_AGENT string.

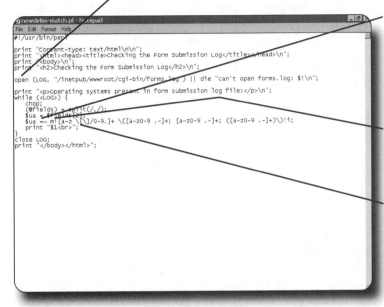

The regular expression has not changed from the previous case-insensitive example. Bind the match operator to the $ua variable.

Now, instead of forward slashes as the delimiters, you use exclamation points.

Notice that now you can remove the escaping backslash in front of the forward slash in this first character class. Because the forward slash is no longer the delimiter, you don't need to escape it to alter its meaning.

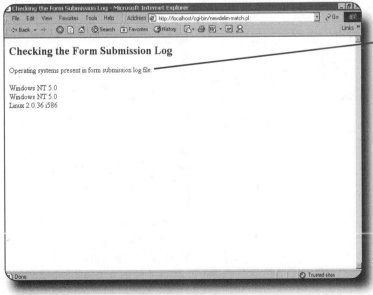

Again, the output is identical. The code changes are for readability and maintainability of the code. No script functionality has been sacrificed for this improvement.

Variable Interpolation

You might find that you don't know exactly what you want to match when you write a regular expression. You might want to match the contents of a variable that is filled in at run-time. To do this, you simply put the variable in the regular expression, with its preceding dollar sign. The regular expression engine in Perl *interpolates* the variable in the expression first, and then proceeds with the matching operation.

In other words, the engine makes a first pass over the expression, looking for variables. If it finds any, it rewrites the expression with the values of the variables in the expression. Then it takes the newly rewritten expression and runs the match operation.

In this example, you provide a form that enables users to select an operating system, which is then searched for in the form submission log. The form decoder script uses the value in the match operator to find matching lines in the log file and to display them in the browser.

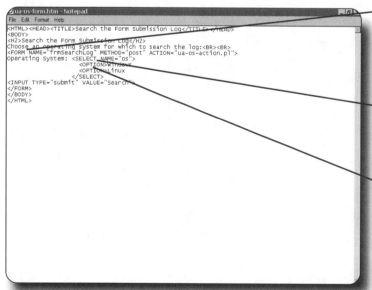

Create a form with the method set to post and the action set to the form decoder script name.

The form has one element, a <SELECT> tag with the name os.

Add two options, Windows and Linux, to the <SELECT> tag. These are the only operating systems that show up in the sample form submission log.

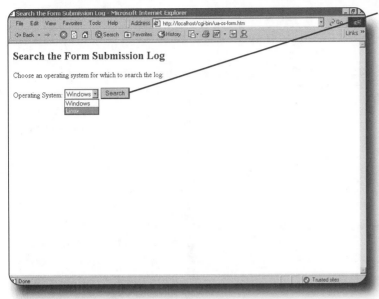

The form submission button has a specific name: Search. Always try to be descriptive about the functions of buttons and links in your forms and Web pages.

Because this script is handling posted information from a form, you need the CGI parsing code from earlier chapters to decode the form fields to Perl variables. The first 20 lines or so of this script take care of this decoding.

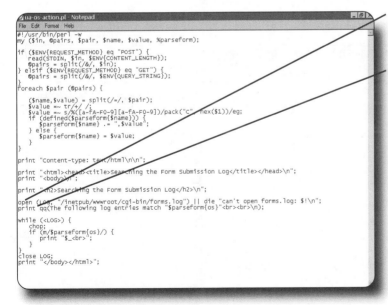

Open the log file and assign it the LOG file handle.

Here is a small Perl bonus. You can use the qq() function to wrap a string with double quotation marks. This enables you to write a string with embedded double quotes without having to escape them. Note that this line reports the user's choice, contained in $parseform{os}, back to the user. This kind of feedback is a good practice to follow.

As before, you read in the log file one line at a time, and chop the trailing newline character.

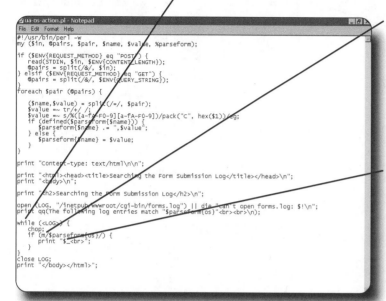

Place the `$parseform{os}` variable in the match operator. Whatever is contained in this variable is matched. To make this a case-insensitive match, you can add the `/i` switch.

If the match operator returns a true value (if it found a match in the current line), the line is displayed to the browser.

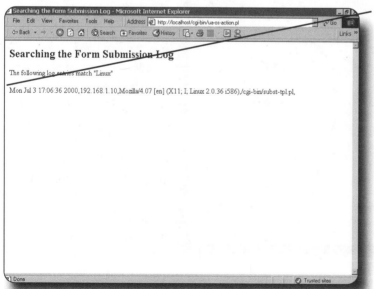

Only one Linux host is represented in the log. You can refine the script to break down the log entry by fields for more readability.

Making Substitutions with Regular Expressions

Pattern matching doesn't end with the matching operator. You can use the substitution operator to replace chunks of text in a pattern with something else. The substitution operator has two operands, the regular expression to match and the replacement expression (which can also be a regular expression).

The substitution operator (s///) has many of the same features as the matching operator. You can change the delimiters to suit your situation. You can use the /i switch to find a case-insensitive pattern match. The first operand of the substitution operator is a regular expression with all the same rules and capabilities of the matching operator's operand. In other words, if you can match a pattern with the matching operator, you can match it with the substitution operator. You can apply the binding operator to a different variable other than the default pattern match space.

```
ua-os-action.pl - Notepad
File  Edit  Format  Help
#!/usr/bin/perl -w
my ($in, @pairs, $pair, $name, $value, %parseform);

if ($ENV{REQUEST_METHOD} eq "POST") {
    read(STDIN, $in, $ENV{CONTENT_LENGTH});
    @pairs = split(/&/, $in);
} elsif ($ENV{REQUEST_METHOD} eq "GET") {
    @pairs = split(/&/, $ENV{QUERY_STRING});
}
foreach $pair (@pairs) {

    ($name,$value) = split(/=/, $pair);
    $value =~ tr/+/ /;
    $value =~ s/%([a-fA-F0-9][a-fA-F0-9])/pack("c", hex($1))/eg;
    if (defined($parseform{$name})) {
        $parseform{$name} .= ",$value";
    } else {
        $parseform{$name} = $value;
    }
}
print "Content-type: text/html\n\n";

print "<html><head><title>Searching the Form Submission Log</title></head>\n";
print "<body>\n";

print "<h2>Searching the Form Submission Log</h2>\n";

open (LOG, "/inetpub/wwwroot/cgi-bin/forms.log") || die "can't open forms.log $!\n";
print qq(The following log entries match "$parseform{os}"<br><br>\n);

while (<LOG>) {
    chop;
    if (m/$parseform{os}/) {
        print "$_<br>";
    }
}
close LOG;
print "</body></html>";
```

You've used the substitution operator already. At the top of the CGI parsing code form, there is a substitution operator that replaces the CGI-encoded characters with their literal counterparts. Take a look at the code in more detail now that you have some background in using regular expressions.

Before the substitution operator works on the encoded variables, you need to translate the plus characters to spaces with the tr/// operator.

The substitution regular expression looks for a percent character followed by a two-character pattern representing a hexadecimal value. The grouping parentheses remember the two hex characters matched.

```
ua-os-action.pl - Notepad
File  Edit  Format  Help
#!/usr/bin/perl -w
my ($in, @pairs, $pair, $name, $value, %parseform);

if ($ENV{REQUEST_METHOD} eq "POST") {
    read(STDIN, $in, $ENV{CONTENT_LENGTH});
    @pairs = split(/&/, $in);
} elsif ($ENV{REQUEST_METHOD} eq "GET") {
    @pairs = split(/&/, $ENV{QUERY_STRING});
}
foreach $pair (@pairs) {

    ($name, $value) = split(/=/, $pair);
    $value =~ tr/+/ /;
    $value =~ s/%([a-fA-F0-9][a-fA-F0-9])/pack("C", hex($1))/eg;
    if (defined($parseform{$name})) {
        $parseform{$name} .= ",$value";
    } else {
        $parseform{$name} = $value;
    }
}

print "Content-type: text/html\n\n";

print "<html><head><title>Searching the Form Submission Log</title></head>\n";
print "<body>\n";

print "<h2>Searching the Form Submission Log</h2>\n";

open (LOG, "/inetpub/wwwroot/cgi-bin/forms.log") || die "can't open forms.log: $!\n";
print qq(The following log entries match "$parseform{os}"<br><br>\n);

while (<LOG>) {
    chop;
    if (m/$parseform{os}/) {
        print "$_<br>";
    }
}
close LOG;
print "</body></html>";
```

The replacement operand is a Perl function that translates the matched hexadecimal value and stores it in $1 to its literal character, thereby decoding the character as encoded by CGI.

Note that the $1 variable contains the two characters matched in the first operand of the substitution operator.

The /e switch instructs the substitution operator to evaluate the expression in the replacement operand. This causes the operator to execute the pack function, which retrieves the actual character represented by the hexadecimal match. The /g switch instructs the operator to perform this substitution everywhere in the target string, not just in the first match.

Advanced Substitutions

The previous form decoding statements are a fairly advanced use of the substitution operator, but you can take it even further. The first several examples in this chapter used a form submission log as the text to process. In this advanced example, you create the log file itself from a template and a regular expression with the substitution operator.

The template is simply a list of CGI variable names enclosed in double angle brackets. A comma separates each of these constructs.

By using a template for the log file, you can change how the log file is laid out at any time. For instance, you might decide that you want a different delimiter in the log.

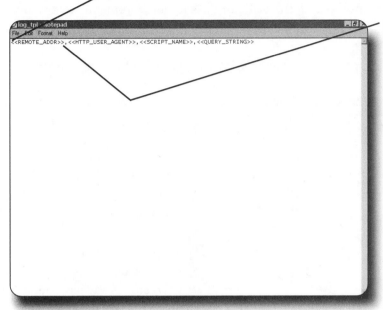

Open the log template file and assign the LOGTPL file handle to it.

The $/ variable controls the input record separator in Perl. By undefining it, you effectively remove the record separator that reads in files. Now when you read in a file, you get the whole file, not just one line!

```
#!/usr/bin/perl
my ($in, @pairs, $pair, $name, $value, %parseform);

if ($ENV{REQUEST_METHOD} eq "POST") {
    read(STDIN, $in, $ENV{CONTENT_LENGTH});
    @pairs = split(/&/, $in);
} elsif ($ENV{REQUEST_METHOD} eq "GET") {
    @pairs = split(/&/, $ENV{QUERY_STRING});
}
foreach $pair (@pairs) {

    ($name,$value) = split(/=/, $pair);
    $value =~ tr/+/ /;
    $value =~ s/%([a-fA-F0-9][a-fA-F0-9])/pack("c", hex($1))/eg;
    if (defined($parseform{$name})) {
        $parseform{$name} .= ",$value";
    } else {
        $parseform{$name} = $value;
    }
}

print "Content-type: text/html\n\n";

print "<html><head><title>CGI Variables</title></head>\n";
print "<body>\n";
print "<h2>Test</h2>";
open(LOGTPL, "/inetpub/wwwroot/cgi-bin/log_tpl");
{
    local undef $/;
    $log_tpl = <LOGTPL>;
}
close LOGTPL;

open(LOG, ">>/inetpub/wwwroot/cgi-bin/forms.log") or print "can't open log file: $!\n<br>";

($logline = $log_tpl) =~ s/<<([^>]+)>>/$ENV{$1}/g;
print LOG scalar localtime(), ",$logline";
close LOG;
print $logline;
print "</body></html>";
```

log_tpl file contents:
```
<<REMOTE_ADDR>>,<<HTTP_USER_AGENT>>,<<SCRIPT_NAME>>,<<QUERY_STRING>>
```

This line stores the entire contents of the file referenced by LOGTPL into the variable $log_tpl. Note also that this line and the previous one are enclosed in curly braces. This ensures that the value of $/ is remembered and reset when the braces are exited.

Open the log file for writing. Don't forget to change the path.

```
subst-tpl.pl - Notepad
File Edit Format Help
#!/usr/bin/perl
my ($in, @pairs, $pair, $name, $value, %parseform);

if ($ENV{REQUEST_METHOD} eq "POST") {
    read(STDIN, $in, $ENV{CONTENT_LENGTH});
    @pairs = split(/&/, $in);
} elsif ($ENV{REQUEST_METHOD} eq "GET") {
    @pairs = split(/&/, $ENV{QUERY_STRING});
}
foreach $pair (@pairs){

    ($name,$value) = split(/=/, $pair);
    $value =~ tr/+/ /;
    $value =~ s/%([a-fA-F0-9][a-fA-F0-9])/pack("C", hex($1))/eg;
    if (defined($parseform{$name})) {
        $parseform{$name} .= ",",$value"
    } else {
        $parseform{$name} = $value;
    }
}

print "Content-type: text/html\n\n";

print "<html><head><title>CGI Variables</title></head>\n";
print "<body>\n";
print "<h2>Test</h2>";
open(LOGTPL, "/inetpub/wwwroot/cgi-bin/log.tpl");
{
    local $/ undef $/;
    $log_tpl = <LOGTPL>;
}
close LOGTPL;

open(LOG, ">>/inetpub/wwwroot/cgi-bin/forms.log") or print "can't open log file: $!\n<br>";

($logline = $log_tpl) =~ s/<<([^>]+)>>/$ENV{$1}/g;
print LOG scalar localtime(), ",$logline";
close LOG;
print $logline;
print "</body></html>";
```

This line does double duty. The first part copies the value of $log_tpl to $logline. Then the substitution operator performs its match and substitution on $logline.

The regular expression matches one or more characters between double angle brackets that are not the right angle bracket itself. The grouping parentheses then remember this value so it can be used in the replacement operand.

The replacement operand is an interpolated variable. The $1 is replaced with the name of the CGI variable in the template file. Then the %ENV hash retrieves the value at the location specified by the CGI variable name. The substitution operator then replaces the template placeholder in $logline with the CGI variable value.

This is a demonstration script. The code presented here is intended to be added to a form decoder script so you can track form submissions in a log file. For the purposes of demonstration, however, the script outputs to the Web browser window as well as to the log file.

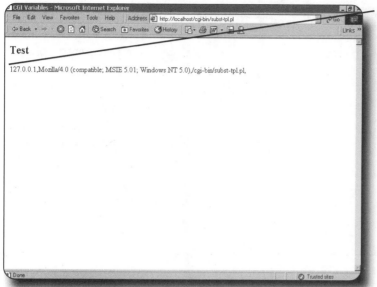

This line of output is written to the log file. By editing the template, you can change what is output to the log file. The code need not be changed.

Using the Split Function

The split function divides a string into pieces as defined by a pattern. In fact, the first argument of the split function is a modified match operator. So you can use a regular expression in the split operation. With careful planning, you can use the split function with a regular expression to divide up large chunks of text for separate processing or extraction.

In this example, you use a regular expression with the split function to divide the contents of a Web page into paragraphs, as defined by the HTML paragraph tag (<P>). You use the sample HTML file included on the CD as the function's target.

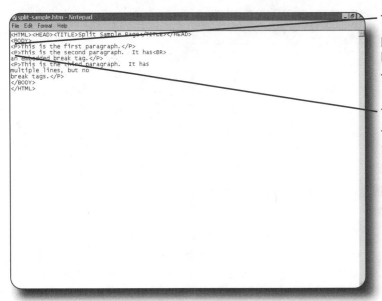

This sample file has three paragraphs in it, as defined by the HTML paragraph tag (<P>).

This paragraph has a break tag (<BR>) in the middle of it. The regular expression ignores anything but the paragraph tag for the split operation.

First, open the sample HTML file for this example. Check the path to make sure it points to the location of the sample file.

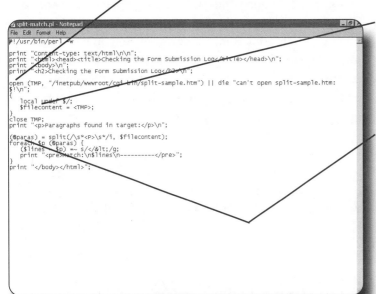

Undefine the input record separator and read the entire file contents into the $filecontent variable, just as in the previous example.

The split function returns an array containing the chunks into which the text was divided. Save this array as @paras.

```
split-match.pl - Notepad
File  Edit  Format  Help
#!/usr/bin/perl -w
print "Content-type: text/html\n\n";
print "<html><head><title>Checking the Form Submission Log</title></head>\n";
print "<body>\n";
print "<h2>Checking the Form Submission Log</h2>\n";

open (TMP, "/inetpub/wwwroot/cgi-bin/split-sample.htm") || die "can't open split-sample.htm:
$!\n";
{
    local undef $/;
    $filecontent = <TMP>;
}
close TMP;
print "<p>Paragraphs found in target:</p>\n";

(@paras) = split(/\s*<P>\s*/i, $filecontent);
foreach $p (@paras) {
    ($lines = $p) =~ s/</&lt;/g;
    print "<pre>Match:\n$lines\n----------</pre>";
}
print "</body></html>";
```

This regular expression uses Perl shortcut classes, mentioned earlier in the chapter. The regular expression matches the HTML paragraph tag with zero or more white-space characters (represented by the \s*) before and after it in the $filecontent variable. The /i switch is used to match <P> or <p> in the tag.

```
split-match.pl - Notepad
File  Edit  Format  Help
#!/usr/bin/perl -w
print "Content-type: text/html\n\n";
print "<html><head><title>Checking the Form Submission Log</title></head>\n";
print "<body>\n";
print "<h2>Checking the Form Submission Log</h2>\n";

open (TMP, "/inetpub/wwwroot/cgi-bin/split-sample.htm") || die "can't open split-sample.htm:
$!\n";
{
    local undef $/;
    $filecontent = <TMP>;
}
close TMP;
print "<p>Paragraphs found in target:</p>\n";

(@paras) = split(/\s*<P>\s*/i, $filecontent);
foreach $p (@paras) {
    ($lines = $p) =~ s/</&lt;/g;
    print "<pre>Match:\n$lines\n----------</pre>";
}
print "</body></html>";
```

Now you loop through each paragraph chunk that the split function found (and stored in the array @paras) by using the foreach control-of-flow function.

The substitution and reassignment statement is for display clean up. It matches any left angle bracket and changes it to the escaped HTML sequence. This prevents the browser from trying to interpret the HTML in the resulting matched strings.

You can display each paragraph found in the sample file and frame the text with HTML formatting to make the display a bit more readable.

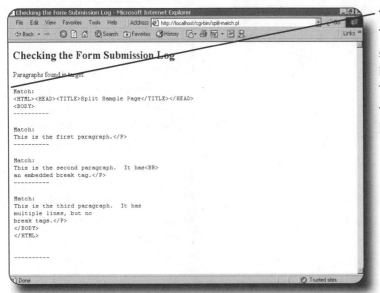

The results are not perfect. The split function only splits a string; it does not interpret it in any way. The first "paragraph" found includes the HTML header tags.

Summary

You now have the basic skills necessary to write regular expressions with Perl. You are acquainted with the match operator, the substitution operator, and the split function and how they use regular expressions. You know what a character class is and how to create one and use it in a regular expression. You can write code to perform case-insensitive pattern matches and group matches. You also learned how to use the substitution operator and a regular expression with file templates to create dynamically generated files. You are now prepared to begin writing regular expressions on your own. You are on your way to a new way of programming.

11

Subroutines

A subroutine is a little section of code or a mini program that performs a specific task or set of tasks. Subroutines are great for handling tasks, either simple or complex ones, which you need to perform more than once in your CGI script. Subroutines can also be stored for later use in new CGI scripts. In this chapter, you'll learn how to:

- Create a subroutine
- Store a subroutine
- Use a subroutine
- Use values returned by subroutines

Creating a Subroutine

In Chapter 5, "Getting the Data Into Your CGI Application," you created the parseform.cgi script. In Chapter 7, "Arrays," you placed the code from this script into a subroutine named Parse_Form in the subparseform.lib. This subroutine was called from the program by using the require "subparseform.lib" and the "&Parse_Form;" statements. You can create a subroutine anywhere within your CGI script, but subroutines are usually placed at the end of your script. Using subroutines will save you time because you won't need to type the same code multiple times. It will also help you keep the overall length of your code shorter, thus making the file size smaller. Now you'll learn how to create a basic subroutine.

A Basic Subroutine

```
Untitled - Notepad
File Edit Search Help
sub Parse_Form {
    if ($ENV{'REQUEST_METHOD'} eq 'GET') {
        @pairs = split(/&/, $ENV{'QUERY_STRING'});
    } elsif ($ENV{'REQUEST_METHOD'} eq 'POST') {
        read (STDIN, $in, $ENV{'CONTENT_LENGHT'});
        @pairs = split(/&/, $in);
    } else {
        print "Content-type: text/html\n\n";
        print "<P>Use Post or Get";
    }

    foreach $pair (@pairs) {
        ($name, $value) = split (/=/, $pair);
        $name =~ s/\+/ /g;
        $name =~ s/%(..)/pack("C", hex($1))/ge;
        $value =~ s/\+/ /g;
        $value =~ s/%(..)/pack("C", hex($1))/ge;
        $value =~ s/<!--(.|\n)*-->//g;

        if ($parseform{$name}) {
            $parseform{$name} .= ", $value";
        } else {
            $parseform{$name} = $value;
        }
    }
}
```

The process of creating a subroutine is very simple. You simply surround the code you want to use in the subroutine as follows.

First type **sub**; this tells Perl that this code is a subroutine.

Next, type the name of the subroutine. This name can contain any combination of alphanumeric characters and underscores. A subroutine name cannot contain any spaces or punctuation. As with variable names, subroutine names are also case sensitive.

Follow this name with an open brace character.

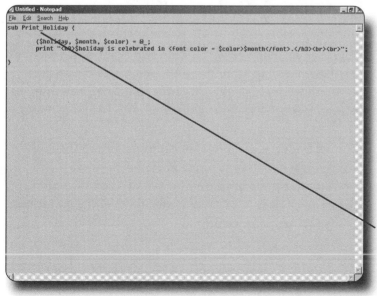

```
Untitled - Notepad
File  Edit  Search  Help
sub Parse_Form {

        if ($ENV{'REQUEST_METHOD'} eq 'GET') {
                @pairs = split(/&/, $ENV{'QUERY_STRING'});
        } elsif ($ENV{'REQUEST_METHOD'} eq 'POST') {
                read (STDIN, $in, $ENV{'CONTENT_LENGHT'});
                @pairs = split(/&/, $in);
        } else {
                print "Content-type: text/html\n\n";
                print "<P>Use Post or Get";
        }

        foreach $pair (@pairs) {
                ($name, $value) = split (/=/, $pair);
                $name =~ s/\+/ /g;
                $name =~ s/%(..)/pack("C", hex($1))/ge;
                $value =~ s/\+/ /g;
                $value =~ s/%(..)/pack("C", hex($1))/ge;
                $value =~ s/<!--(.|\n)*-->//g;

                if ($parseForm{$name}) {
                        $parseForm{$name} .= ", $value";
                } else {
                        $parseForm{$name} = $value;
                }
        }
```

And finally, type a closing brace character at the end of the subroutine.

The code for this subroutine can be found in the subparseform.lib file. This basic type of subroutine does not require any input in order to use it. It just performs a specific function (in this case, it parses form input). There's no way for you to control or alter which data is processed when you call this type of subroutine.

You are now ready to learn how to create a subroutine that requires input.

```
Untitled - Notepad
File  Edit  Search  Help
sub Print_Holiday {

        ($holiday, $month, $color) = @_;
        print "<h3>$holiday is celebrated in <Font color = $color>$month</Font>.</h3><br><br>";

}
```

A Subroutine that Requires Input

In Chapter 7, you created a script that printed the month in which certain holidays occur. You will now learn how to modify parts of that script to create a subroutine that requires input.

As in the previous example, type **sub**, the name of the subroutine, and an open brace.

Any data passed to a subroutine is contained in a special array called the *subroutine arglist*. It is denoted by the @_ characters.

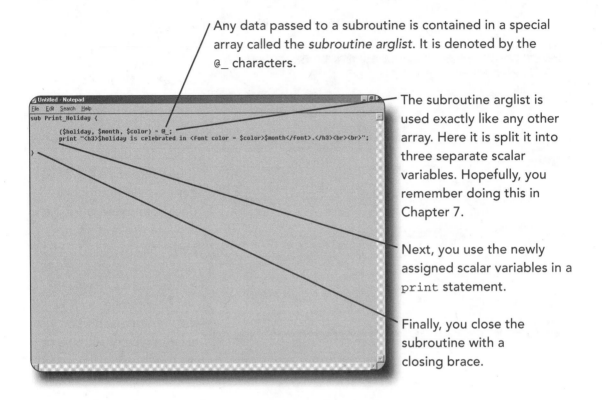

The subroutine arglist is used exactly like any other array. Here it is split it into three separate scalar variables. Hopefully, you remember doing this in Chapter 7.

Next, you use the newly assigned scalar variables in a print statement.

Finally, you close the subroutine with a closing brace.

Storing a Subroutine

Now that you know how to create two types of subroutines, you'll learn how to store the subroutines you create in a *library*. A library is simply a text file containing one or more subroutines.

Most of the time, a subroutine is proprietary to the specific CGI script for which you wrote it. However, some subroutines can be used over in new CGI scripts. Storing these subroutines in a library makes them easily accessible to any CGI script you write.

As I mentioned earlier, subroutines are stored in libraries, which are simply text files. Libraries usually have a .lib or .pl extension.

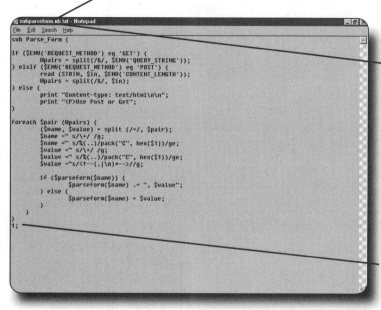

```
subparseform.nb.txt - Notepad
File  Edit  Search  Help
sub Parse_Form {

if ($ENV{'REQUEST_METHOD'} eq 'GET') {
        @pairs = split(/&/, $ENV{'QUERY_STRING'});
} elsif ($ENV{'REQUEST_METHOD'} eq 'POST') {
        read (STDIN, $in, $ENV{'CONTENT_LENGTH'});
        @pairs = split(/&/, $in);
} else {
        print "Content-type: text/html\n\n";
        print "<P>Use Post or Get";
}

foreach $pair (@pairs) {
        ($name, $value) = split (/=/, $pair);
        $name =~ s/\+/ /g;
        $name =~ s/%(..)/pack("C", hex($1))/ge;
        $value =~ s/\+/ /g;
        $value =~ s/%(..)/pack("C", hex($1))/ge;
        $value =~s/<!--(.|\n)*-->//g;

        if ($parseform{$name}) {
                $parseform{$name} .= ", $value";
        } else {
                $parseform{$name} = $value;
        }
    }
}
1;
```

NOTE

See the section entitled "Creating Your Application Using a PC" in Chapter 3, "Your First CGI Application," for instructions on renaming a file and removing the .txt extension.

The only special thing that you need to do is add the number 1, followed by a semicolon, to the bottom of the file. The last statement of any Perl library must evaluate to "true". Your statement can be anything that evaluates to "true" such as "1 + 1"; However, a simple 1 and a semicolon is most commonly used.

Then save the file as subparseform.lib.

Calling a Subroutine

To use a subroutine, you create a call to the subroutine in your CGI script. As you know, there are two types of subroutines: ones that don't require any input and ones that do. Either of these two types can be contained within a CGI script or stored in an external library. Next you learn how to call each of these types of subroutines.

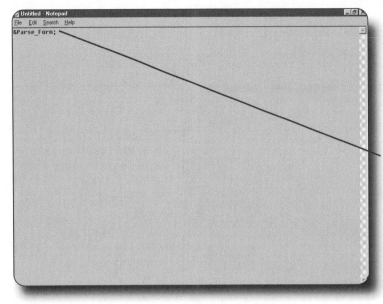

Calling a Basic Subroutine

A subroutine call is simple. You've already seen them used in previous chapters.

To call a subroutine, type an ampersand, followed by the name of the subroutine and a semicolon.

NOTE

When Perl encounters a subroutine call during execution of a CGI script, the code within the subroutine is executed. Execution continues with the next line of code after the subroutine call.

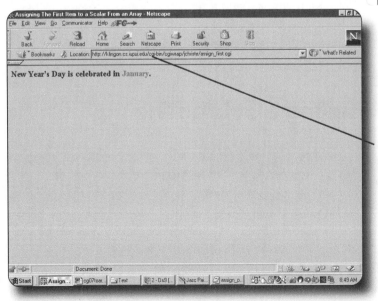

Calling a Subroutine that Requires Input

In Chapter 7 you saw a script that printed the month in which a holiday occurs.

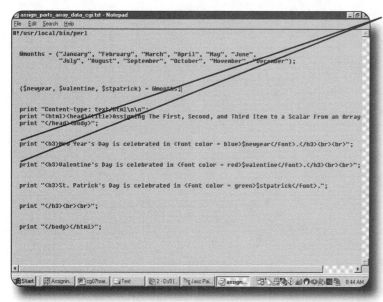

Later, you added more print statements to print multiple holidays.

Because every print statement contains the same basic elements, you can write a subroutine containing one print statement that will produce the same results.

You now learn how to create a subroutine that can take any holiday, month, and font color as input. The subroutine then prints the data in the same format as the previous scripts you've seen. The advantages are that you can use the same subroutine to print any holiday you choose, and you can also specify the font color.

The only difference in calling a subroutine that requires input is that you need to include the input data when you call it.

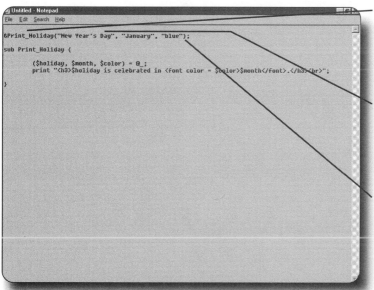

You start with an ampersand, the name of the subroutine, and an opening parenthesis.

Next you include the data you want to send to the subroutine, separated by commas.

Finally, close the subroutine call with an end parenthesis and a semicolon.

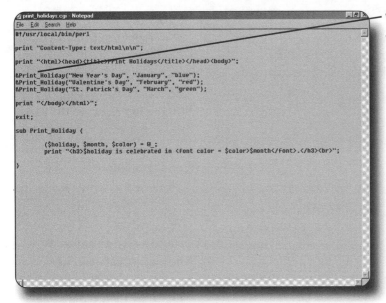

When called correctly from within a CGI application as in print_holidays.cgi...

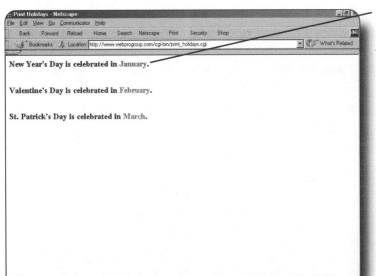

...this subroutine creates the same results as the script that used three separate print statements.

Calling a Subroutine from an External File

You call a subroutine from an external library in exactly the same way you call a subroutine that is within your CGI script. The only difference is that you must use a *require* statement. The require statement uses the `require` function. You've seen a require statement before, but here it is again.

The require statement appropriately starts with the word `require`.

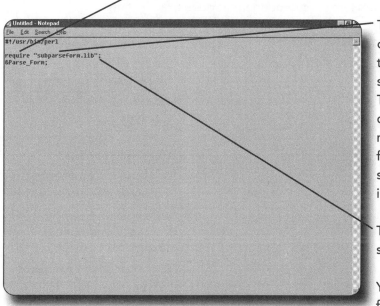

This is followed by the name of the library that contains the subroutine or subroutines you want to use. The library name must be in double or single quotation marks. The `require` function allows your CGI script to use the subroutines in the specified library.

The statement ends with a semicolon, of course.

You can call sub parse_form from any of your CGI applications as described above. This makes it so that you only have to include two lines of code in your scripts to parse form input rather than 23!

NOTE

See the section entitled "Evaluating without Comparisons" in Chapter 9, "Conditional Statements," for information on true/false comparisons.

Subroutine Return Values

All subroutines return some value. The value returned from the subroutine is determined by the last statement or expression that is executed. If the expression evaluates to `true`, the value 1 is returned. If the expression evaluates to `false`, the value 0 is returned.

A simple example of a subroutine that returns a useable value is one that determines whether one number is larger than another number.

Here's a subroutine that does exactly that.

```
Untitled - Notepad
File  Edit  Search  Help

sub Compare_Numbers {

    ($first_number, $second_number) = @_;

    $first_number > $second_number;

}
```

You should be familiar with the first line in the subroutine. It splits the input data into two scalar variables.

The last line of this subroutine is an expression that evaluates whether the first number is greater than the second number.

If this statement evaluates to true, the return value is 1. Otherwise, the return value is 0.

Using the Subroutine Return Value

To use the return value from a subroutine, you can assign that value to a variable as in the compare_numbers.cgi script on the CD-ROM. Here's how to do it:

Type the variable name you want to use followed by an equals sign, just like you do when assigning a value to any other variable.

Then you call the subroutine by typing an ampersand and the name of the subroutine, followed by an open parenthesis.

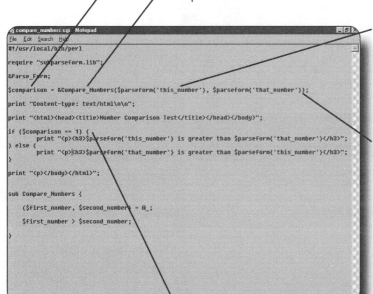

```
#!/usr/local/bin/perl

require "subparseform.lib";

&Parse_Form;

$comparison = &Compare_Numbers($parseform{'this_number'}, $parseform{'that_number'});

print "Content-type: text/html\n\n";

print "<html><head><title>Number Comparison Test</title></head></body>";

if ($comparison == 1) {
        print "<p><h3>$parseform{'this_number'} is greater than $parseform{'that_number'}</h3>";
} else {
        print "<p><h3>$parseform{'that_number'} is greater than $parseform{'this_number'}</h3>";
}

print "<p></body></html>";

sub Compare_Numbers {

    ($first_number, $second_number) = @_;

    $first_number > $second_number;

}
```

Then you type the names of the variables that contain the numbers you want to compare, separated by a comma.

End the call with a closing parenthesis and a semicolon.

When this expression is evaluated, the variable to the left of the equals sign will have a value of either 1 or 0.

Now you can use this variable in a simple if/else conditional statement to print the results of the comparison.

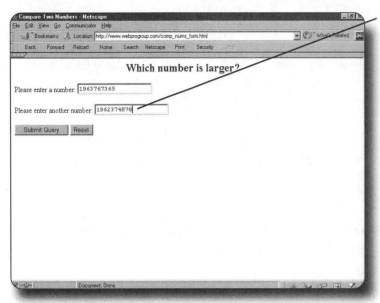

The form that calls the compare_numbers.cgi application (comp_nums_form.html) has two text input fields for submitting two numbers.

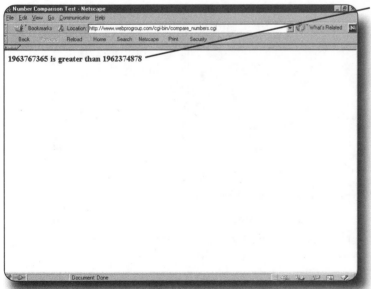

The page generated by the application displays the results of the number comparison.

Although this example is quite simple, you can see the usefulness of using subroutine return values.

Manually Setting the Return Value

Although regular true/false return values are helpful, sometimes they are not enough. In some circumstances, you will want to set the return value yourself. To do this, you must use a return statement. As you can probably guess, you use a `return` function to set the return value manually. Here's another simple example to demonstrate how this is done from the compare_numbers2.cgi script on the CD-ROM. The first difference to note is in the subroutine.

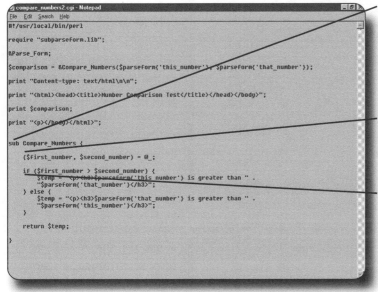

The first line of the subroutine is exactly the same. It starts with `sub`, the name of the subroutine, and an opening brace.

The second line is also the same. The subroutine input is split into scalar variables.

In this version, you move the if/else comparison to the subroutine. The `if` statement contains the comparison that determines whether the first number is greater than the second.

If this statement evaluates to true, you set the value of a new variable to the output string you want to print like so: Include the name of the variable, the equals sign, and then the string you want to print enclosed in quotation marks. End the line with a semicolon.

Next, there's the beginning of the `else` statement.

If the `else` block is executed, the new variable is set to an alternative version of the output string.

Finally, you return the value of the new variable with the return statement. Type **return** followed by the new variable. End the line with a semicolon.

```
#!/usr/local/bin/perl

require "subparseform.lib";

&Parse_Form;

$comparison = &Compare_Numbers($parseform{'this_number'}, $parseform{'that_number'});

print "Content-type: text/html\n\n";

print "<html><head><title>Number Comparison Test</title></head></body>";

print $comparison;

print "<p></body></html>";

sub Compare_Numbers {

    ($first_number, $second_number) = @_;

    if ($first_number > $second_number) {
        $temp = "<p><h3>$parseform{'this_number'} is greater than " .
        "$parseform{'that_number'}</h3>";
    } else {
        $temp = "<p><h3>$parseform{'that_number'} is greater than " .
        "$parseform{'this_number'}</h3>";
    }

    return $temp;
}
```

After the subroutine is executed, the variable to the left of the equals sign will have the value of one of the output strings.

To print the output in this version, you simply need to print the variable.

```
#!/usr/local/bin/perl

require "subparseform.lib";

&Parse_Form;

$comparison = &Compare_Numbers($parseform{'this_number'}, $parseform{'that_number'});

print "Content-type: text/html\n\n";

print "<html><head><title>Number Comparison Test</title></head></body>";

print $comparison;

print "<p></body></html>";

sub Compare_Numbers {

    ($first_number, $second_number) = @_;

    if ($first_number > $second_number) {
        $temp = "<p><h3>$parseform{'this_number'} is greater than " .
        "$parseform{'that_number'}</h3>";
    } else {
        $temp = "<p><h3>$parseform{'that_number'} is greater than " .
        "$parseform{'this_number'}</h3>";
    }

    return $temp;
}
```

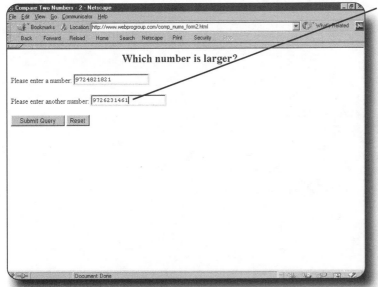

The form that calls the compare_numbers2.cgi application (comp_nums_form2.html) has two text input fields for submitting two numbers—exactly like the previous form.

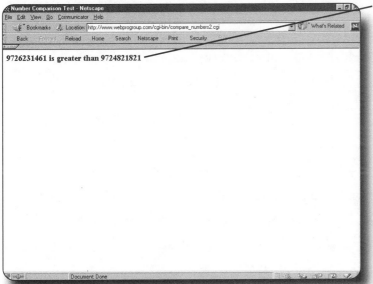

The page generated by the application also displays the results of the number comparison in exactly the same way.

Summary

The knowledge you gained in this chapter will help shorten your CGI scripts by enabling you to place redundant code into subroutines. You know the difference between a basic subroutine and a subroutine that requires input and how to call both types. The job of creating new CGI applications will be much easier now because you can save reusable subroutines in your own library to use over again and again. You now understand how to use a subroutine return value, how to manually set the return value, and the importance of both.

12

Retaining Visitor Data

In the scripts you've created so far, if you resubmit a form, the server processes the request as if you never submitted it before. The form must be filled out again. This is what is known as a *stateless* connection. If you need some way of retaining the data submitted in the first form while gathering new data from the second form, hidden fields enable you to do that.

What if you want visitors to register the first time they visit your Web site? Also, when visitors return to your site, you want them to be able to skip the registration and go directly to a login page. If you need some way to remember that a visitor has registered and to recognize them when they return, cookies help you to do that. In this chapter, you'll learn how to:

- Create hidden fields
- Use hidden fields
- Set cookies
- Use cookies

Creating Hidden Fields

A hidden field is another way to pass input data to your script. Because there is no reason for your users to view it, this input data is hidden from the direct view of the users. Hence the name "hidden." However, hidden fields can be viewed in the HTML source of your form. Hidden fields can be included in static HTML forms, such as to pass the recipient e-mail address to a feedback script. Hidden fields also provide a way for you to manage collected data from users during a multi-form input process.

Adding Hidden Fields to Your Form

In appearance, a hidden field is similar to all other form fields. You create a hidden field as follows.

First type a less than sign (<) and the word **input**, just like the beginning of any other form field.

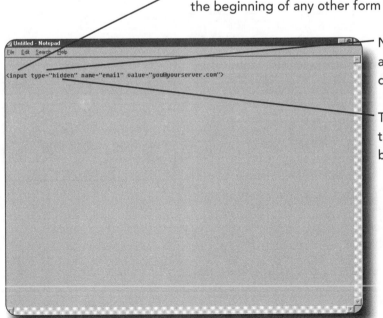

Next, type the word **type**, an equals sign, and opening quotation marks.

The type is hidden, so type the word **hidden**, followed by closing quotation marks.

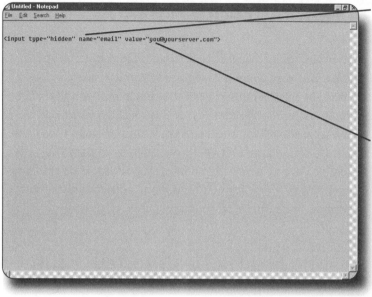

Next, type the word **name**, an equals sign, opening quotation marks, and the name you want to give this field followed by closing quotation marks.

To end it, type the word **value**, an equals sign, opening quotations marks, and the value you want to give this field. Add the closing quotation marks and a greater than sign (>).

Although this field does not show up in your form, you can rest assured that the value will be passed to your CGI script when the form is submitted. You can use this value just like the input from any other form field.

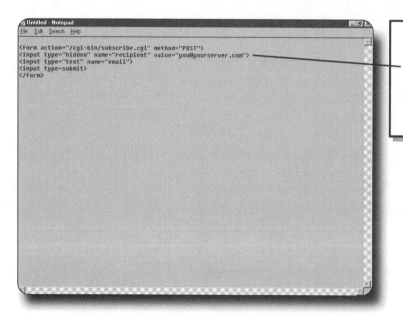

NOTE

Hidden fields must be placed within the opening and closing form tags.

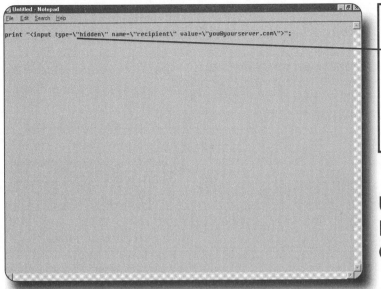

```
print "<input type=\"hidden\" name=\"recipient\" value=\"you@yourserver.com\">";
```

TIP

When printing a hidden field from within a CGI script, quotation marks within the tag should have a backslash in front of them.

Using a Hidden Field to Store Collected Data

As I mentioned in the beginning of this chapter, there will be times when you'll want to require your users to submit two or more forms in succession. Hidden fields can be used to retain the input data between forms, as shown in the following example.

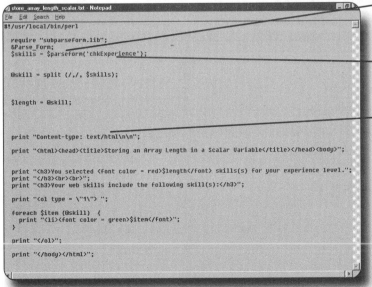

store_array_length_scalar.txt - Notepad
File Edit Search Help

```
#!/usr/local/bin/perl

require "subparseform.lib";
&Parse_Form;
$skills = $parseform{'chkExperience'};

@skill = split (/,/, $skills);

$length = @skill;

print "Content-type: text/html\n\n";

print "<html><head><title>Storing an Array Length in a Scalar Variable</title></head><body>";

print "<h3>You selected <font color = red>$length</font> skills(s) for your experience level.";
print "</h3><br><br>";
print "<h3>Your web skills include the following skill(s):</h3>";

print "<ol type = \"1\"> ";

foreach $item (@skill) {
   print "<li><font color = green>$item</font>";
}

print "</ol>";

print "</body></html>";
```

In previous scripts, you parsed form input.

Then you processed the form input.

And finally, you printed some results to the browser.

In this new script (use_hidden_fields.cgi script on the CD-ROM), you parse the form as you've done before.

The second form contains a hidden field that identifies it as the final form. So, rather than processing the input right away, you want to perform a test to determine whether the second or final form has been submitted.

To determine whether the final form has been submitted, you use a simple if/else block.

If the final form has been submitted, you process the form data and print the final results.

```perl
#!/usr/local/bin/perl

require "subparseform.lib";
&Parse_Form;

if ($parseform{'Form_name'} eq "Final") {

    $skills = $parseform{chkExperience};

    @skill = split (/,/, $skills);

    $length = @skill;

    print "Content-Type: text/html\n\n";
    print "<html><head><title>Using Hidden Fields</title></head>";
    print "<body bgcolor=white>";
    print "<h3>Your real name is <font color=blue>$parseform{'FirstName'}</font>, ";
    print "but people call you <font color=navy>$parseform{'NickName'}</font>.</h3><p>";
    print "<h3>You're from <font color=gray>$parseform{'Country'}</font> and you claim to ";
    print "be only <font color=maroon>$parseform{'Age'}</font> ";
    print "years old.</h3><p>";
    print "<h3>You selected <font color=red>$length</font> skill(s) for your experience level.";
    print "</h3>\n<P>\n";
    print "<h3>Your Web skills include the following skill(s):</h3>\n";
    print "<ol type =\"1\">\n";
    foreach $item (@skill) {
        print "<li><font color=green>$item</font>\n";
    }
    print "</ol>\n";
    print "</body></html>\n";

} else {

    print "Content-Type: text/html\n\n";
    print "<html><head><title>Using Hidden Fields</title></head>\n";
    print "<body bgcolor=white>\n";
```

If the final form has not been submitted, you print the second form.

As mentioned previously, this form includes a hidden field that identifies it as the final form.

The second form also includes hidden fields containing all the data that was collected in the first form.

```perl
    print "<h3>You selected <font color=red>$length</font> skill(s) for your experience level.";
    print "</h3>\n<P>\n";
    print "<h3>Your Web skills include the following skill(s):</h3>\n";
    print "<ol type =\"1\">\n";
    foreach $item (@skill) {
        print "<li><font color=green>$item</font>\n";
    }
    print "</ol>\n";
    print "</body></html>\n";

} else {

    print "Content-Type: text/html\n\n";
    print "<html><head><title>Using Hidden Fields</title></head>\n";
    print "<body bgcolor=white>\n";
    print "<h2>What areas do you have experience in?</h2>\n";
    print "<form action=\"/cgi-bin/use_hidden_fields.cgi\" method=\"POST\">\n";
    print "<input type=\"hidden\" name=\"Form_name\" value=\"Final\">\n";
    while (($key, $value) = each %parseform) {
        print "<input type=\"hidden\" name=\"$key\" value=\"$value\">\n";
    }
    print "<input type=\"checkbox\" NAME=\"chkExperience\" value=\"HTML\">HTML<br>\n";
    print "<input type=\"checkbox\" name=\"chkExperience\" value=\"DHTML\">DHTML<br>\n";
    print "<input type=\"checkbox\" name=\"chkExperience\" value=\"JavaScript\">JavaScript<br>\n";
    print "<input type=\"checkbox\" name=\"chkExperience\" value=\"CGIPerl\">CGI/Perl<br>\n";
    print "<input type=\"checkbox\" NAME=\"chkExperience\" VALUE=\"Java Applets\">Java Applets";
    print "\n<p>\n";
    print "<input type=submit>\n";
    print "<input type=reset>\n";
    print "</form>\n";
    print "</body></html>\n";

}
```

NOTE

See the section entitled "Retrieving Each Key and Value" in Chapter 8, "Hashes," for more information on using a `while` loop to retrieve the data in key-value pairs.

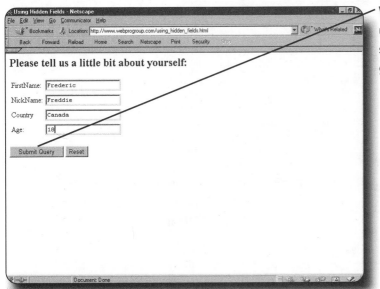

When the form used to call use_hidden_fields.cgi is submitted, a new form is generated.

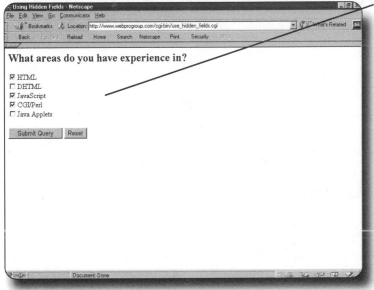

This is the new form.

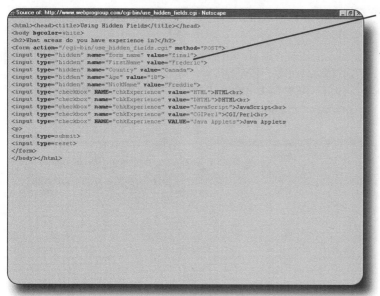

This new form contains the input data from the previous form stored as hidden fields.

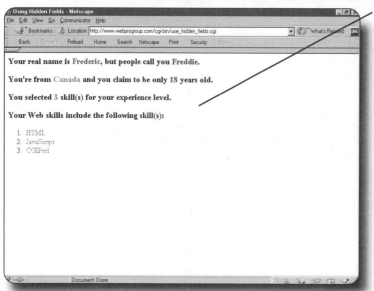

After the final form is submitted, the final results are printed.

Understanding Cookies

As I mentioned earlier, using cookies is another valuable way to retain visitor data. You'll now learn all about cookies and how to use them.

A *cookie* is simply a piece of information stored on a user's hard drive. This bit of information can then be retrieved when the user returns to the same Web site. Cookies have a size limit of 4K. Browsers allow only 20 cookies per domain and will store a maximum of 300 cookies at any given time. After these limits are reached and a new cookie is sent, the oldest cookie in the jar gets eaten to make room for the new one.

Cookies can store any piece of data that you want to be able to retrieve when users return to your Web site. Cookies can help you personalize a visitor's experience at your Web site. By gathering and storing information about a user's preferences, your CGI applications can tailor the output to each user. You can store a visitor's information and save them time because they don't have to log in each time they return. Cookies are also used in e-commerce to track the contents of a visitor's shopping cart. Cookies are used in sales groups to track which affiliate gets credit for a sale. Cookies can also simply count the number of times someone visits your site.

Setting Cookies

A cookie is set by printing or sending a Set-Cookie header to the browser. In the section entitled "Outputting Text to a Browser" of Chapter 3, "Your First CGI Application," you learned about printing a Content-Type header to tell the browser that the output that follows is text or html. The Set-Cookie header is sent to the browser in the same way; it tells the browser that the information included is "cookie dough" or the stuff that cookies are made of. Setting a cookie requires only two pieces of information: the name you choose for the cookie and the content or value of the cookie.

To set a cookie, type the beginning of a normal `print` statement, including an open quotation mark.

Then type **Set-Cookie** and a colon (**:**).

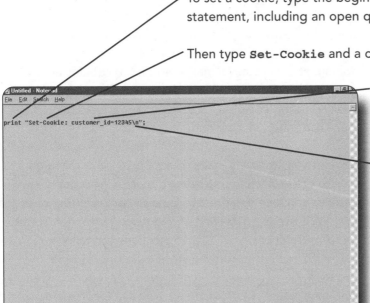

Next, type the name and value of the cookie, separated by an equals sign.

Finally, type a backslash (****), the letter **n**, a closing quotation mark, and a semicolon.

Recall that \n is the newline character. It tells the Perl interpreter to go to a new line before printing anything else and signifies the end of the Set-Cookie header.

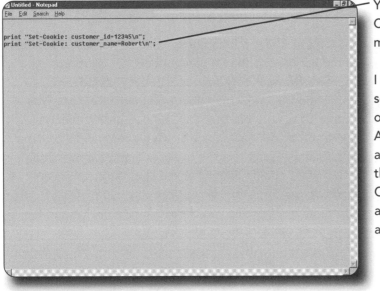

You can print multiple Set-Cookie headers and thus set multiple cookies.

I stated previously that setting a cookie requires only a name and a value. Although this is true, there are additional parameters that you can set in the Set-Cookie header. These additional parameters are as follows:

- **Expires.** This is the date you want the cookie to expire.

- **Domain.** This is the domain/server to which the cookie can be returned.

- **Path.** This is the path to which the cookie can be returned.

- **Secure.** If set, the cookie can be returned only using a secure connection.

You'll now learn how to use each of these parameters.

Setting the Expiration Date

To set an expiration date for the cookie, add the following to the "Set-Cookie" content header.

First, add a semicolon and a space after the name parameter.

Add the word **expires**, an equals sign, and the date that you want the cookie to expire.

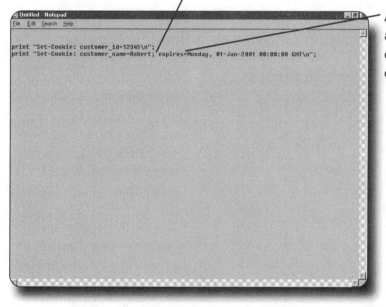

```
print "Set-Cookie: customer_id=12345\n";
print "Set-Cookie: customer_name=Robert; expires=Monday, 01-Jan-2001 00:00:00 GMT\n";
```

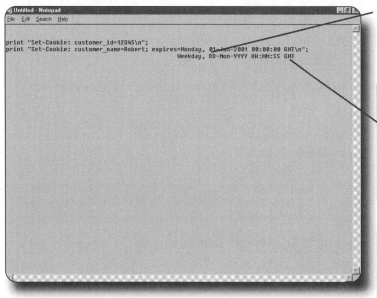

The date needs to be in this exact format: Weekday, DD-Mon-YYYY HH:MM:SS GMT.

NOTE

The only time format that is accepted is the Greenwich Mean Time Zone.

NOTE

If an expiration date is not set, the cookie expires when the users close their browsers.

Limiting Cookies to a Specific Domain

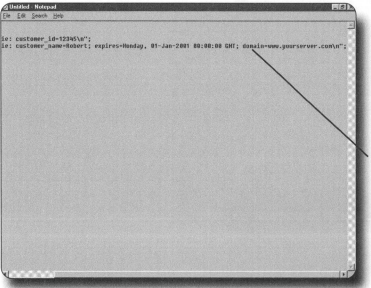

You can limit the domain or server that is allowed to retrieve a cookie by setting the `domain` parameter. Here's how to limit the domain to www.yourserver.com as an example.

Add another semicolon, a space, the word **domain**, an equals sign, and the domain name of your server to the Set-Cookie header.

A cookie with the domain set manually like this is returned only to www.yourserver.com. It will not be returned to members.yourserver.com, cgi.yourserver.com, and so on. To allow a cookie to be returned to any server in .yourserver.com, set the `domain` parameter as follows.

Add another semicolon, the word **domain**, and an equals sign. This sets the Set-Cookie header just like in the previous example.

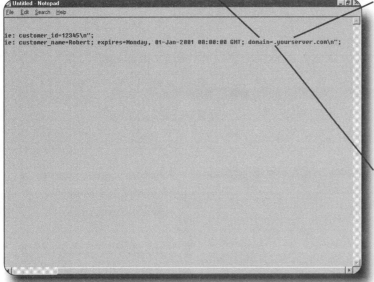

However, the domain name of your server cannot contain www.

This cookie returns to www.yourserver.com, members.yourserver.com, and so on.

Notice the period at the beginning of the domain name.

The period at the beginning of the domain name is not a typo. There is a reason for it.

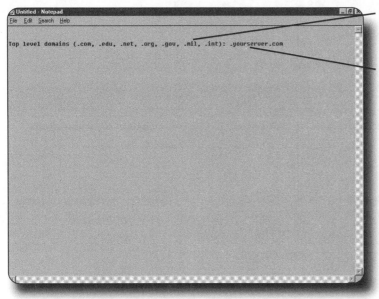

Here, the domain is one of the seven top-level domains.

Therefore, the domain name sent to the cookie must contain at least two periods.

All other domain names set manually in a cookie must contain three periods.

If the domain parameter is not set manually, the domain is automatically set to equal the HTTP host name of the server that sets the cookie.

Limiting Cookies to a Specific Section of Your Server

In addition to limiting a cookie to a specific domain, you can limit them to a specific area of your server by setting the `path` parameter. The `path` parameter is set the same way as the previous parameters.

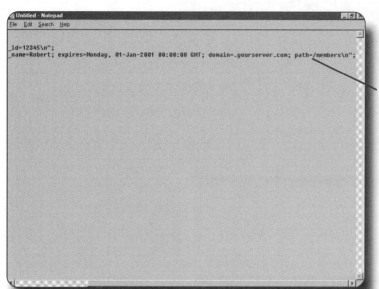

First, add another semicolon after the previous parameter, followed by the word **path**, an equals sign, and then the path to which you want to limit the cookie.

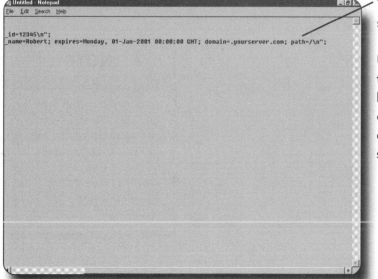

The most common path is a simple forward slash (/).

Using a forward slash to set the path allows this cookie to be retrieved from anywhere on the server that set the cookie. This might not seem significant at first glance.

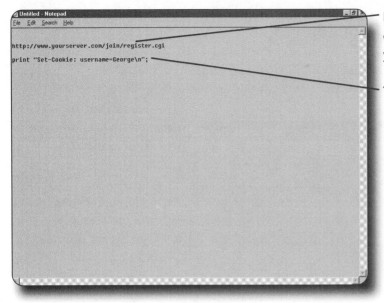

However, suppose you have one CGI script in one area of your server.

This CGI script sets a cookie.

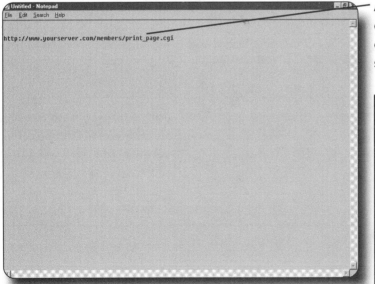

A second CGI script in a different area of your server cannot retrieve and use the same cookie.

NOTE

If all your CGI applications that use cookies are stored in the same location, the cgi-bin for example, you don't have to worry about the problem I just described.

Limiting Cookies to a Secure Server

Limiting your cookies to a secure server guarantees the privacy of the cookie data. It ensures that the information is encrypted until it arrives safely at its destination.

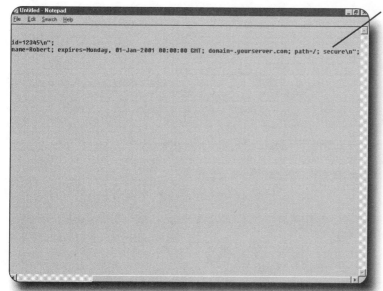

You can limit your cookie to a secure connection (SSL) by adding another semicolon, a space, and the word **secure** to the end of your Set-Cookie header.

A secure cookie is sent only to a secure URL (https://).

Reading Your Cookies

In order to retrieve and use your cookies, you need to understand how the cookie data is stored in its variable and how to separate it into usable parts.

In Chapter 4, "Getting the Data from Visitors to Your Web Page," you learned all about environmental variables that are set whenever information is exchanged between a browser and a server.

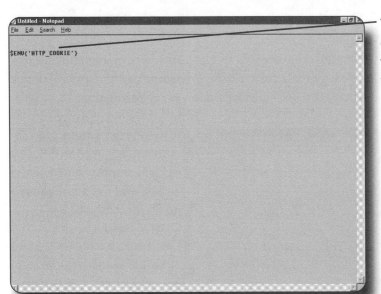

The `'HTTP_COOKIE'` environmental variable holds the cookie or cookies that were sent from the browser.

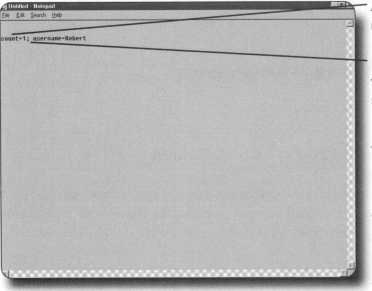

An equals sign separates the name and value of the cookie.

If there are multiple cookies, they are separated by semicolons and spaces.

Tossing Your Cookies

The `HTTP_COOKIE` environmental variable can be used and manipulated just like any other scalar variable. In Chapter 7, "Arrays," you learned how to split a scalar variable into an array. To separate the string into separate cookies, you split the `HTTP_COOKIE` environmental variable at a semicolon and space and place the parts into an array.

First type the name of the array, followed by an equals sign.

This is the array that holds the separate cookies after the split.

Next, type the word **split**, an open parenthesis, a forward slash, a semicolon followed by a space, another forward slash, and then a comma.

This tells the Perl interpreter to split the string at each semicolon and space.

```
Untitled - Notepad
File  Edit  Search  Help

@cookies = split (/; /, $ENV{HTTP_COOKIE});

foreach $cookie (@cookies) {
    ($name, $value) = split (/=/, $cookie);
    $cookies{$name} = $value;
}
```

Finally, type the HTTP_COOKIE environmental variable, which contains the string of cookies you want to split by typing a dollar sign, the word **ENV**, an open brace, the name of the variable (**HTTP_COOKIE**) and a closing brace. Follow this with a closing parenthesis and a semicolon.

You now have an array that contains all the separated cookies. However, each of the cookies is still in two parts: the name and the value separated by an equals sign. You now need to split the cookies into their separate parts and assign them as key-value pairs to a hash.

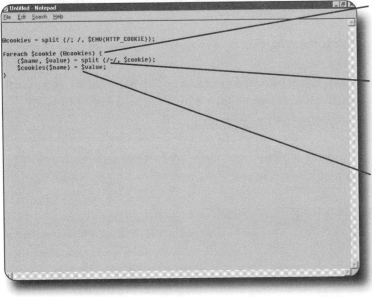

```
Untitled - Notepad
File  Edit  Search  Help

@cookies = split (/; /, $ENV{HTTP_COOKIE});

foreach $cookie (@cookies) {
    ($name, $value) = split (/=/, $cookie);
    $cookies{$name} = $value;
}
```

To do this, loop through each cookie contained in your array using a `foreach` loop.

You want to split each cookie into a name and a value by splitting it at the equals sign.

After the cookie is split, you can assign each part to a hash.

You now have each cookie stored as key-value pairs in a hash.

Putting It All Together

It would be helpful for you to put all the knowledge learned in this chapter together into an example script. This example script helps you better understand how cookies work. This example script (cookie_counter.cgi can be found on the CD-ROM) uses a cookie to set a simple counter, which keeps track of how many times someone calls the script.

```
cookie_counter.cgi - Notepad
File  Edit  Search  Help
#!/usr/local/bin/perl

@cookies = split (/; /, $ENV{HTTP_COOKIE});

foreach $cookie (@cookies) {
    ($name, $value) = split (/=/, $cookie);
    $cookies{$name} = $value;
}

$counter = $cookies{counter} + 1;

print "Set-Cookie: counter=$counter\n";

print "Content-Type: text/html\n\n";
print "<html><head><title>Cookie Counter</title></head>\n";
print "<body bgcolor=white>\n";

if ($cookies{counter} > 0) {
    print "<h3>Welcome back!  You've been here $cookies{counter} time(s) before.</h3>";
}
else {
    print "<h3>Welcome!  This is your first time here!</h3>";
}
print "</body></html>\n";

exit;
```

The first thing you do is split any cookies in the `HTTP_COOKIE` environmental variable into an array.

The first time the script is called, there will not be any cookies.

Then you loop through each of the cookies, separate the individual cookies into a name and a value, and assign the parts in a hash.

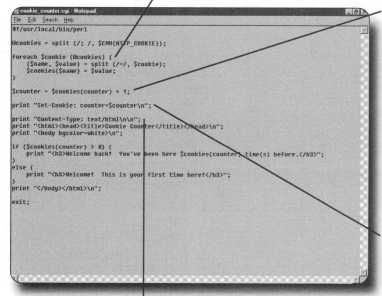

Because this is a counter script, you need to increment a counter. To do this, set the value of a counter variable to equal the value stored in the counter cookie, plus one.

If there aren't any cookies, the counter variable equals one.

Now that you've incremented the counter, you can set the counter cookie.

NOTE

The Set-Cookie header must be printed before the Content-Type header. Otherwise the cookie header and content are treated as plain text and the cookie will not be set.

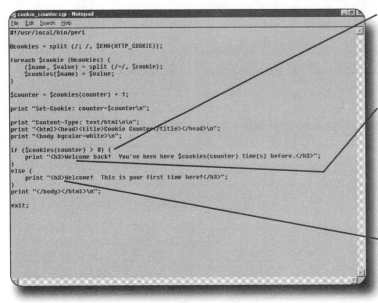

```
#!/usr/local/bin/perl

@cookies = split (/; /, $ENV{HTTP_COOKIE});

foreach $cookie (@cookies) {
    ($name, $value) = split (/=/, $cookie);
    $cookies{$name} = $value;
}

$counter = $cookies{counter} + 1;

print "Set-Cookie: counter=$counter\n";

print "Content-Type: text/html\n\n";
print "<html><head><title>Cookie Counter</title></head>\n";
print "<body bgcolor=white>\n";

if ($cookies{counter} > 0) {
    print "<h3>Welcome back!  You've been here $cookies{counter} time(s) before.</h3>";
}
else {
    print "<h3>Welcome!  This is your first time here!</h3>";
}
print "</body></html>\n";

exit;
```

Next, you perform an `if` test to determine whether the value of the counter cookie is greater than zero.

If the value of the counter cookie is greater than zero, you know the user has called the script before so you print a `Welcome back!` message.

Otherwise, it's their first time calling the script, so you print a `Welcome!` message.

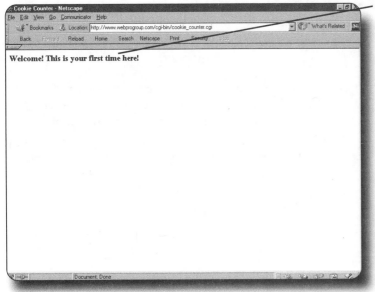

Welcome! This is your first time here!

The first time the script is called, there is no cookie set. The value of the counter is set to 1 and stored in the counter cookie. The `Welcome` message is then printed.

The second time the script is called, the counter cookie has the value of 1. The counter is incremented to 2 and stored in the counter cookie again. Then the `Welcome back!` message is printed, which shows that the user has been here before.

The third time the script is called, the counter cookie has the value of 2. The counter is incremented to 3 and stored in the counter cookie again. Then the `Welcome back!` message is printed, which shows that the user has been there before—and so on, and so on.

Summary

You now know how to add hidden fields to static forms and forms that are output by your CGI applications. You know how to use hidden fields to store collected data during a multiform input process. You also know how to set, retrieve, and use cookies. You should now have a full understanding of how hidden fields and cookies help you bridge the gap in the stateless connection.

13

Outputting Data

You will have to output data to the browser sooner or later (usually sooner). Perl gives you many options for displaying data from your CGI application. The number of tools is small but the options are many. You can pick and choose how to use the tools depending on your situation. Perl enables you to output the same data many ways. After you have learned the basics of using these tools, you'll be able to output your data any way you want. In this chapter, you'll learn how to:

- Use STDOUT output
- Use `print` to output raw and formatted data
- Output HTML tags, links, and images
- Create headers and footers
- Output hashes and arrays with HTML tags
- Format numbers and strings for output with `sprintf`

Generating STDOUT Output

Output from Perl is based on file handles. A *file handle* is a reference to a particular output stream. An output stream can be a file on disk, a network socket, or a console window, for instance. The default output file handle for most Perl output functions is STDOUT, or standard output. This file handle usually refers to the current console window, but for your CGI application, STDOUT refers to output being sent to the requesting Web browser.

The basic output function in Perl is the `print` function. The `print` function takes two arguments: a file handle to send the output to and a list of expressions to output. Because STDOUT is the default file handle, you usually don't see it referenced in code; if you don't specify a file handle for `print`, Perl assumes you want to print to STDOUT. Use STDOUT for anything you want to send to the browser for display.

Normal Output Using print

You can specify the strings and variables to output in different ways for the `print` function. You can use the concatenation operator for strings, a period (.), to add literal strings and variables together into a single string. You can list several literals or variables, separated by commas. If you are printing to STDOUT, you can omit the file handle argument to the `print` function.

Create a variable named $title, which holds the title string for the page.

Note that the print statement for the content-type does not specify the file handle argument. Thus, you know the line is being printed to the default STDOUT.

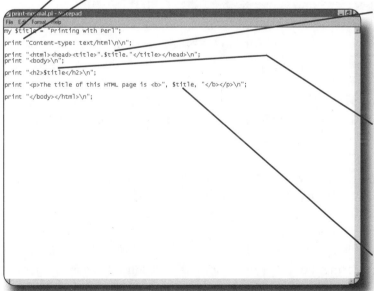

You can concatenate strings and variables by joining them with periods. Note that the variable, $title, has no quotes around it.

You can embed variables inside string literals. Perl will interpolate the variable in the string before handing it to the print statement for output.

You can provide a comma-separated list of literal strings and variables to the print function, as well. This is slightly faster than concatenating multiple strings together.

The value of the $title variable is displayed in the browser's title bar.

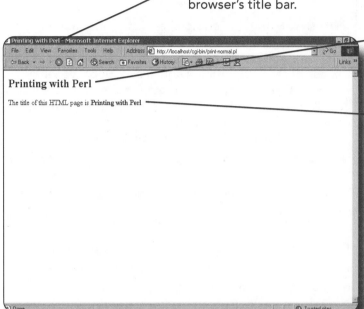

The value of the $title variable is displayed in the HTML header output.

The text of the page is output as a single, seamless string. There is no indication that the print statement included a list of separate strings and variables.

Formatted Output Using printf

You can format a string for output by specifying numeric and string formats with the printf function. The printf function takes three arguments: a file handle (defaults to STDOUT), a format string that specifies how the text be formatted, and a list of variables or strings to be output with the specified format.

The format string uses a special formatting syntax to describe how the values in the following list should be formatted. You can output values as characters (%c), decimal integers (%d), exponential floating-point numbers (%e), fixed-point format floating-point numbers (%f), compact-format floating-point numbers (%g), long decimal integers (%ld), long octal integers (%lo), long unsigned decimal integers (%lu), long hexadecimal integers (%lx), octal integers (%o), strings (%s), unsigned decimal integers (%u), hexadecimal numbers (%x), and hexadecimal numbers with uppercase characters (%X). Whew! That's a lot of options.

The format syntax is as follows: %a.bx, where a and b are optional size specifications (usually padding and decimal point precision, respectively, but there is variation depending on x), and x is a character representing one of the previous output formats listed.

In this example, you create a decimal-to-hexadecimal lookup chart for the decimal numbers from 0 to 63. You use the printf function inside a for loop to output the decimal/hex pairs and display the result in preformatted HTML mode.

You need to provide a descriptive label for the output in an HTML header tag.

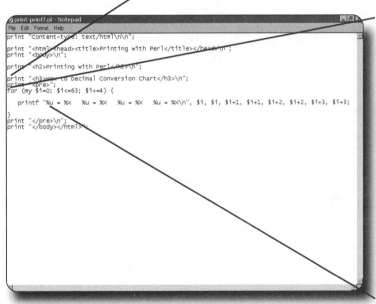

Inside the for loop arguments, you create a variable $I as the loop index in the first argument. The second argument sets the conditions for the loop index. The loop processes as long as the value of $I is less than or equal to 63. The third argument sets the increment for the loop index each time through the loop. Here, the index increases by four each time.

The format string is a picture of how the string should look after the values have been formatted and output to the file handle (using the default STDOUT). The format string has four pairs of numbers. The first pair contains an unsigned decimal integer and the second pair contains a hexadecimal number with capitals. Therefore, there are eight fields that need to have values in the value list following the format string.

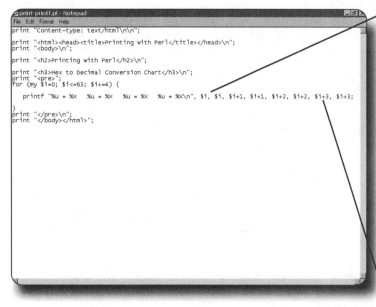

```
print-printf.pl - Notepad
File  Edit  Format  Help
print "Content-type: text/html\n\n";

print "<html><head><title>Printing with Perl</title></head>\n";
print "<body>\n";

print "<h2>Printing with Perl</h2>\n";

print "<h3>Hex to Decimal Conversion Chart</h3>\n";
print "<pre>";
for (my $i=0; $i<=63; $i+=4) {

    printf "%u = %X    %u = %X    %u = %X    %u = %X\n", $i, $i, $i+1, $i+1, $i+2, $i+2, $i+3, $i+3;

}
print "</pre>\n";
print "</body></html>";
```

Each pair of numbers represents the decimal and hexadecimal equivalent of the loop index. To achieve a table layout of the values, four numbers are placed in a row to produce a table of four columns. Add one to $i for each spot farther from the first value. This produces a sequence of four increasing numbers across each table row.

The result of the printf function is a string with four decimal numbers converted to hexadecimal format. Each iteration of the for loop produces a new row of numbers.

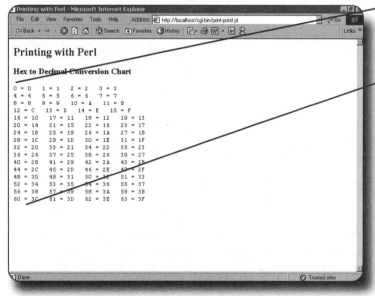

The chart is laid out in four columns, reading across from left to right.

You can see, for instance, that the hexadecimal representation of 60 is 3C. The printf function has simply output the number 60 as a hexadecimal number. This is an easy way to perform decimal-to-hex and hex-to-decimal conversions.

The output in the Web browser is not the best. The HTML preformatting is literal. This chart would probably look better in an HTML table.

Generating HTML Formatted Output

You can output HTML formatting tags directly with the `print` or `printf` functions. Because the browser receives whatever you send to STDOUT from your CGI application, it interprets this output as whatever content-type you specify. Then you simply need to put the HTML tags inside double quotation marks in the list arguments to the `print` function and in the format argument to the `printf` function. The `print` and `printf` functions output them as text to the browser, which in turn interprets them as HTML tags (if the content-type is `text/html`).

Adding HTML Formats to Output

In this example, you rework the output of the decimal-to-hex conversion chart to use an HTML table instead of HTML preformatting.

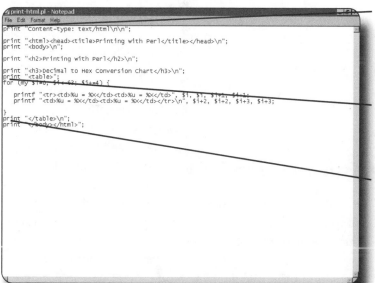

Make sure you specify the content-type as `text/html` for the output of the CGI application.

Start an HTML table by using `print` to output a string with the HTML tag.

Start the table row in the format string of the first `printf` statement. I've separated the output of the single line into two for readability. You can use a single `printf` statement here.

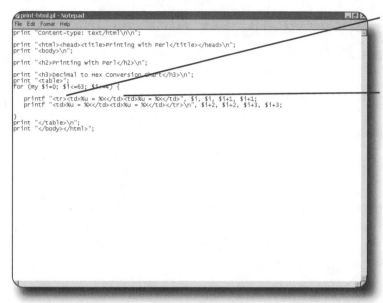

Between each number pair, place your beginning and ending table cell tags.

Use `print` to output the end table tag, which closes the HTML table.

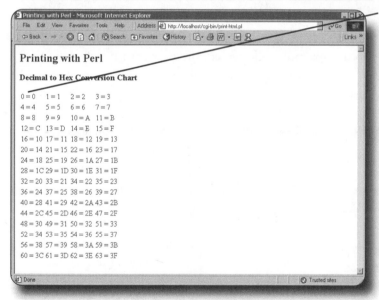

This is a little better. The columns align better than the HTML preformatting.

Printing Multiple Lines

The `print` function has multiple line mode; so you can print lines verbatim from your script. This mode involves the use of a label. A *label* is simply a marker in your script. In multiline mode of `print`, after the file handle argument, you use `<<`, followed by a label, instead of using the list of literals and variables. This tells the `print` statement to treat each following line as an argument to be printed. All the lines down to the label are printed. A benefit of using the multiline mode is that you do not need to use double quotes on lines.

In this example, you use the multiline mode to output a
section of a Web page that displays some CGI variables.

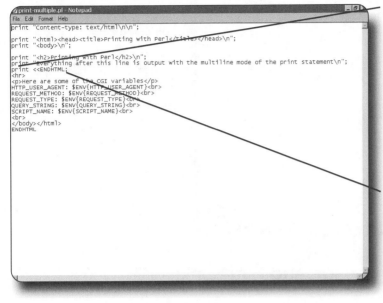

Use the print function with
the default file handle. Use a
label named ENDHTML to
mark the end of the lines to
be output. You can use
anything you like as the
label, except Perl keywords.
A common convention is to
use all capitals for the label.

You might be tempted to
omit the semicolon at the
end of the print command;
don't. It is required, even
though you might think that
the following output lines
are part of the argument list.

Everything from this line
down to the end label will
be printed as you see it,
except that the variables will
be interpolated for output.

To include variables to be
output in these lines, simply
type them in the desired
position, as you do for any
other string with an
embedded Perl variable.

The ending label must be on
a line by itself in order for Perl
to recognize it. In this case,
don't include the semicolon
at the end of the line.

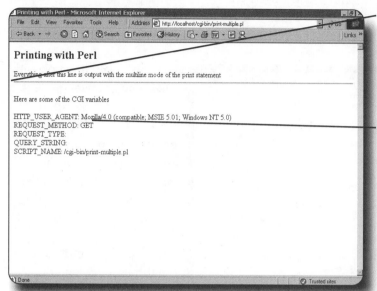

Starting with this horizontal rule, everything else on this page was outputted by the `print` function in multiline mode.

Note that the CGI variable values are output to the browser window.

Image and Path Links

Image and link paths in HTML are included in tags as quoted values to tag arguments. In the `<IMG>` tag, this attribute is `src` and in the `<A>` tag this attribute is the `<href>` tag. Properly formatted HTML denotes the values to these attributes with double quotation marks. Because double quotation marks happen to be the string delimiters for the `print` function, this presents a problem for your code.

You have three ways to handle this situation. You can escape the HTML attribute double quotes in your Perl string. You escape the quote character by preceding it with a backslash. You can use the Perl function, `qq`, to handle the quoting and escaping for you. You can also use the multiline mode of the `print` statement, as demonstrated in the previous section.

In this example, you use each of these three techniques to handle the double quotes in HTML image and link tags.

To include a double quote inside a double-quoted string, escape the double-quote character by preceding it with a backslash.

Use the qq function to quote a string. In the parentheses of the qq function, type the string to be quoted, including any embedded double quotes, such as the attribute values of the <A> tag.

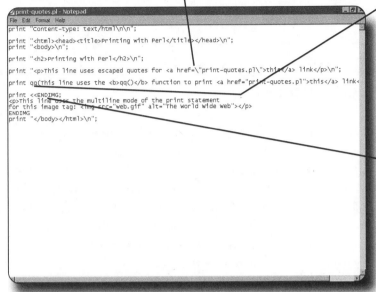

Use the multiline mode of print to print lines verbatim. This line can include double quotes with no escaping necessary.

Check the source of this Web page to convince yourself that this link is displayed with double quotes.

Perl is again flexible about how you can solve a problem. Pick and choose the right solution for your particular situation or coding style.

Generating Header and Footer Subroutines

You can save yourself a lot of typing by encapsulating the header and footer code for your pages in subroutines. This technique is particularly useful for maintaining a consistent style for all pages on a Web site or in a single CGI application. The greatest advantage to using subroutines, discussed in Chapter 11, "Subroutines," for these formatting choices is the capability to separate the "look and feel" of a site from the content. With separate files that contain the header and footer code, you can change the entire Web site simply by changing either of these two files.

Creating Header and Footer Subroutines

Creating a file containing subroutines is simple. There are a few rules you need to follow, but this process is simple. Open a new file and write your subroutine code. At the end of the file, after the last subroutine has been defined, place a 1, followed by a semicolon. This is important because Perl evaluates the code in the included file, and this process must return a true value. You can achieve this requirement by using the 1 at the end of the file.

In this example, you create a file that contains the header information necessary for the Web browser to properly parse the file. You also do the same thing for the HTML footer code.

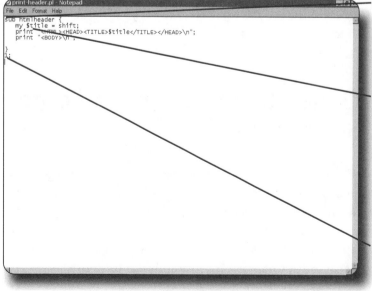

Create a `sub` function and call it `htmlheader`. Start the block of code for the `sub` function with a curly brace.

This function is expecting a value passed in. This value is expected to be a string holding the name (or title) of the Web page. This value is output in the `<TITLE>` tag for the page.

Don't forget the closing line of the file containing the 1.

If this is missing, Perl returns an error when this file is included in another file.

In this example, you create a footer subroutine that displays an arbitrary string passed to the function and the last modified date and time of the including file. To get this information, you use the stat command to retrieve information about the file from the file system, such as last modified time, creation time, size, and so on.

Save the passed-in string value in the variable $footertext.

Save the array returned by the stat function in the array variable @statinfo. The $0 special variable contains the full path and file name of the currently executing script.

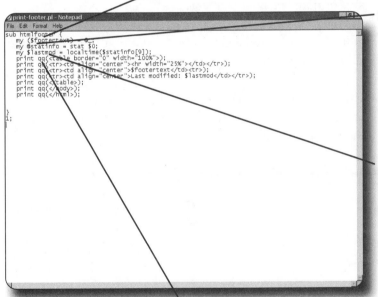

The last modified date information is in the tenth position of the @statinfo array. You can use the localtime function to return a human-readable date and time from this value.

Now you output an HTML table containing the passed-in string and the last modified date in different cells. Feel free to experiment with how you want this footer information displayed. I've used the qq function to make the code easier to read.

Calling Header Subroutines

Calling subroutines is a two-step process. First, you must make the subroutine available to the script. Because you have created the routines in separate files to be shared among all your CGI application files, you need to inform Perl where it can find the files containing the subroutines. Perl maintains an array, @INC, which contains a list of search paths for included files. If the file you want to include is not in one of these paths, you have to add the path to the @INC array. Second, you call the subroutine you want with the appropriate arguments, if any.

In this example, you create a CGI script that calls the header subroutine you created in the previous example.

The push function adds an element to the end of an array. The arguments include the array to which to append and the element to append.

```
print-include.pl - Notepad
File Edit Format Help
#!/usr/local/bin/perl
push(@INC, "e:/inetpub/wwwroot/cgi-bin");
require "print-header.pl";

print "Content-type: text/html\n\n";

htmlheader("Including a Header Subroutine");

print "<h2>Including a Header Subroutine</h2>\n";
print "<p>You have lots of options when printing data from Perl.</p>\n";

print "This page includes a header library and calls the <b>htmlheader</b>\n";
print "subroutine to display the HTML document header tags.</p>\n";
print "</body></html>";
```

The current directory is not in the @INC search path array, so you need to add it here with the push function. Your path might vary from the one listed here. Change it accordingly.

Use the require function to include another Perl script file in the current script. This function brings the subroutines defined in the print-header.pl file into the current script and makes them available for use. Specify the filename to include in double quotes.

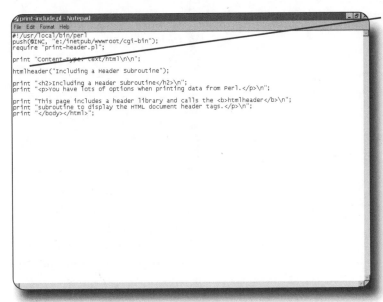

Call the `htmlheader` subroutine from the print-header.pl file. The subroutine expects one argument: the title of the HTML page produced by the script.

The parentheses around the argument are optional. I have included them for readability.

Calling Footer Subroutines

The steps required to call the footer subroutine that you created are the same as when you call the header routine.

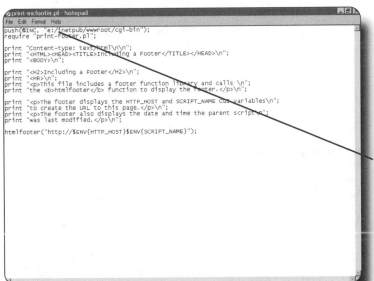

In this example, you create a CGI script that includes the footer script. You also use variable interpolation to include CGI variables in the configurable text that shows up in the footer.

The current directory is not in the `@INC` search path array, so you need to add it here with the `push` function. Your path might vary from the one listed here. Change it accordingly.

Use the `require` function to include another Perl script file in the current script.

Use the `print` function to output your Web page contents.

Call the `htmlfooter` function with one argument in parentheses. Use the `HTTP_HOST` and `SCRIPT_NAME` CGI variables to create a string of the URL to the current page.

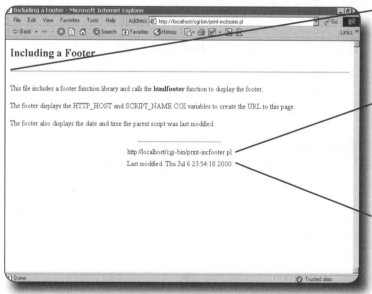

Everything from the horizontal rule down was displayed from the `htmlfooter` subroutine.

Here is the URL of the current page. This should match the URL in the address line of the browser, above.

This line shows the date and time when the script was last modified.

Generating Table and List Outputs

Displays of data on the Web often take the form of tables and lists. HTML is adept at formatting data in this way. You have now learned enough about Perl data output to make short work of displaying hashes and arrays with HTML formatting commands. In this section, you write Perl scripts to display a hash as an HTML table and an array as an HTML list.

Outputting a Hash as a Table

A hash is similar in structure to a two-column table. The first column contains the hash key value and the second column contains the hash element value. The two values together form a pair much like a table row.

In this example, you create a Perl script to display a hash of keys and values as an HTML table using data output techniques learned earlier in the chapter. You use the %ENV environment hash to display to the browser.

Start by adding the current directory to the search array @INC. Then require the header and footer script files in order to access the htmlheader and htmlfooter subroutines.

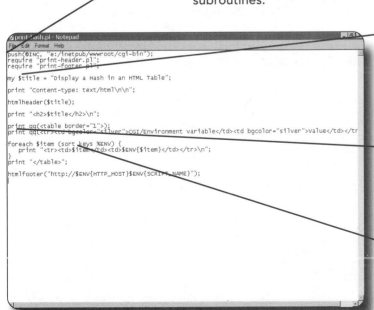

Create a variable, $title, to hold the title string of the page. Use this variable in the next line in a call to the htmlheader subroutine.

Start the HTML table with the <TABLE> tag and one table row. This holds the column header labels.

Use the keys function to extract the keys from the %ENV hash and the sort function to sort the result of

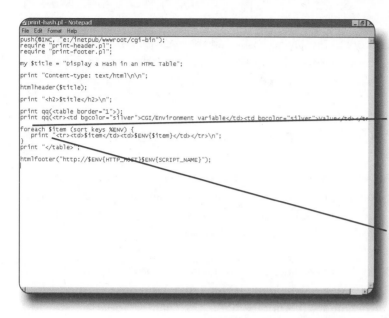

the `keys` function. The resulting sorted array provides the list of values for the `foreach` loop.

Loop through each value in the resulting array from the `sort` function with the `foreach` control-of-flow command.

Using the `print` function, output the HTML tags for a table row with two cells. In the first cell, place the `foreach` loop control variable, `$item`. This variable holds the name of the next CGI variable in the list. In the second cell, place the hash reference to the `%ENV` hash to retrieve the value of the CGI variable.

Don't forget to close the HTML table with an end table tag. Close the page with a call to the `htmlfooter` subroutine.

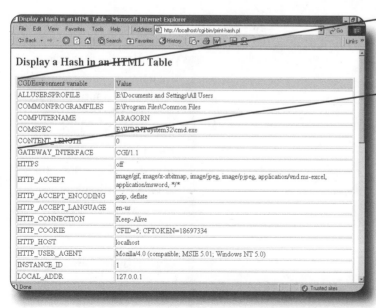

Each column has a header label that describes the contents of the column.

The CGI variable names are sorted alphabetically in the first column, and the associated values appear in the second column.

That's a lot of output for a few lines of code. With some simple techniques and a judicious use of Perl data output functions, you have sent a large amount of information to the client's browser. But hashes are not the only data structure you can output easily from your CGI applications—you can also output arrays.

Outputting an Array as a List

An array is similar to a simple list of values, ordered or unordered. HTML has two list tags that display these kinds of lists. You can follow the same basic logic for outputting an array as you did when outputting a hash.

In this example, you create a CGI script that outputs the values of an unordered list of values stored in an array.

Set up the script for the inclusion of the header and footer subroutines, just as you did in the previous example.

Create an array named @crewlist and populate it with the names of a famous starship crew. You can change the order of the names if you like.

Start the HTML unordered list with the <UL> tag.

In a foreach loop, step through each of the values of the @crewlist array.

Use print to display each name in the list, as represented by $item, inside HTML list element tags (<LI></LI>).

After the foreach loop, don't forget to close the unordered list with the closing tag (</UL>).

```
print-array.pl - Notepad
File Edit Format Help
push(@INC, "e:/inetpub/wwwroot/cgi-bin");
require "print-header.pl";
require "print-footer.pl";

my $title = "Display an Array in an HTML List";
my @crewlist = ('Kirk','Spock','McCoy','Sulu','Scott','Uhura','Chekov','Chapel');

print "Content-type: text/html\n\n";

htmlheader($title);

print "<h2>$title</h2>\n";

print "Here is the main crew list of a starship you might recognize:<br><br>\n";
print "<ul>\n";

foreach $item (@crewlist) {
    print "<li>$item</li>\n";
}
print "</ul>";

htmlfooter("http://$ENV{HTTP_HOST}$ENV{SCRIPT_NAME}");
```

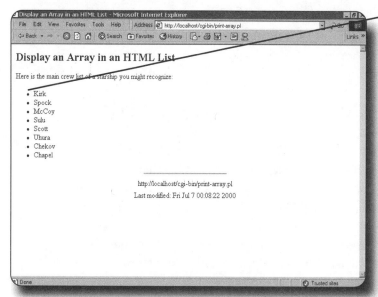

Here is the unordered HTML list. If this was an ordered list, the bullets would be numbers.

You are now armed with enough information to use Perl data structures and output functions to print large amounts of data from your CGI applications with little effort. Fewer lines of code mean faster development time and less code maintenance.

Formatting Numbers and Strings

You have already seen how to print formatted numbers and strings with the `printf` function. This is fine when you want to send the formatted line to a file handle immediately. But what if you need to format a large amount of numbers and strings and output them later in the code? What if you want to save a formatted string to use in another section of the CGI application? With Perl, you can do just that with the `sprintf` function. The `sprintf` function is similar to the `printf` function, but instead of sending the formatted result to a file handle, the `sprintf` simply returns the formatted string to the calling line of code. In this way, you can save the return value of the `sprintf` function in a variable for use or output later.

The `sprintf` function takes two arguments: a format string that specifies how the text should be formatted and a list of variables or strings to be output with the specified format.

Printing Formatted Data

In this example, you improve on the decimal-to-hexadecimal conversion chart by adding a third value to the chart: the character value of the decimal number. You build an HTML table of the values using `sprintf` and save the result in a single variable to be output later in the script.

Set up the script for the inclusion of the header and footer subroutines, just as you did in previous examples.

Create a variable called `$hextable` to store the conversion table text. Initialize it with the beginning tags to display an HTML table.

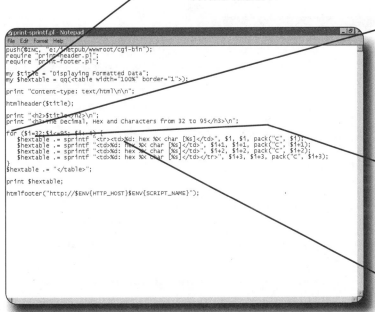

In a `for` loop, loop from 32 to 95 in steps of four. Most of the characters between 32 and 95 are printable, so this range is a good choice for this chart.

Use the shortcut concatenation operator (`.=`) to add the result of the `sprintf` to the `$hextable` variable.

The format string of this example is similar to the second decimal-to-hex chart example, but this time, you add a third format specification of `%s` to display the string value of the decimal number.

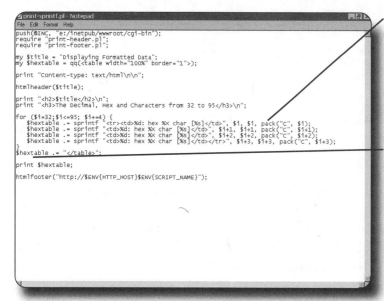

```
print-sprintf.pl - Notepad
File Edit Format Help
push(@INC, "e:/inetpub/wwwroot/cgi-bin");
require "print-header.pl";
require "print-footer.pl";

my $title = "Displaying Formatted Data";
my $hextable = qq(<table width="100%" border="1">);

print "Content-type: text/html\n\n";

htmlheader($title);

print "<h2>$title</h2>\n";
print "<h3>The Decimal, Hex and Characters from 32 to 95</h3>\n";

for ($i=32;$i<=95; $i+=4) {
    $hextable .= sprintf "<tr><td>%d: hex %x char [%s]</td>", $i, $i, pack("C", $i);
    $hextable .= sprintf "<td>%d: hex %x char [%s]</td>", $i+1, $i+1, pack("C", $i+1);
    $hextable .= sprintf "<td>%d: hex %x char [%s]</td>", $i+2, $i+2, pack("C", $i+2);
    $hextable .= sprintf "<td>%d: hex %x char [%s]</td></tr>", $i+3, $i+3, pack("C", $i+3);
}
$hextable .= "</table>";

print $hextable;

htmlfooter("http://$ENV{HTTP_HOST}$ENV{SCRIPT_NAME}");
```

Use the pack function to convert the decimal number to a character. This character is then formatted as a string by the sprintf function for display.

Close the HTML table by appending the end table tag to the $hextable variable. Then, simply print the $hextable variable to display all the hard work of sprintf.

Now you have a table that shows the decimal, hexadecimal, and character equivalents side by side.

Formatting Numbers as Dollars and Cents

Displaying currency formats on Web pages is common with the growth of electronic commerce Web sites. You can use the Perl sprintf function to handle this kind of display.

In this example, you use sprintf to convert a list of sample numbers of various types to U.S. currency values and save them as a string. You then display the string with a standard print function.

Create an array of sample numbers for conversion.

Declare a variable to hold the return values of the `sprintf` functions (called `$currencylist` here).

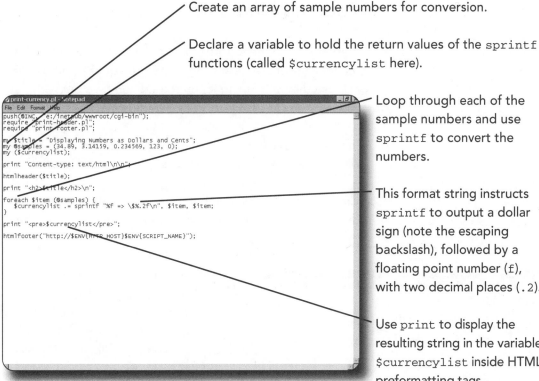

Loop through each of the sample numbers and use `sprintf` to convert the numbers.

This format string instructs `sprintf` to output a dollar sign (note the escaping backslash), followed by a floating point number (`f`), with two decimal places (`.2`).

Use `print` to display the resulting string in the variable `$currencylist` inside HTML preformatting tags.

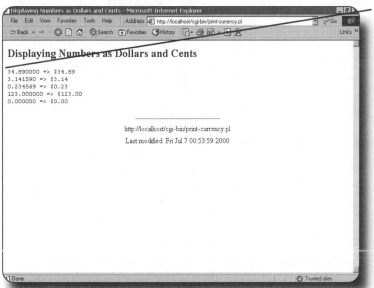

In this display, you can see how `sprintf` rounded the numbers and displayed them with precision to the hundredths place.

The `sprintf` function can make short work of converting and rounding currency numbers in your CGI applications. If you are writing mathematical or engineering CGI applications, `sprintf` can help with this type of floating point precision formatting.

Padding Numbers

Sometimes you need to space out numbers in order to line up columns or create space for the growth of a number. You can use the `sprintf` function to pad numbers out with spaces. You can also justify the numbers displayed.

In this example, you convert a list of sample numbers and display them with various types of padding and justification.

Create some sample numbers in an array after setting up the page for the subroutine script inclusions, just as in the previous examples.

```
print-padding.pl - Notepad
File Edit Format Help
push(@INC, "c:/inetpub/wwwroot/cgi-bin");
require "print-header.pl";
require "print-footer.pl";

my $title = "Displaying Numbers as Dollars and Cents";
my @samples = (34.89, 3.14159, 0.234569, 123, 0);
my ($currencylist);

print "Content-type: text/html\n\n";

htmlheader($title);

print "<h2>$title</h2>\n";

foreach $item (@samples) {
    $currencylist .= sprintf "%f => \$%.2f\n", $item, $item;
}
print "<h3>Without Padding</h3><pre>$currencylist</pre>";
$currencylist = "";

foreach $item (@samples) {
    $currencylist .= sprintf "%.8f => \$%-10.2f\n", $item, $item;
}
print "<h3>With Padding, Left Justified</h3><pre>$currencylist</pre>";
$currencylist = "";

foreach $item (@samples) {
    $currencylist .= sprintf "%.8f => \$%10.2f\n", $item, $item;
}
print "<h3>With Padding, Right Justified</h3><pre>$currencylist</pre>";

htmlfooter("http://$ENV{HTTP_HOST}$ENV{SCRIPT_NAME}");
```

This is the same `foreach` loop and `sprintf` call from the currency example. I present it here for contrast with the following displays.

Display the resulting string variable with an appropriate header to describe the output. After you have displayed the `$currencylist`, reset it to an empty string for use by the next loop. Repeat this process after each `foreach` loop.

This format string pads the number display to 10 columns left of the decimal and two places after the decimal. The negative sign in front of the 10 instructs `sprintf` to left-justify the resulting number.

This format string pads the number display to 10 columns left of the decimal and two places after the decimal. The number is right-justified in the resulting formatted display.

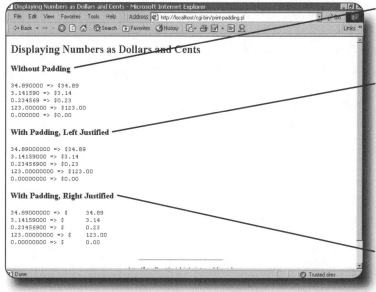

This section displays the numbers as ordinary currency figures with no padding.

This section displays the numbers as currency, but the numbers are left-justified in the output. Note that this does not appear to be any different from the previous section. The padding is to the right and not visible.

This section shows the same numbers, but now they are justified to the right. Now the padding between the left-most digit and the dollar sign is apparent in each number.

You can use padding and HTML preformatting to display justified columns of numbers and strings with the sprintf function. You find even more ways of displaying data in this manner in the next chapter.

Summary

You have learned in this chapter how to use the print, printf, and sprintf output functions in Perl to display data in different ways from your CGI applications. You have learned that the default file handles for these functions is STDOUT and that STDOUT is the output file handle that sends data to the client browser for viewing. You have output HTML formatting tags, printed multiple lines, and learned how to handle embedded quotes in output strings. You have also learned how to create standard header and footer subroutines to use in multiple CGI application pages for consistency. You have output Perl hashes and arrays in HTML tables and lists, respectively, and you have learned how to format numbers and strings with great flexibility.

In the next chapter, you will learn even more about formatting your output in Perl.

14

Formats

Perl excels at manipulating data. One of the most common text-manipulation tasks that Perl is called upon to perform is *report generation*. The creators of Perl knew that this would be a common-place task, so they included a few special formatting functions and syntax to make your life easier. Perl formats are a little out of the ordinary with the rest of Perl's functions, but you'll be glad you took a few moments to acquaint yourself with these formats.

In this chapter, you'll learn:

- What a format is
- How to define a format
- How to use a format
- How to use text and numeric fields
- How to use multiline fields
- How to use a top-of-page format
- How to change a format's defaults

Using Formats

A *format* in Perl is a template of how output should look. The template is declared as part of your Perl application, or it can be included from another file. The format itself is simply a set of lines of text containing variable placeholders called *fields*, interspersed with other static text elements, such as labels, lines, tabs, newlines, and so on. Embedded in the format along with the fields are Perl variable names representing the values to be placed in the fields when you invoke the format for output. You can think of a format much like a mail-merge letter template in your word processor.

Formats use a special syntax for the fields to be output. You can have text fields, numeric fields, or multiline fields. You can justify the values in the fields to the left, to the right, or to the center. You can embed decimal points in numeric fields and align columns of numbers on the decimal.

Formats were designed to create report templates for reporting on large amounts of data when you don't need the specialized formatting commands of your word processor or database report generator. Formats are great for reporting on log files of many types. One pertinent example is Web server log files.

You can also use formats to create e-mail templates used by your CGI application. This is the equivalent of a CGI mail merge system. E-mail templates can be created to provide automated, customized e-mail responses to user queries, e-mail notifications to the system administrator about application events (such as errors) in your CGI application, or as the basis for mass mailings about new products, Web site updates, and so on.

From a Web perspective, formats have a somewhat limited use for display in a browser. Because the literal text formatting of the format is crucial in, for instance, aligning numbers by the decimal point, you are forced into using the HTML preformatting tags (<PRE></PRE>) to maintain the original layout of the format. You can, however, use formats to create HTML templates to be filled in at run-time, with standard HTML tags and Perl variables.

Mastering formats takes some practice because they are so flexible. There are two simple steps to using a format. First, define the format and declare it somewhere in your code. Second, invoke the format by using the write function.

Formats must be associated with a file handle in Perl in order to work. Thus, whenever you write to that particular file handle, you get the output formatted as declared in the associated Perl format. By default, if you do not specify a file handle when declaring a format, STDOUT is assumed.

Defining a Format

You define a format by using the format declaration function, followed by a file handle name and an equals sign. On the following line, you begin the actual format layout with fields and static text elements. When you're done, end the format specification by placing a period in the first position on a line by itself.

NOTE

Although a format can be declared anywhere in your Perl script, I've declared all formats in this chapter in separate files from the scripts that use them. In the examples, you simply require these files, just as you did with the subroutine files in Chapter 13, "Outputting Data."

Start the declaration with the `format` command, followed by a file handle name. Whenever you write to this file handle, this declared format is used.

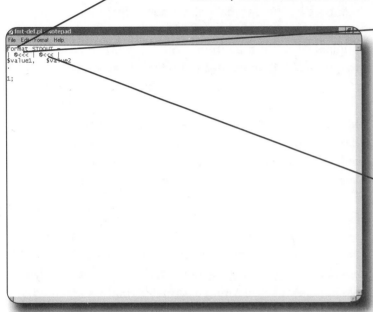

This is a field specification. The @ signifies that the following text is a field. The <'s are literal placeholders for characters in the field. Thus, this field is four characters in length (the @ counts too).

The <'s also signify that when the field is filled in with a value, that value should be left-justified in the field. To right-justify a field, you use the > character, and to center a value in the field, you use the | character.

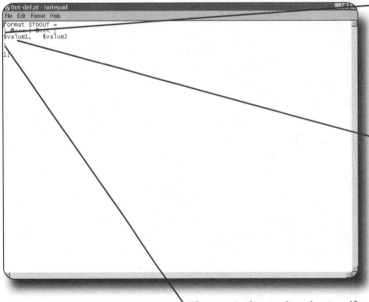

Note that the |'s in this text are static text, because they are separated from the @ fields by spaces. These static text elements create a border around the values.

Place the variable names corresponding to the previous fields on the next line, separated by commas. Extra spaces are ignored, and it helps readability to line up the variables with their associated fields.

The period on a line by itself ends the declaration of the format specification.

Invoking a Format

Invoking a format is also simple. You simply write to the associated file handle. In this example, the file handle is `STDOUT` to make things simple. Prior to the call to the `write` function, you should make sure that the format has access to the variables specified in the format. If the variables do not exist or they are empty, the format won't display anything in their associated fields. No error will be generated.

In this example, you output a hash of simple values with the format you previously declared.

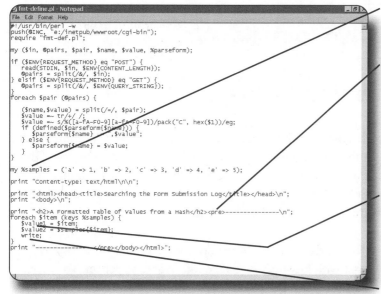

Declare a hash and give it some keys and values.

Because the layout would be destroyed by simply outputting it to a Web page, use the `<PRE></PRE>` HTML tags to preserve the plain text formatting.

Set the `$value1` and `$value2` variables with the hash key and hash value, respectively.

Use the `write` command to send the key and value to `STDOUT`. Because you named the format `STDOUT`, writing to `STDOUT` uses the format specification included at the top of the script.

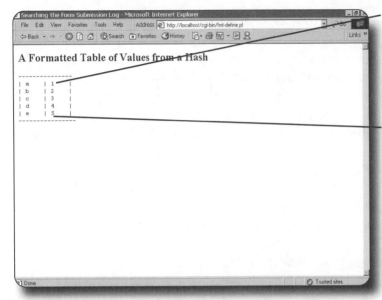

Note that the browser has displayed the text in a monospace font because of the HTML preformatting tags.

Note that the pattern of each row in the table matches the single line of the format specification.

That's all there is to it. The real power of formats comes in designing the declaration itself.

Using Fields

The heart of a format declaration is the field. Without fields, the format is nothing more than a bunch of static text. The fields enable you to design a format that fills in dynamically at run-time. This flexibility results in dynamic reports or documents based on live data.

The fields come in three varieties. The text field displays text with justification set to left, right, or center. The numeric field displays numbers with optional decimal placement. The text-block field displays multiline, variable-length records of text data, with justification set to left, right, or center.

This example uses all three types of fields on the same format specification. The example presents an HTML form that elicits feedback from Web customers. Upon submission, a text file based on a format is written to the Web server for later processing.

Create an HTML form with the appropriate document tags and set the action attribute of the <FORM> tag to "fmt-feedback-action.pl." This form processor invokes the format.

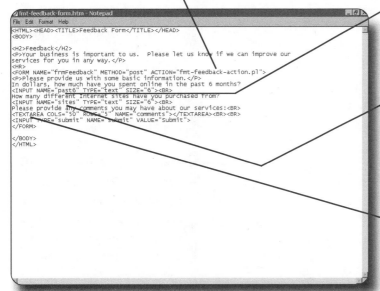

You ask the users how much they have spent online in the past six months with an <INPUT> field named past6.

Ask the users from how many Web sites they have purchased merchandise in the past six months with an <INPUT> field named sites.

Ask the users to provide some comments on how to improve your Web site and name the field comments.

This is just a basic feedback form. I have only included enough questions to provide a good representation of field types for the format specification. Feel free to elaborate on this design.

Make sure the text box is large enough for your customers to type comfortably. You can adjust the cols and rows attributes of the <TEXTAREA> tag to change the text box size.

The format declarations are placed in a separate script file to enable easier reuse. Use the `push` function to add the location of the format declaration file to the search path and then `require` the file.

```
fmt-feedback-action.pl - Notepad
File Edit Format Help
#!/usr/bin/perl
push(@INC, "e:/inetpub/wwwroot/cgi-bin");
require "fmt-formsave.pl";

my ($in, @pairs, $pair, $name, $value, %parseform);

if ($ENV{REQUEST_METHOD} eq "POST") {
    read(STDIN, $in, $ENV{CONTENT_LENGTH});
    @pairs = split(/&/, $in);
} elsif ($ENV{REQUEST_METHOD} eq "GET") {
    @pairs = split(/&/, $ENV{QUERY_STRING});
}
foreach $pair (@pairs) {

    ($name,$value) = split(/=/, $pair);
    $value =~ tr/+/ /;
    $value =~ s/%([a-fA-F0-9][a-fA-F0-9])/pack("c", hex($1))/eg;
    if (defined($parseform{$name})) {
        $parseform{$name} .= ",$value";
    } else {
        $parseform{$name} = $value;
    }
}

local $today = scalar localtime();
local $past6, $numsites, $usercomments, $ua, $ip;
$ua = $ENV{HTTP_USER_AGENT};
$ip = $ENV{REMOTE_ADDR};
$past6 = $parseform{past6};
$numsites = $parseform{sites};
$usercomments = $parseform{comments};

my $formid = time;
open(FORMSAVE, ">e:/inetpub/wwwroot/cgi-bin/$formid-$ip.txt") || die "can't open file: $!\n";
write FORMSAVE;
close FORMSAVE;

print "Content-type: text/html\n\n";
print <<ENDHTML
<html><head><title>Thank You!</title></head>
<body>
```

Save the date and time as a string for use in the format declaration. The next line declares the variables used by the format. You'll see these variables when you create the format file.

Now assign values to these variables. Grab the user agent string and the remote client address from the CGI variables and save the variable values from the `%parseform` hash.

You need a unique name for each feedback submission you receive. An easy way to get a unique number is to save the number returned from the `time` function (the number of seconds since January 1, 1980).

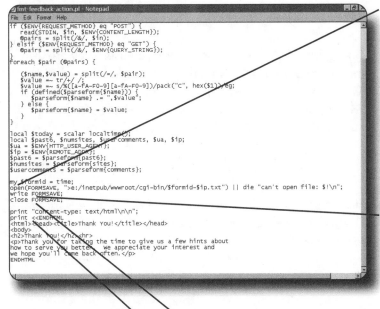

Open a file handle for writing named FORMSAVE. The format in the fmt-formsave.pl file is associated with this file handle name. Note the > preceding the filename and path. This > signifies that the script is writing to the file handle as opposed to reading it.

With all the variables set with values and the file handle open, the only thing left to do is write to the file with the format specification.

Don't forget to close the file handle.

Up to this point, nothing has been sent back to the client browser. Using the multiline mode of the print function, you can display a short note of appreciation to the users.

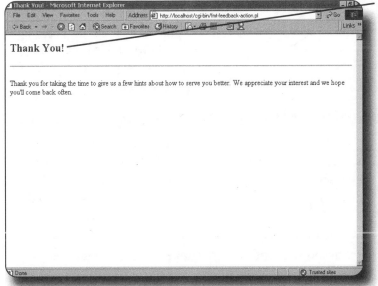

By the time the users see this message, their responses have been recorded in a file on the Web server.

As with the opening example, invoking the format is quite easy. Now it's time to create the format for saving this submission and see what it looks like.

Text Fields

Text fields are the most basic fields you use. They are also the most common. You've already been given the basics of what constitutes a text field, so you can jump right in to the FORMSAVE format. In this section, you focus on the text fields only.

Declare the format and give it the name FORMSAVE.

First, create a label for the remote client address variable. The square brackets that follow frame the field specification for this variable.

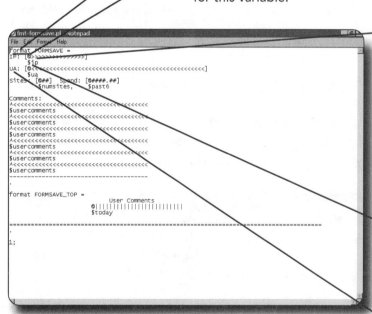

Create a text field by starting with the @ sign. Because this is an IP address, the field has to accommodate 15 characters. Right-justify the field by adding 15 > characters. This leaves an extra space in the field for good measure.

In the line immediately following this field, place the variable name that holds the remote client address, $ip.

Follow the same procedure for the user agent field specification, except left-justify this field by using the < character. The user agent value can be fairly long, so be sure to provide enough characters in the field specification.

You will work with the other fields in this format in the following sections. For now, take a look at the output of this format.

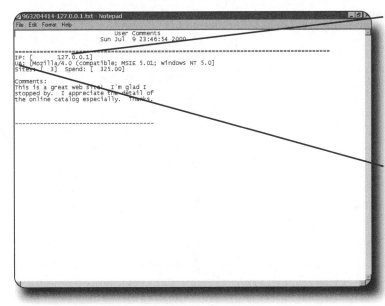

Here is the remote client address for this submission. Note that the IP address is right-justified inside the square brackets, just as you specified in the format declaration.

The user agent string is long, as you suspected. If the string is too long for the field specification, the format truncates the string. And this has indeed happened here; the trailing parenthesis of this string is missing.

Numeric Fields

You specify numeric fields by starting with the @ character, just like text fields. But instead of using >, <, or l to fill out the field, you use the pound sign. You can also include a period as the location of the decimal point. In the feedback example, you have two numbers to display in the format, a currency figure and an integer.

Create a numeric field for the number of visited sites by following the same procedure as you used for the remote address and user agent text fields. This time, use the pound sign to create

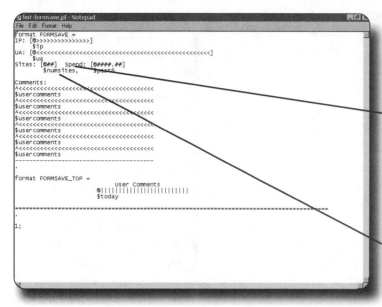

a numeric field of three digits. Don't forget that the at sign counts as a character column in the field.

Do the same thing for the amount spent in the past six months, but add a decimal followed by two pound signs to display the number in dollars and cents.

On the next line, place the variables $numsites and $past6 separated by a comma to provide the values for the numeric fields when the format is invoked.

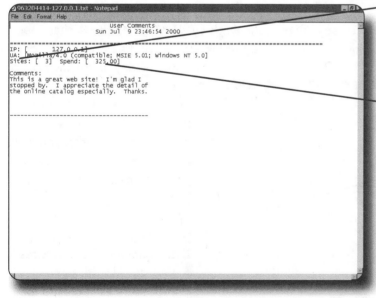

You can see from this display that this user visited three Web sites and spent $325 in the last six months.

Note that both numeric fields are right-justified inside the square brackets.

Multiline Fields

Sometimes you need to display a value that spans multiple lines. You can use the multiline field in those circumstances. The multiline field starts with a caret symbol (^) and uses the <, >, and pipe (|) symbols for justification.

To specify multiple lines, repeat the field specification and the variable assignment lines as many times as necessary.

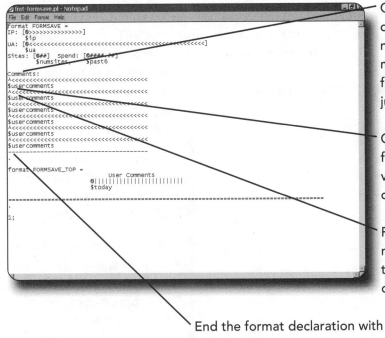

Create a label for the user comments section. On the next line, start a new multiline field with a ^ followed by 40 left-justification characters.

On the next line after the field specification, place the variable for the user comments from the form.

Repeat this pattern five more times to produce six total lines to hold the user comments.

End the format declaration with a dotted line for clarity. Be sure to add the period on a line by itself.

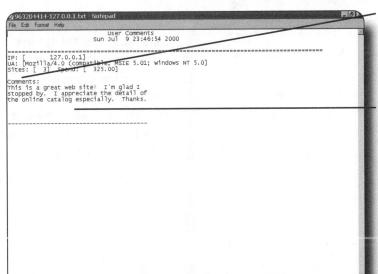

Here are the comments from the form. Note that they have spread out over three lines in the format output.

Note there are three blank lines because these comments only consumed three of the six lines in the format.

Filled Fields

In the previous example, the comments section was padded with blank lines because the user comments did not fill all six lines. Perl formats are a little smarter than that. You can instruct the format to suppress these blank lines when there is no data to put in them by placing a tilde symbol (~) somewhere on the same line as the field specification.

The only difference between this format declaration and the last example is the inclusion of the tilde symbol.

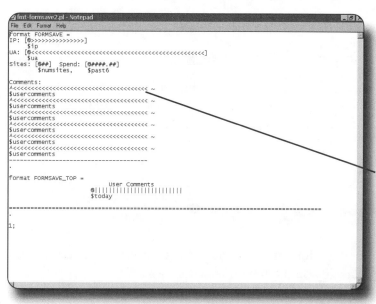

Place a tilde at the end of each field specification for the user comments data. This suppresses each line when the value of the $usercomments variable does not reach that line.

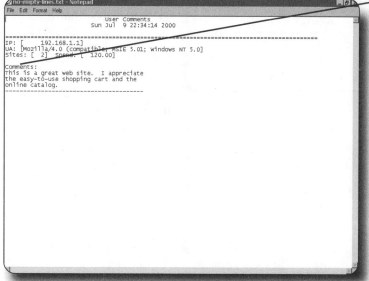

Here is another form submission that did not use all six lines in the format. Note this time, however, that there are no blank lines between the comments and the dotted line at the end of the format specification.

Using the Top-of-Page Format

Formats also have the capability to perform some simple page formatting. You can specify a report page header with the top-of-page format declaration. A top-of-page format declaration is associated with a particular file handle, just like a normal format. By default, Perl will look for a top-of-page format declaration with the same name as the current file handle appended with _TOP. If Perl finds such a declaration, it will process that format for the top of each page output on that file handle. After one page of output has been reached on a given file handle, Perl outputs the top-of-page format again. You learn how to change the number of lines on a page later in the chapter.

Using the Top-of-Page Format

To use a top-of-page format, you need to declare a second format that defines how you want the top of the page to look. Perl takes care of including this format specification in the output; you do not need to make any additional calls to write.

In this example, you create a report for the form submission log file you created in Chapter 10, " Handling Data with Regular Expressions." You specify a standard format declaration and a top-of-page declaration for the report to be output to STDOUT. These declarations reside in a separate file.

Declare the standard format for the STDOUT default file handle.

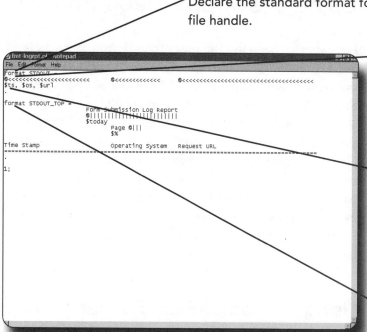

Each line of the report has three left-justified fields for a timestamp, the operating system, and the URL of the submitted form.

Don't forget to specify the variables on the line following the field specifications. Be sure to separate the variables with commas.

Declare the top-of-page format by appending _TOP to the STDOUT format name.

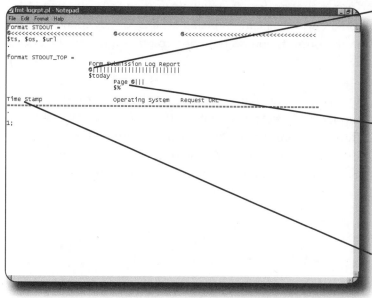

Center-justify a field just below the report title. This field holds the date and time of the report as represented by $today.

Perl formats can also track page numbers in the special variable called $%. Place a small centered field below the report date to display the current page number.

Now create some static text labels for the column headers of each field represented in the standard format declaration.

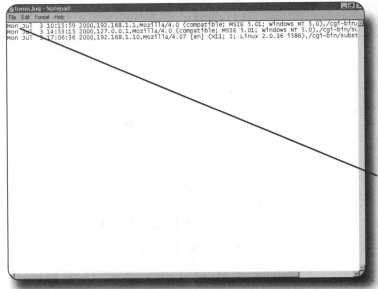

It is always helpful, if not absolutely necessary, to see the data before you attempt to manipulate it. The form submission log from Chapter 10 is included with this chapter to refresh your memory of the log format.

Each line in the log consists of a timestamp, the remote client address, the user agent string, the URL submitted, and the query string.

Be sure to include the file with the formats. This procedure is identical to the previous examples.

Open the form submission log file for reading.

Loop through each line of the log file and extract each element with the split function.

Because the operating system is embedded in the user agent string, you need to extract it. This regular expression from Chapter 10 (the expression in the match operator) performs that operation.

Save the matched pattern from the regular expression as the operating system string, and then write to STDOUT to produce a line on the report.

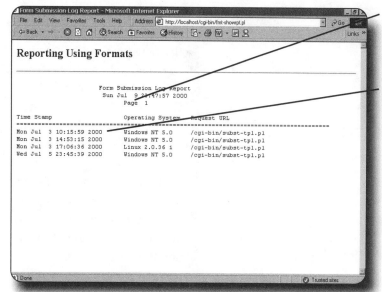

Here is the page number. This is a pretty short report, so you only have the one page.

Here are the individual lines as specified by the standard format declaration.

Changing Format Defaults

Because Perl assigns formats to individual file handles, you can change some of the format parameters used by a file handle. You can change the name of the standard format and the name of the top-of-page format used by a file handle. In other words, you don't have to name your formats with the same name as the file handle; you can reassign the formats associated with a file handle. You can also change the page length for a format from the default of 60 lines. These options give you some extra flexibility with your formats.

Changing the Format Names

The names of the output formats associated with a given file handle are stored in special variables: $~ for the standard format and $^ for the top-of-page format. To change the values of these variables, select the file handle first. You can change the current file handle by using the `select` function.

In this example, you create formats with names that do not match the file handles you use to output the format. You then use the `select` function to select the appropriate file handle and change the names of the standard format and the top-of-page format for the file handle. The basis of the example is the feedback example covered previously in this chapter.

```
fmt-formsave3.pl - Notepad
File  Edit  Format  Help
format FORMSAVE_NOBLANKS =
IP: [@>>>>>>>>>>>>>]
       $ip
UA: [@<<<<<<<<<<<<<<<<<<<<<<<<<<<<<<<<<<<<<<<<<<<<<<<<<<<]
       $ua
Sites: [@##]  Spend: [@####.##]
        $numsites,    $past6

Comments:
^<<<<<<<<<<<<<<<<<<<<<<<<<<<<<<<<<<< ~
$usercomments
^<<<<<<<<<<<<<<<<<<<<<<<<<<<<<<<<<<< ~
$usercomments
^<<<<<<<<<<<<<<<<<<<<<<<<<<<<<<<<<<< ~
$usercomments
^<<<<<<<<<<<<<<<<<<<<<<<<<<<<<<<<<<< ~
$usercomments
^<<<<<<<<<<<<<<<<<<<<<<<<<<<<<<<<<<< ~
$usercomments
^<<<<<<<<<<<<<<<<<<<<<<<<<<<<<<<<<<< ~
$usercomments
^<<<<<<<<<<<<<<<<<<<<<<<<<<<<<<<<<<< ~
$usercomments
------------------------------------------
.

format FORMSAVE_NOBLANKS_TOP =
                    User Comments
                @||||||||||||||||||||||||||
                $today
---------------------------------------------------------------
.

1;
```

This format is the same as the multiline format in previous sections. The only difference here is that you give it the name FORMSAVE_NOBLANKS.

Do the same for the top-of-page format. Note that you don't have to use the suffix _TOP here.

```
fmt-feedback-action2.pl - Notepad
File  Edit  Format  Help
#!/usr/bin/perl
push(@INC, "e:/inetpub/wwwroot/cgi-bin");
require "fmt-formsave.pl";

my ($in, @pairs, $pair, $name, $value, %parseform);

if ($ENV{REQUEST_METHOD} eq "POST") {
    read(STDIN, $in, $ENV{CONTENT_LENGTH});
    @pairs = split(/&/, $in);
} elsif ($ENV{REQUEST_METHOD} eq "GET") {
    @pairs = split(/&/, $ENV{QUERY_STRING});
}
foreach $pair (@pairs) {

    ($name,$value) = split(/=/, $pair);
    $value =~ tr/+/ /;
    $value =~ s/%([a-fA-F0-9][a-fA-F0-9])/pack("C", hex($1))/eg;
    if (defined($parseform{$name})) {
        $parseform{$name} .= ",$value";
    } else {
        $parseform{$name} = $value;
    }
}

local $today = scalar localtime();
local $past6, $numsites, $usercomments, $ua, $ip;
$ua = $ENV{HTTP_USER_AGENT};
$ip = $ENV{REMOTE_ADDR};
$past6 = $parseform{past6};
$numsites = $parseform{sites};
$usercomments = $parseform{comments};

my $formid = time;
open(FORMSAVE, ">e:/inetpub/wwwroot/cgi-bin/$formid-$ip.txt") || die "can't open file: $!\n";
my $oldfh = select FORMSAVE;
$~ = "FORMSAVE_NOBLANKS";
$^ = "FORMSAVE_NOBLANKS_TOP";
select ($oldfh);

write FORMSAVE;
close FORMSAVE;
```

Save the old current file handle while selecting the FORMSAVE file handle, which you opened previously. This preserves the state of the script while you make the format variable changes.

Change the value of the $~ variable (the standard format) to FORMSAVE_NOBLANKS.

```
fmt-feedback-action2.pl - Notepad
File Edit Format Help
#!/usr/bin/perl
push(@INC, "e:/inetpub/wwwroot/cgi-bin");
require "fmt-formsave.pl";

my ($in, @pairs, $pair, $name, $value, %parseform);

if ($ENV{REQUEST_METHOD} eq "POST") {
    read(STDIN, $in, $ENV{CONTENT_LENGTH});
    @pairs = split(/&/, $in);
} elsif ($ENV{REQUEST_METHOD} eq "GET") {
    @pairs = split(/&/, $ENV{QUERY_STRING});
}
foreach $pair (@pairs) {

    ($name,$value) = split(/=/, $pair);
    $value =~ tr/+/ /;
    $value =~ s/%([a-fA-F0-9][a-fA-F0-9])/pack("c", hex($1))/eg;
    if (defined($parseform{$name})) {
        $parseform{$name} .= ",$value";
    } else {
        $parseform{$name} = $value;
    }
}

local $today = scalar localtime();
local $past6, $numsites, $usercomments, $ua, $ip;
$ua = $ENV{HTTP_USER_AGENT};
$ip = $ENV{REMOTE_ADDR};
$past6 = $parseform{past6};
$numsites = $parseform{sites};
$usercomments = $parseform{comments};

my $formid = time;
open(FORMSAVE, ">e:/inetpub/wwwroot/cgi-bin/$formid-$ip.txt") || die "can't open file: $!\n";
my $oldfh = select FORMSAVE;
$~ = "FORMSAVE_NOBLANKS";
$^ = "FORMSAVE_NOBLANKS_TOP";
select ($oldfh);

write FORMSAVE;
close FORMSAVE;
```

Change the value of the $^ variable (the top-of-page format) to FORMSAVE_NOBLANKS_TOP.

Restore the old default file handle.

Now, when you write to the FORMSAVE file handle, you will be using the new format, FORMSAVE_NOBLANKS, instead.

Changing the Page Length

Changing the page length default is just as easy. You follow the same procedure as for changing the format names. In this example, you continue with the example from the previous section and change the number of lines per page along with the format names.

```
fmt-feedback-action3.pl - Notepad
File Edit Format Help
#!/usr/bin/perl
push(@INC, "e:/inetpub/wwwroot/cgi-bin");
require "fmt-formsave.pl";

my ($in, @pairs, $pair, $name, $value, %parseform);

if ($ENV{REQUEST_METHOD} eq "POST") {
    read(STDIN, $in, $ENV{CONTENT_LENGTH});
    @pairs = split(/&/, $in);
} elsif ($ENV{REQUEST_METHOD} eq "GET") {
    @pairs = split(/&/, $ENV{QUERY_STRING});
}
foreach $pair (@pairs) {

    ($name,$value) = split(/=/, $pair);
    $value =~ tr/+/ /;
    $value =~ s/%([a-fA-F0-9][a-fA-F0-9])/pack("c", hex($1))/eg;
    if (defined($parseform{$name})) {
        $parseform{$name} .= ",$value";
    } else {
        $parseform{$name} = $value;
    }
}

local $today = scalar localtime();
local $past6, $numsites, $usercomments, $ua, $ip;
$ua = $ENV{HTTP_USER_AGENT};
$ip = $ENV{REMOTE_ADDR};
$past6 = $parseform{past6};
$numsites = $parseform{sites};
$usercomments = $parseform{comments};

my $formid = time;
open(FORMSAVE, ">e:/inetpub/wwwroot/cgi-bin/$formid-$ip.txt") || die "can't open file: $!\n";
my $oldfh = select FORMSAVE;
$~ = "FORMSAVE_NOBLANKS";
$^ = "FORMSAVE_NOBLANKS_TOP";
$= = 40;
select ($oldfh);

write FORMSAVE;
```

Save the old current file handle while selecting the FORMSAVE file handle, which you opened previously. This preserves the state of the script while you make the format variable changes.

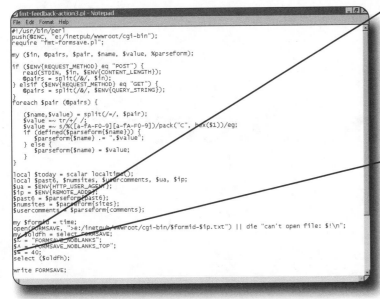

Change the value of the $~ variable (the standard format) to FORMSAVE_NOBLANKS and change the value of the $^ variable (the top-of-page format) to FORMSAVE_NOBLANKS_TOP.

Change the value of the $= variable (the number of lines per page) to 40 (the default is 60).

Now, the write operation to the FORMSAVE file handle uses the new formats and the page length is limited to 40 lines.

Summary

In this chapter, you learned what a Perl format is and in what circumstances formats are of use. You learned how to define a standard format and invoke the format with the write function. You learned about field specifications in formats and how to create text, numeric, and multiline fields. You also learned how to justify fields to the left, right, center, and on a decimal point. Finally, you learned how to implement top-of-page formats for reports, as well as how to change the formats associated with a given file handle and change the default page length. Formats can be beneficial to your CGI applications when you need only basic formatting for your reports or other output. The format is another example of how Perl gives you many choices for data formatting and output.

15

Files and Directories

Throughout the previous chapters you have mastered the process of inputting data to your application using an HTML form, and you possess the skills needed to send data, in the form of output, to a browser. You will now gain the knowledge needed to retrieve and send data to files on the server. You will also gain the skills that enable you to access and modify directories located on the server. This is more advanced than simple input and output to a browser; however, it is a process that you will find useful and beneficial to have in your arsenal of CGI tools. In this chapter, you will learn about:

- Using files
- Using directories
- Using file and directory operations

Using Files

You use files to store data that you will use in later applications or in repeated executions of the same application. In order to use a file in Perl, you have to create a label for the file you want to use. This label is referred to as a file handle and is used when you open, modify, or close any file from your application. With that in mind, you need to know how to open a file.

Opening Files

Before you can perform any modifications to a file, you need to open it from within your application. This process is simple and requires only one line of code to perform the function. There are three ways that you can open a file: the first writes to the file, overwriting any existing data; the second writes to the file, appending the new data to the end of the existing data; and the third reads the file, or inputs the data to your application. You see the code for each method in the next examples.

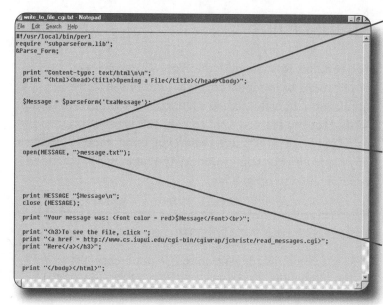

To open a file that you want to write to without preserving the existing data, type the open command, followed directly by an opening parenthesis.

You then type the name of the file handle you will use for your file, followed by a comma.

Type an opening double quotation mark, followed by the greater than sign.

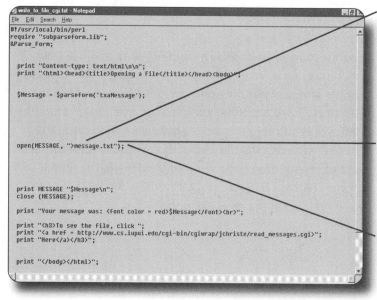

Next, you type the name of the file to which you are writing the data. If the file is in a different directory than the script, you need to include the entire file path.

You then type the closing double quotation mark, followed by a closing parenthesis.

End this line with a semicolon.

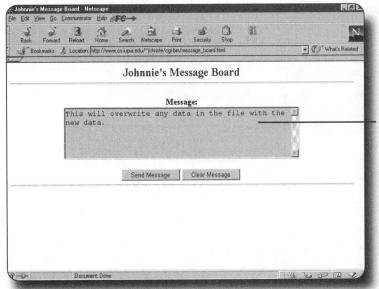

The complete code for the form in this example, open_file_html.txt, can be found on the CD in the examples for this chapter.

The users type their message into the form and submit it.

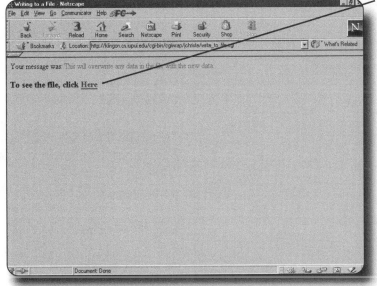

The application generates a display that shows the users their message and includes a link to enable them to view the file.

The complete code for the form in this example, read_messages_cgi.txt, can be found on the CD in the examples for this chapter.

When the users click on the link, they see the entire file.

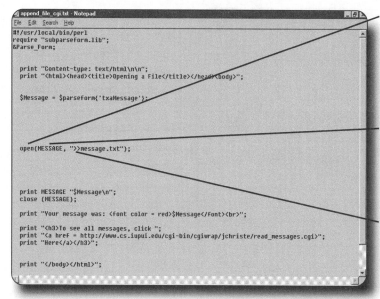

To open a file and append new data to it, type the **open** command, followed directly by an opening parenthesis.

You then type the name of the file handle you use for your file, followed by a comma.

Next, type an opening double quotation mark, followed by two greater than signs.

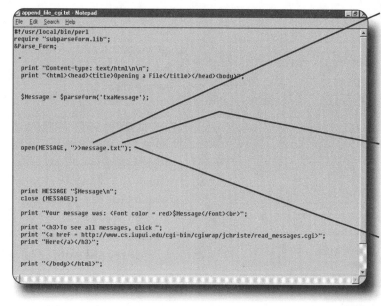

Next, type the name of the file to which you are writing the data. If the file is in a different directory than the script, you need to include the entire file path.

Then type the closing double quotation mark, followed by a closing parenthesis.

End this line with a semicolon.

The users type their messages into the form and submit it.

The application generates a display that shows the users their message and includes a link to enable them to view the file.

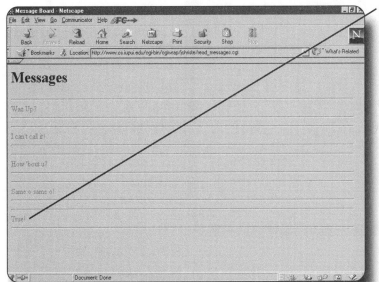

When the users click on the link, they see the entire file. This method appends their message to the existing data in the file.

The complete code for the form in this example, append_file_html.txt, can be found on the CD in the examples for this chapter.

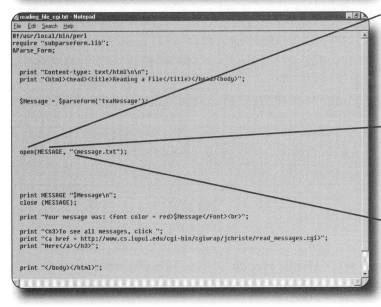

To open a file and read or input its data into your application, type the **open** command, followed directly by an opening parenthesis.

You then type the name of the file handle you will use for your file, followed by a comma.

Type an opening double quotation mark, followed by a less than sign. Perl does not require the less than sign in this instance; however, you might want to use it just so you don't think that you forgot to include a character when you debug the application.

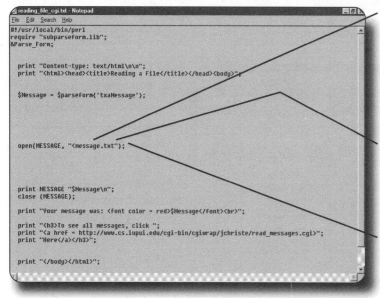

Next, type the name of the file to which you are writing the data. If the file is in a different directory different than the script, you need to include the entire file path.

You then type the closing double quotation mark, followed by a closing parenthesis.

End this line with a semicolon.

Closing Files

It makes sense that if you open a file, it will need to be closed at some point. In the following sections, you learn how to perform numerous functions while the file is open. You generally never open a file and then close it without performing some type of operation; however, the following examples begin with opening a file and end with closing it. Therefore, you learn how to close a file here.

NOTE

Perl automatically closes a file when you exit the script; however, it is a good habit to close a file when you are finished with it. This helps eliminate problems when two applications try to access the file at the same time.

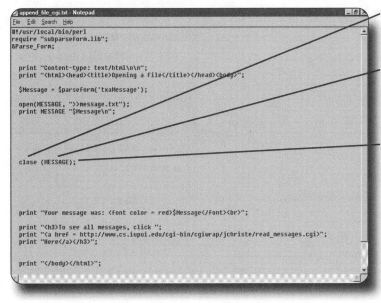

To close a file, type the **close** command.

This is followed by the file handle enclosed in parentheses.

End this line with a semicolon.

Writing to Files

In the previous examples, the users' messages were written to a file that they were able to view. You now learn how to get the data to the file so that it can be stored for later use.

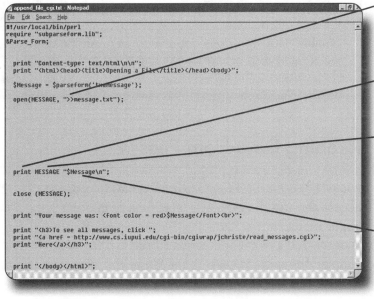

To write data to a file, first open the file using the write to or append symbols.

You then type the **print** command.

You follow this command with the file handle of the file to which you want to write the data (in this case, MESSAGE).

You then type an opening double quotation mark and the data you want to write to the file. This can be a string or a variable. A variable does not need to be enclosed in quotation marks; however, you might want to do so anyway in order to remain in the habit.

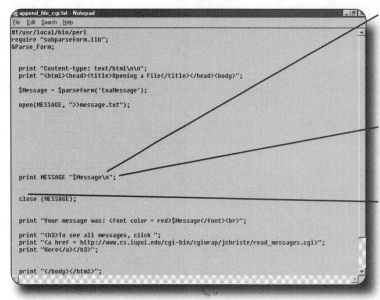

If you want to separate the messages from each other, you can include the newline character (\n) after the data you are writing to the file.

You then close the quotation marks and end the line with a semicolon.

You need to close the file when you are finished writing to it.

CAUTION

Remember that the single greater than symbol overwrites any existing data in the file. Make certain that you use the correct symbol or you can lose valuable data. Perl does not display any warning that you are about to overwrite existing data, so be careful when choosing the symbol.

Reading Data from Files

You will find it useful to store data in files in order to access and use the data at a later time or in other applications. In the "Opening Files" section of this chapter, you saw the messages stored in a file that enabled the users to view them. Here, you learn how to retrieve the stored data from a file.

To begin, you need to open the file from which you want to retrieve the data. Because you are only reading the file, use the less than sign.

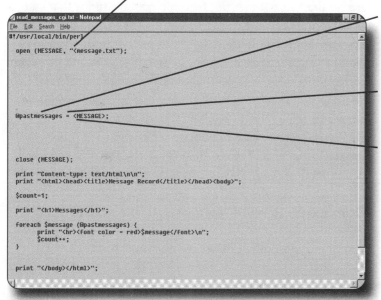

You then type the array in which you will store the lines from the file.

Follow this array name with an equals sign.

Then type a less than sign.

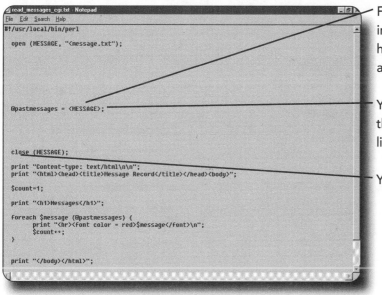

Follow the less than sign immediately with the file handle of the file you are accessing.

You follow this with a greater than sign and then end the line with a semicolon.

You then close the file.

Exclusive File Access

Earlier, you learned that you should close a file as soon as you are finished with it in order to avoid complications that can arise from multiple users accessing it at the same time. You do not want multiple users trying to overwrite or append a file at the same time; it will cause complications and can even corrupt the file. To prevent this from occurring, Perl has designed a function to enable your users to gain exclusive access to a file. The `flock` function gives the users exclusive access when they open a file and then releases the exclusive access when they close the file. You will use both functions together to properly execute this process.

Open the file to which you want exclusive access.

You then type the exclusive access command (**flock**).

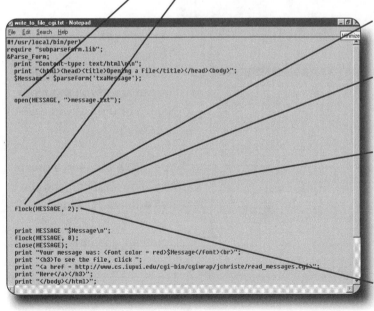

Then you type an opening parenthesis.

You then type the file handle of the file you are accessing, followed by a comma.

You then type the exclusive access code (**2**)—the code for gaining exclusive access—for the function followed by a closing parenthesis.

End this line with a semicolon.

Next, modify the file you opened.

You then type the exclusive access command.

Then you type an opening parenthesis.

You then immediately type the file handle of the file you are accessing followed by a comma.

Type the release exclusive access code (8)—the command for releasing exclusive access—for the function followed by the closing parenthesis.

You will end this line with a semicolon.

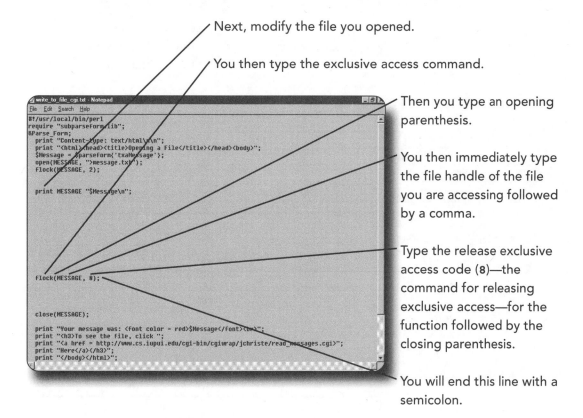

```
write_to_file_cgi.txt - Notepad
File  Edit  Search  Help
#!/usr/local/bin/perl
require "subparseform.lib";
&Parse_Form;
    print "Content-type: text/html\n\n";
    print "<html><head><title>Opening a File</title></head><body>";
    $Message = $parseform{'txaMessage'};
    open(MESSAGE, ">message.txt");
    flock(MESSAGE, 2);

    print MESSAGE "$Message\n";




    flock(MESSAGE, 8);


    close(MESSAGE);

    print "Your message was: <Font color = red>$Message</Font><br>";
    print "<h3>To see the file, click ";
    print "<a href = http://www.cs.iupui.edu/cgi-bin/cgiwrap/jchriste/read_messages.cgi>";
    print "Here</a></h3>";
    print "</body></html>";
```

During the time that your application has the file in `flock` mode, other users cannot gain access to the file. So, you will want to open and close the `flock` function and the file as soon as you are finished with the modification.

Now that you have mastered opening, writing to, and closing a file, it is time to learn how to make other modifications to files.

Renaming Files

There might be times when you will want to change the name of a file. Perhaps you have a better name for the file that makes more sense, or maybe you routinely change the message board filename to keep track of the message during certain times (months, weeks, and so on). Whatever your reason for changing the filename, the process is the same and can be accomplished from within your application.

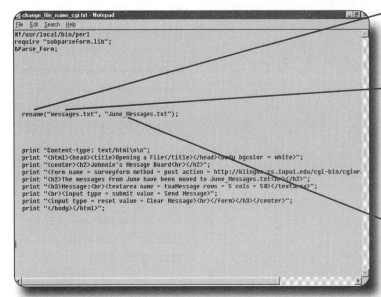

```
change_file_name_cgi.txt - Notepad
File  Edit  Search  Help
#!/usr/local/bin/perl
require "subparseform.lib";
&Parse_Form;



   rename("messages.txt", "June_Messages.txt");


print "Content-type: text/html\n\n";
print "<html><head><title>Opening a File</title></head><body bgcolor = white>";
print "<center><h2>Johnnie's Message Board<hr></h2>";
print "<form name = surveyform method = post action = http://klingon.cs.iupui.edu/cgi-bin/cgiwr
print "<h2>The messages from June have been moved to June_Messages.txt<hr></h2>";
print "<h3>Message:<br><textarea name = txaMessage rows = 5 cols = 50></textarea>";
print "<br><input type = submit value = Send Message>";
print "<input type = reset value = Clear Message><hr></form></h3></center>";
print "</body></html>";
```

To rename a file, use the `rename` command, followed by an opening parenthesis.

Then type the name of the file you want to change followed by a comma. Remember that if it is a string, you need to enclose it in double quotation marks.

Type the new filename, followed by a closing parenthesis and end the line with a semicolon.

CAUTION

If a file currently exists with the same name, your file will overwrite the original file's data. Therefore, be certain to check the new name you are assigning to the file before you run the application. This process also removes the old file from its existing location, so be sure to change the path in any applications that access this file.

The complete code for the form in this example, change_file_html.txt, can be found on the CD in the examples for this chapter. You can create an application or link that displays the URL for this example.

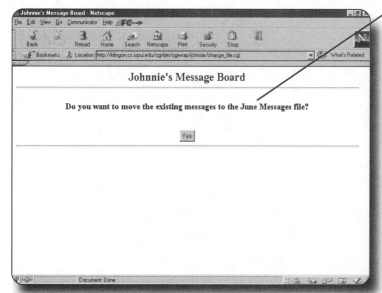

I have created an HTML page that enables the users to move the messages to a different folder.

When the users click on the Submit button, the script will display an updated message board page, which informs them that the old messages have been moved to a new file.

The complete code for the application in this example, change_file_cgi.txt, can be found on the CD in the examples for this chapter. You can create an application or link that displays the URL for this example.

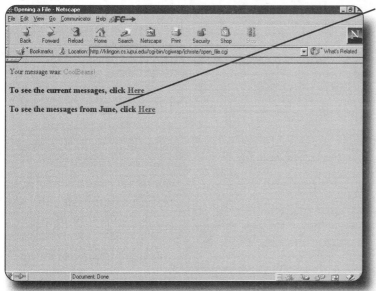

When the users send their messages, they see a page that displays their message as well as links to the current message file and the renamed message file.

If the users click on the current messages link, they only see the messages posted since the file was renamed.

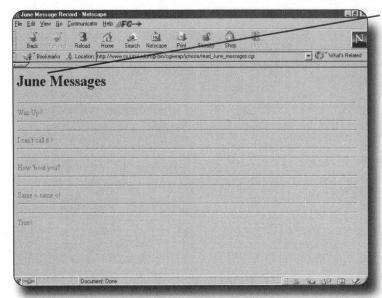

The complete code for the application in this example, read_June_messages_cgi.txt, can be found on the CD in the examples for this chapter.

When the users click on the June messages link, they see the messages that were previously in the renamed file.

Removing Files

There might be instances in which you want to remove old files from a directory. They can be obsolete files, or they might be temporary files that you no longer need.

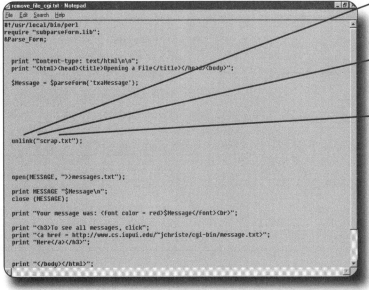

To remove a file, first type the Perl **unlink** operator.

You then type an opening parenthesis.

This is followed by the name of the file you want to remove. If it is a string, you need to enclose it in quotation marks. Then type a closing parenthesis and end the line with a semicolon.

The complete code for the applications and HTML pages in this example can be found on the CD in the examples for this chapter. They are named, in order of use,

remove_file_html.txt, remove_file_cgi.txt,
removed_file_cgi.txt, and read_message_cgi.txt.

Checking the Status of Files

There are times when you will want to determine whether a
file exists or find out what the permissions are on a file.
There are simple processes that enable you to check the file
and retrieve such information.

> **NOTE**
>
> In order to display the results of the file status checks, I
> have used an `if` statement in the following example.
> Therefore, the line that the check is on ends in an opening
> curly bracket ({). This is not always the case, and if the
> check was not located in an `if` statement, it would end
> with a semicolon. Also, the check statement is enclosed in
> parentheses only because of the `if` statement.

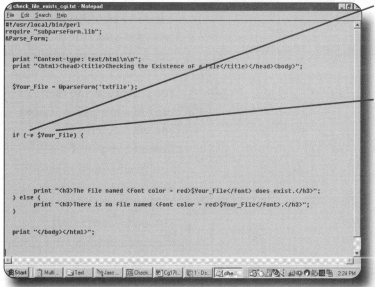

To determine whether a file
exists, type the operator
that checks for a file's
existence.

Then type the name of the
file whose existence you want
to check. Remember that if it
is a string, you need to
enclose it in quotation marks.

The complete code for the
HTML page in this,
check_file_exists_html.txt,
can be found on the CD in
the examples for this chapter.

The generated HTML response informs you of the status of the existence of the file.

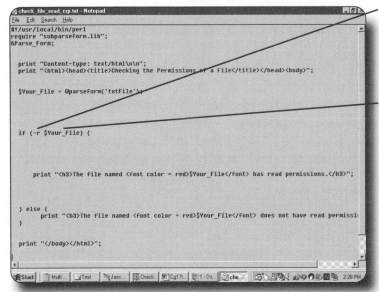

To determine whether a file has read permissions, you type the operator that checks for this permission.

You then type the name of the file whose permissions you want to check. Remember that if it is a string, you need to enclose it in quotation marks.

The generated HTML response tells you the read permission of the file.

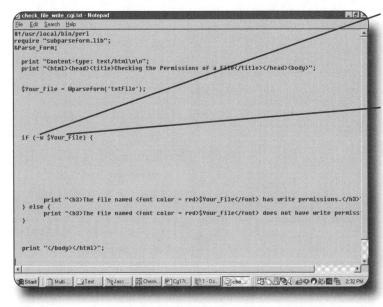

To determine whether a file has write permissions, you type the operator that checks for this permission.

You then type the name of the file whose permissions you want to check. Remember that if it is a string, you need to enclose it in quotation marks.

The generated HTML response tells you the status of the write permission of the file.

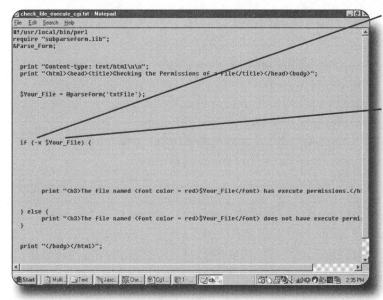

To determine whether a file has execute permissions, you type the operator that checks for this permission.

You then type the name of the file whose permissions you want to check. Remember that if it is a string, you need to enclose it in quotation marks.

The generated HTML response tells you the status of the execute permission of the file.

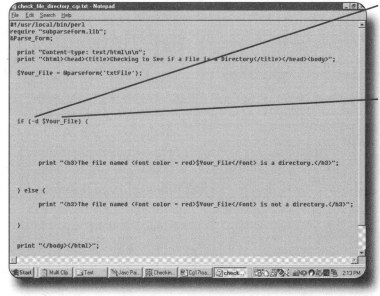

To determine whether a file is a directory, you type the operator that checks for a directory.

You then type the name of the file that you want to check. Remember that if it is a string, you need to enclose it in quotation marks.

The generated HTML response informs you of the directory status of the file.

Now that you have mastered using and modifying files, you are ready to move ahead and learn how to use and modify directories.

Using Directories

You saw the benefits of using files in your applications in the previous section. In this section, you learn to use directories in your applications. This is useful in that it enables you to view the files contained in a directory, change directories, create directories, and remove directories from within your application.

Opening Directories

You generally start directory modification by opening the directory, as you did with files in the previous section. The process is similar; however, you use different operators.

The complete code for the form in this example, open_dir_html.txt, can be found on the CD in the examples for this chapter.

To open a directory, type the **opendir** operator.

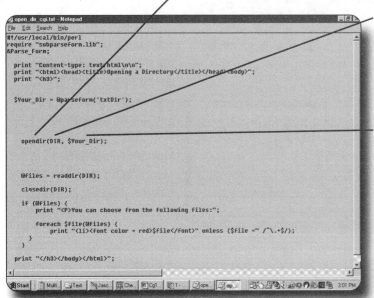

```perl
#t/usr/local/bin/perl
require "subparseform.lib";
&Parse_Form;

    print "Content-type: text/html\n\n";
    print "<html><head><title>Opening a Directory</title></head><body>";
    print "<h3>";

    $Your_Dir = @parseform{'txtDir'};


    opendir(DIR, $Your_Dir);


    @files = readdir(DIR);

    closedir(DIR);

    if (@files) {
        print "<P>You can choose from the following files:";

        foreach $File(@files) {
            print "<li><font color = red>$File</font>" unless ($file =~ /^\.+$/);
        }
    }

    print "</h3></body></html>";
```

You then type an opening parenthesis and the label—basically the same as a file handle, but for a directory—followed by a comma.

Then you type the name of the directory you want to open. If you are opening the directory you are working in, simply type a period in quotation marks. If it is another directory, you need to provide the entire path to the directory. Remember

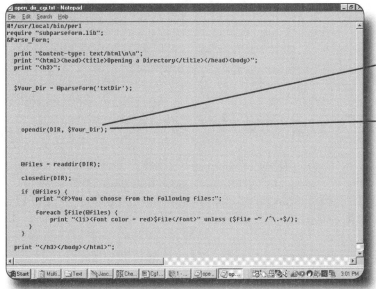

that strings need to be enclosed in quotation marks.

You then type a closing parenthesis.

End this line with a semicolon.

Close the directory as soon as you can after you have opened it, just as you do with files.

Closing Directories

The process of closing a directory is similar to closing a file, and like a file, you should close the directory as quickly as possible after you have accessed the directory data you need.

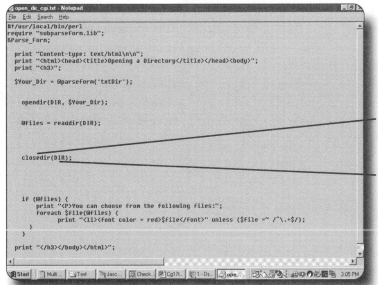

The complete code for the form in this example, open_dir_html.txt, can be found on the CD in the examples for this chapter.

To close a directory, type the `closedir` operator.

You then type an opening parenthesis, followed by the label you used to open the directory. Then type a closing parenthesis and end this line with a semicolon.

Now that you have mastered opening and closing directories, it is time to learn how to use this to your advantage. The first function you learn is how to view the files and directories in a directory.

Viewing Directory Contents

One of the primary reasons you open a directory is to view the contents of the directory, both files and subdirectories. This is a simple process and can be accomplished in a single line of code.

The complete code for the form in this example, open_dir_html.txt, can be found on the CD in the examples for this chapter.

Begin by opening the directory.

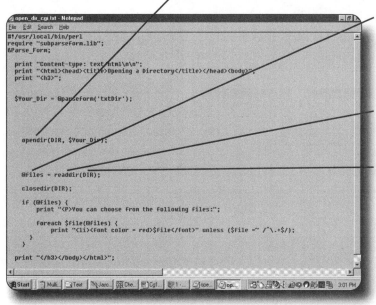

You then type the array in which you will store the file and directory names of the directory you opened.

Then type an equals sign and the **readdir** operator.

Type the label, enclosed in parentheses, which you used to open the file and end the line with a semicolon.

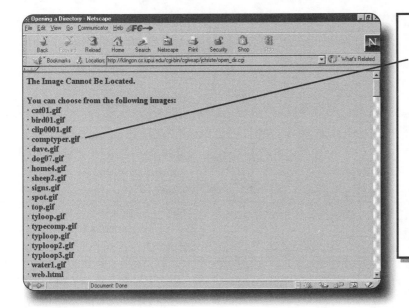

NOTE

The code for this example shows you how to display the directory contents. It is the same process you used before when displaying the keys and values of an array. The code for this process appears after the line of code that closes the directory.

Changing the Directory

You can work in the directory where the script is located or you can move to a different directory to access files and directories. This process is useful when you want to access multiple files that are not located in your cgi-bin.

The complete code for the form in this example, change_dir_html.txt, can be found on the CD in the examples for this chapter.

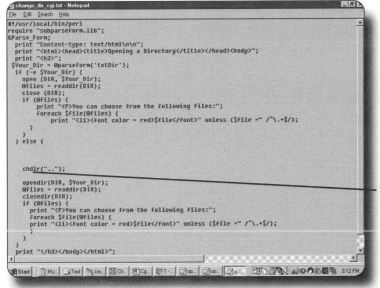

You first type the **chdir** operator.

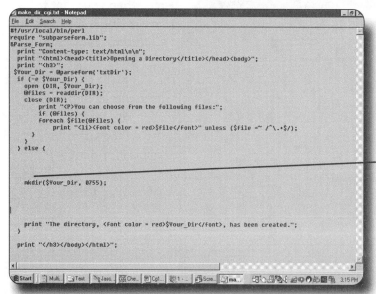

```
change_dir_cgi.txt - Notepad
File Edit Search Help
#!/usr/local/bin/perl
require "subparseform.lib";
&Parse_Form;
  print "Content-type: text/html\n\n";
  print "<html><head><title>Opening a Directory</title></head><body>";
  print "<h3>";
$Your_Dir = @parseform('txtDir');
  if (-e $Your_Dir) {
    open (DIR, $Your_Dir);
    @Files = readdir(DIR);
    close (DIR);
    if (@files) {
       print "<P>You can choose from the following files:";
       foreach $file(@files) {
          print "<li><font color = red>$file</font>" unless ($file =~ /^\.+$/);
       }
    }
  } else {

    chdir("..");

    opendir(DIR, $Your_Dir);
    @files = readdir(DIR);
    closedir(DIR);
    if (@files) {
      print "<P>You can choose from the following files:";
      foreach $file(@files) {
        print "<li><font color = red>$file</font>" unless ($file =~ /^\.+$/);
      }
    }
  }
  print "</h3></body></html>";
```

You then type an opening parenthesis, followed by the path of the directory to which you want to change. Remember that if it is a string, you need to enclose it in quotation marks. In this example, you are changing to a directory in the parent directory of the current directory. You use the two periods to access the parent directory.

Type a closing parenthesis and end the line with a semicolon.

Creating New Directories

You might need to store files in a directory that does not exist. In instances like this, you can create a new directory from within your application.

```
make_dir_cgi.txt - Notepad
File Edit Search Help
#!/usr/local/bin/perl
require "subparseform.lib";
&Parse_Form;
  print "Content-type: text/html\n\n";
  print "<html><head><title>Opening a Directory</title></head><body>";
  print "<h3>";
$Your_Dir = @parseform('txtDir');
  if (-e $Your_Dir) {
    open (DIR, $Your_Dir);
    @files = readdir(DIR);
    close (DIR);
       print "<P>You can choose from the following files:";
       if (@files) {
       foreach $file(@files) {
          print "<li><font color = red>$file</font>" unless ($file =~ /^\.+$/);
       }
    }
  } else {

    mkdir($Your_Dir, 0755);


    print "The directory, <font color = red>$Your_Dir</font>, has been created.";
  }
  print "</h3></body></html>";
```

The complete code for the form in this example, make_dir_html.txt, can be found on the CD in the examples for this chapter.

Begin by typing the **mkdir** operator.

You then type an opening parenthesis, followed by the name of the directory you want to create as well as the path, if necessary. Remember that if this is a string, you need to enclose it in quotation marks.

Type a comma.

Next, you type the permissions for the directory you are creating. Directories generally have their permissions set to 0755. This is the permission for owner readable, writeable, and executable; owner's group readable and executable; and world readable and executable.

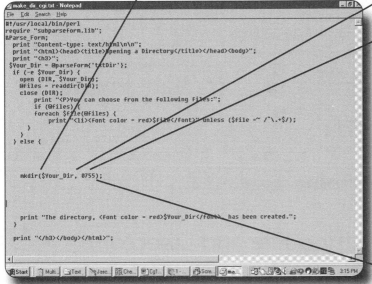

```perl
#!/usr/local/bin/perl
require "subparseform.lib";
&Parse_Form;
    print "Content-type: text/html\n\n";
    print "<html><head><title>Opening a Directory</title></head><body>";
    print "<h3>";
$Your_Dir = @parseform{'txtDir'};
    if (-e $Your_Dir) {
       open (DIR, $Your_Dir);
       @files = readdir(DIR);
       close (DIR);
          print "<P>You can choose from the following files:";
          if (@files) {
          foreach $file(@files) {
              print "<li><Font color = red>$file</Font>" unless ($file =~ /^\.+$/);
       }
    }
    } else {

    mkdir($Your_Dir, 8755);

    print "The directory, <font color = red>$Your_Dir</Font> has been created.";
    }

    print "</h3></body></html>";
```

A closing parenthesis and a semicolon follow the permissions and end the line.

Removing Directories

Perl enables you to remove empty directories from within your application. If the directory contains any files or subdirectories, you cannot remove the directory from inside your application.

The complete code for the form in this example, remove_dir_html.txt, can be found on the CD in the examples for this chapter.

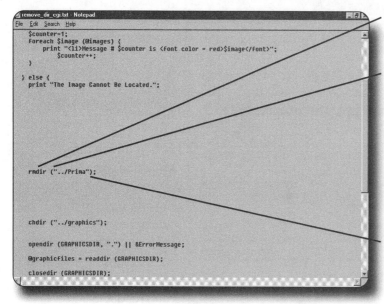

```
remove_dir_cgi.txt - Notepad
File  Edit  Search  Help
      $counter=1;
      Foreach $image (@images) {
          print "<li>Message # $counter is <font color = red>$image</font>";
              $counter++;
      }

} else {
print "The Image Cannot Be Located.";




rmdir ("../Prima");




chdir ("../graphics");

opendir (GRAPHICSDIR, ".") || &ErrorMessage;

@graphicfiles = readdir (GRAPHICSDIR);

closedir (GRAPHICSDIR);
```

To remove a directory, type the **rmdir** operator.

You then type an opening parenthesis, followed by the name of the directory that you want to remove, along with the path if necessary. Remember that if it is a string, you need to enclose it in quotation marks.

You then type a closing parenthesis and end the line with a semicolon.

Using File and Directory Operations

There are a few operations that you will probably perform on files and directories that were not covered in the previous sections. You need to understand how to use these operations because you will often come across them in borrowed and modified code.

NOTE

The error subroutine appears at the bottom of the open_dir_error_cgi.txt code in the following example. It also appears on the CD-ROM.

Verifying Files and Directories

If you have an application that is accessing a file or directory that it cannot open, Perl will keep running the script without the file or directory. This can create problems. The main concern is that the application continues to use the server resources and wastes time waiting for an application that is not functioning correctly. In order to eliminate this potential problem, you can use a subroutine that sends a message and exits the application when a problem occurs.

Begin by typing the function you want to perform: In this case, you are opening a directory.

Following the open directory command, you type the logical or operator (| |). This operator determines whether one or the other operations is true; therefore, if the open directory function fails, the function after the logical or operator will execute.

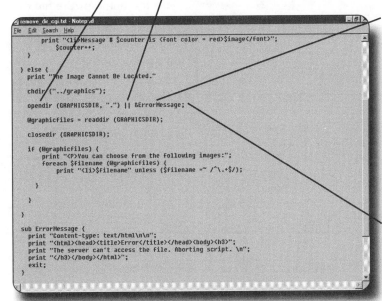

You then type the name of the subroutine that you created to handle this situation. Subroutine calls usually begin with the ampersand; however, Perl 5 enables you to use empty parentheses after the subroutine name—such as `ErrorMessage()`.

End this line with a semicolon.

Changing Permissions in Your Application

If the permissions of a file or directory are not set correctly, your application might not be able to open it. This can create problems when your application depends on the data in the file to continue executing correctly. Luckily, Perl enables you to change permissions from inside your applications.

The complete code for the form in this example, new_perm_html.txt, can be found on the CD in the examples for this chapter.

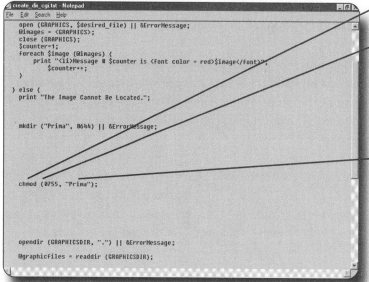

Type the **chmod** operator.

Then type an opening parenthesis and the new permissions you want for the file or directory followed by a comma.

Type the name of the file or directory, along with the path, if necessary, whose permission you are changing. Remember that if it is a string, you need to enclose it in quotation marks. Then end the line with a closing parenthesis and a semicolon.

Eliminating Characters

Data that is input from your forms or from files might contain extra spaces or returns. You will now learn how to eliminate these extra characters.

Eliminating Ending Characters on a String

You can remove any character at the end of a string with a simple process designed specifically for this task.

The complete code for the form in this example, chop_html.txt, can be found on the CD in the examples for this chapter.

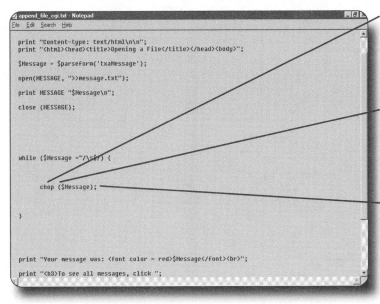

Start by typing the **chop** operator. It removes characters from the end of strings.

You then type an opening parenthesis followed by the variable that contains the data in question.

You then type the closing parenthesis and end the line with a semicolon.

Eliminating Newline Characters from a String

You can remove newline characters at the end of a string with a simple process designed specifically for this task.

The complete code for the form in this example, chomp_html.txt, can be found on the CD in the examples for this chapter.

Start by typing the **chomp** operator. You use it to remove newline characters from the end of strings.

You then type an opening parenthesis followed by the variable that contains the data in question.

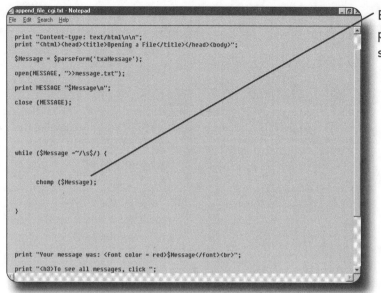

End the line with a closing parenthesis followed by a semicolon.

```
print "Content-type: text/html\n\n";
print "<html><head><title>Opening a File</title></head><body>";

$Message = $parseform{'txaMessage'};

open(MESSAGE, ">>message.txt");

print MESSAGE "$Message\n";

close (MESSAGE);




while ($Message =~/\s$/) {


    chomp ($Message);


}


print "Your message was: <font color = red>$Message</font><br>";

print "<h3>To see all messages, click ";
```

Summary

This chapter is full of material that enables you to create and modify applications that are powerful and that set you apart from Web developers who only know the basic CGI operators and functions. You are now prepared to develop powerful and useful Web applications that can perform operations on files and directories. You are no longer limited to the novice stage of being able to get information from forms, manipulate it, and display it on an HTML page. You have the power and skills to create applications that your clients need in the Web market today. You should be pleased with the level of knowledge you possess, and you should enjoy using it in your future Web development projects.

PART IV

Appendixes

A

Debugging Your Application

Up until now, this book has focused on helping you write CGI applications. This appendix focuses on what happens after you've written the CGI application when you need to solve problems within the application. In this appendix, you'll learn:

- Why debugging is an essential part of programming
- How to decipher error messages
- Various debugging techniques
- How to create and use an error subroutine

Understanding Debugging

So, you've programmed your first complete CGI application, you upload it to your server, call the script in your browser, and wait. It doesn't work!

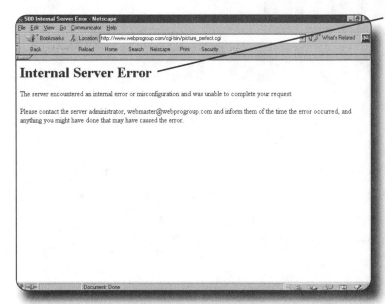

Instead of executing, you receive an Internal Server Error.

This means that there is a bug or an error in the code of your script. What do you do now? Don't panic! All it takes is a little debugging to make it work. Debugging means testing your application and then carefully going back through your script to "squash" the bugs or to find and fix the errors.

If you're going to write CGI applications with more than a few lines of code, you're going to have errors. This is why good debugging skills are an essential part of programming. Learning the correct debugging skills saves you a lot of time and unnecessary frustration.

You should always debug your application. "Wait a minute!" you might say. "Why do I *always* need to debug my application? What about when I run it the first time and it runs without any problem? Why do I need to debug it then?" Even though your script appears to run fine, there can be hidden errors that you don't know about. There can be errors in your logic. These errors might not be evident at first.

Recall that debugging is testing your application and then carefully going back through the code of your script to find and fix the errors. Part of the definition of debugging includes testing. Even when your script appears to run fine, always test it under different situations and with different input. If your script performs mathematical calculations, try entering several sets of data and make sure that you receive the desired output every time. Of course, the more straightforward the function of the application is, the less testing it requires.

Deciphering Error Messages

With every bug that you have, there are clues as to what the problem is and how to fix it. At first glance, these clues you receive might not appear to be very useful. Most of the bugs that aren't hidden have specific error messages associated with them. These bugs are not hidden because you receive a definite error message for each one of these types of bugs. You'll know up front that there's something wrong. These error messages are returned through your browser when you try to run a script.

The hardest part of debugging can be figuring out what these error messages are trying to tell you. Some tell you right away exactly what's wrong. Others can indicate one of several problems. That's why I call them *clues*. They give you a clue as to what's wrong and you have to decipher the rest. This appendix lists each of the major error messages you'll encounter along with an explanation of what each one means and how to fix it.

So what about the bugs that don't have an error message associated with them? The other bugs you encounter that don't have specific error messages associated with them are obvious bugs that show up in the output of your script. This appendix also lists some of the more common of these errors and solutions for each of them.

The Dreaded 500 Internal Server Error

Nothing can make your heart sink lower than finishing a CGI application that you're proud of, running it, and receiving this error. It is dreaded because it doesn't tell you exactly what's wrong. It can point to a number of problems in your script. You've already seen what this error looks like in Netscape in the first figure.

Although error messages are formatted differently in Internet Explorer, they mean the same thing. If you look closely, you can recognize them in either browser.

Here are the things to check when you receive an Internal Server error.

Incorrect Path to Perl

In Chapter 3, "Your First CGI Application," you learned about the special format of the first line of your Perl applications. Recall that this line contains the path to the Perl interpreter. If this line is incorrect, you will get an Internal Server error.

Less-Than-Picture-Perfect Punctuation

As you know, Perl is particular about punctuation. Something as small as a missing semicolon or an extra quotation mark can cause an Internal Server Error. Scan your code closely to check for punctuation errors. Be sure to check for comment lines, mismatched quotation marks, and missing semicolons and backslashes.

Watch for comment lines in which you forgot the pound sign at the beginning.

Mismatched quotation marks, such as a single quote and double quote used in the same expression, are problematic.

```
picture_perfect.cgi - Notepad
File  Edit  Search  Help
#!/usr/local/bin/perl

Path to sendmail on your server
$sendmail = '/bin/sendmail";

require "subparseform.lib;

&Parse_Form

print "Content-Type: text/html\n\n";

print "<html><head><title>Picture Perfect Punctuation</title></head>";
print "<body bgcolor="#FFFFFF">";
print "<p><h3>This Perl code has picture perfect punctuation!</h3>";
print "</body></html>";

exit;
```

Missing quotation marks cause problems.

Missing semicolons at the end of your lines cause code to fail.

Missing backslashes in front of quotation marks in your HTML code also cause problems.

If your eyes grow tired, you still can't find all the punctuation errors, and you still get an Internal Server Error, there is hope! You can comment out lines of code and run the script again to pinpoint the problem. You can even jump directly to this step if you like and save the strain on your eyes.

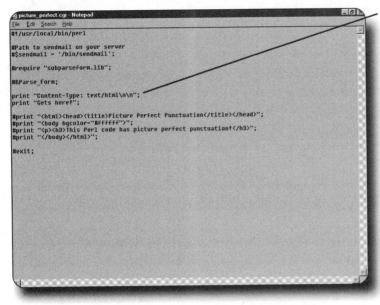

Comment out every line of code except the line that prints the content header and add one other temporary `print` statement below it. Inspect these two lines closely to make sure they are okay.

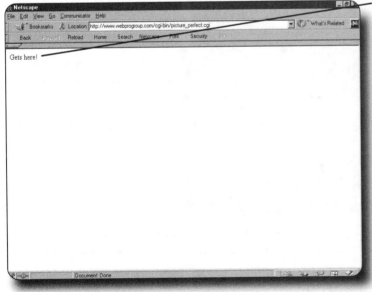

Test the script again and, if the two lines are okay, the script will print the temporary `print` statement.

Now, start uncommenting lines of code one by one and testing the script in between. If, after you've uncommented a line of code and tested it in your browser, you get an Internal Server error, you know you've found the line that contains the bug.

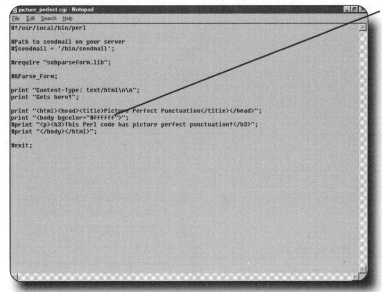

This is the line that contains the bug.

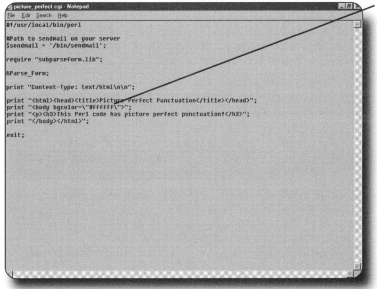

You can now squash the bug contained in this line and remove the temporary `print` line.

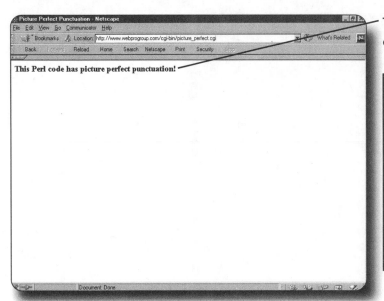

Test the script again to confirm that it's fixed.

TIP

If you still receive an Internal Server error after uncommenting the remaining lines of code, repeat the commenting out/ debugging procedure until you've squashed all the bugs.

Faulty Format

Perl is just as particular about format as it is about punctuation. Incorrectly formatted statements in your CGI application also cause an Internal Server error. The two most common problems to watch out for are mismatched braces and mismatched parentheses.

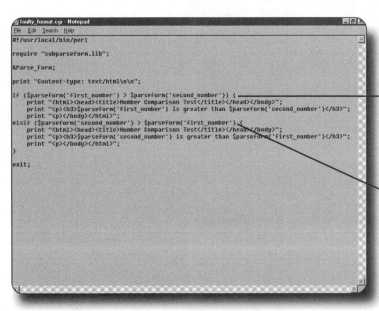

Mismatched braces occur when you have an open brace without a matching closing brace or vice versa.

Mismatched parentheses occur when you have an open parenthesis without a matching closing parenthesis or vice versa.

Both of these problems can be found and fixed using the commenting-out/debugging method.

403 Forbidden

This message can make you feel like a kid with your hand caught in the cookie jar.

All this message means is that the permissions of your CGI application are not set correctly in order for it to execute.

NOTE

Refer to the section entitled "Changing the Permissions of Your Application" in Chapter 3 for information about how to change the file permissions and fix this problem.

The Document Contained No Data

Suppose you had a script that used an `if`/`elsif` clause to compare two numbers and determine which one was larger.

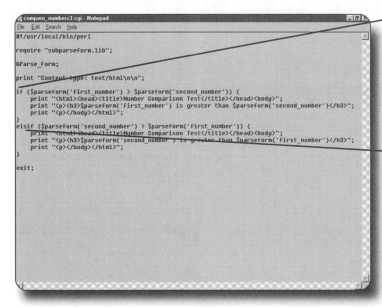

The `if` clause performs a simple test to determine whether the first number is greater than the second number. If this statement is true, it prints the results.

If the first statement is false, the `elsif` clause performs another simple test to determine whether the second number is greater than the first number. If this statement is true, it prints the results.

This script works fine when one of the numbers submitted is always larger than the other. However, if you ever have two identical numbers, you'll get a Document Contained No Data error.

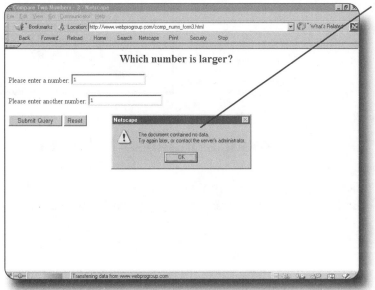

This is the Document Contained No Data error.

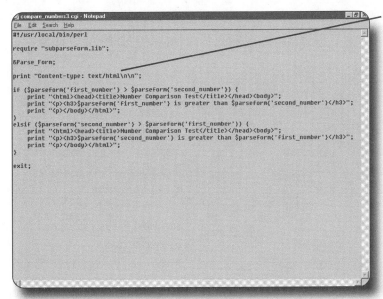

This type of error occurs when the content header is printed but nothing else is printed after that. Because neither the `if` or the `elsif` statements were true, nothing else was printed.

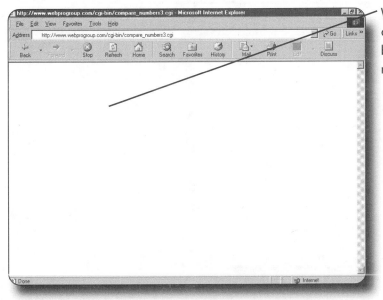

When this type of error occurs in Internet Explorer, a blank page is returned and no error is reported.

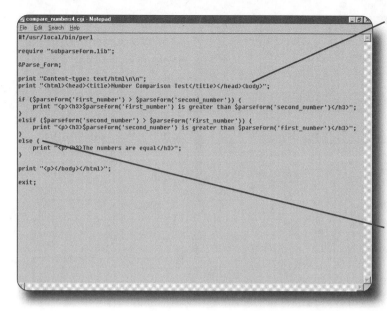

```
#!/usr/local/bin/perl

require "subparseform.lib";

&Parse_Form;

print "Content-type: text/html\n\n";
print "<html><head><title>Number Comparison Test</title></head><body>";

if ($parseform{'first_number'} > $parseform{'second_number'}) {
    print "<p><h3>$parseform{'first_number'} is greater than $parseform{'second_number'}</h3>";
}
elsif ($parseform{'second_number'} > $parseform{'first_number'}) {
    print "<p><h3>$parseform{'second_number'} is greater than $parseform{'first_number'}</h3>";
}
else {
    print "<p><h3>The numbers are equal</h3>";
}

print "<p></body></html>";

exit;
```

This error is easily avoided by printing something else after the content header.

This problem illustrates the need to test your applications thoroughly. Through testing, you can find areas where your logic is not complete.

You find areas that need to be expanded.

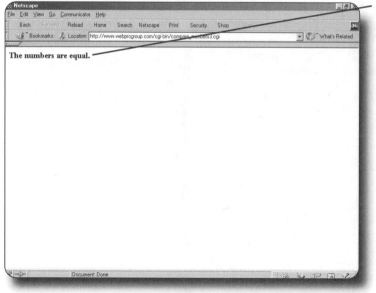

The numbers are equal.

Now, the code covers all possible outcomes.

404 File Not Found

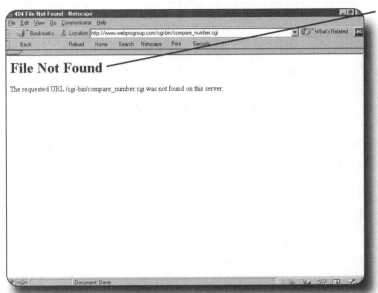

If after submitting a form, you receive a 404 File Not Found error, it means exactly what it says. The browser could not find the CGI script that your form was trying to submit to.

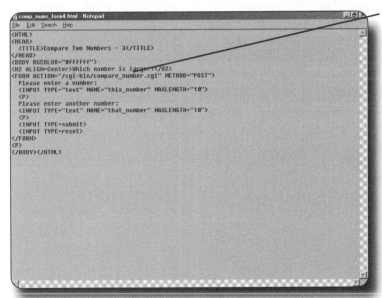

This means that the path to your CGI application in the action attribute of your <FORM> tag is incorrect.

The name of the application might be misspelled or the path might not point to the correct location. To prevent or fix this error, make sure that the path to your script is correct and that it is updated as you move files.

Using Other Valuable Debugging Tools

You've learned what certain error messages mean and how to fix the bugs that cause them. However, you might also encounter problems whereby the output from your script is not what you expected. The output of your script might be incomplete or incorrect. In these cases, you do not receive any error messages. In this section, you learn about a couple of debugging tools that help you in these situations.

Using Error Subroutines

An *error subroutine* is a simple subroutine that prints an HTML page that tells you an error has occurred in your CGI application. You can also use error subroutines to send messages to users who submit a form with incomplete or incorrect information.

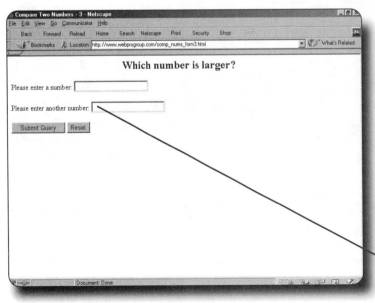

To demonstrate the value of using an error subroutine, the following examples illustrate a few situations where you'll find them useful. You previously learned about adding an additional `else` clause to cover all possible input situations. However, here is another scenario that you haven't yet considered.

Suppose someone submits your form without filling in any of the fields.

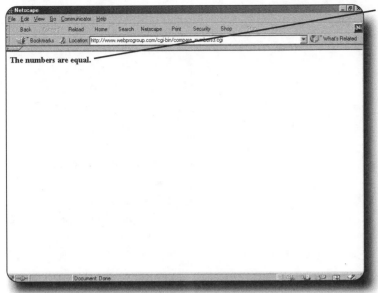

The output is not correct.

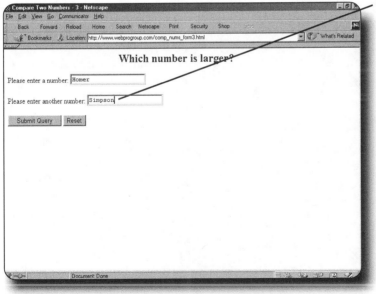

Now suppose someone submits your form with data other than what the form was intended for.

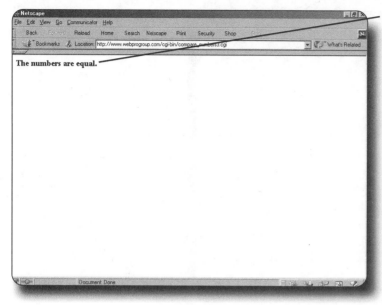

The script still works; however, once again the output is not correct.

To prevent this from happening, you need to use a technique called *form validation*. It means that you first validate the data that was submitted to verify that the required information was indeed entered. You can also verify that the data is in the correct format. For example, you can verify that a number was submitted in a number field and not other text.

If the data does not pass the validation testing, you can use an error subroutine to tell the users that they must submit correct information. This might not seem too important for a few form submittals. However, if you were receiving hundreds or thousands of submittals per day, you'd need this assurance.

Perhaps you have another script that opens a file and reads the contents of the file into an array.

Then it prints each line of the file.

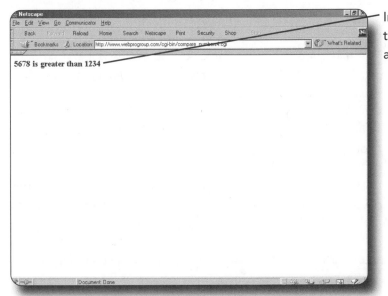

In some cases, it is difficult to tell whether the file was actually opened.

It is also sometimes difficult to tell whether the contents of the file were printed.

Unless you use an error subroutine, that is. In this simple example, it is easy to determine that the file was not being opened and printed. However, if you had a CGI application containing a few hundred or thousand lines of code and many places where files are opened, you'd need this check. Including an error subroutine in your CGI applications is not only smart; it's good programming practice. People who use and maintain your CGI applications after you will thank you for it!

Creating an Error Subroutine

You learned earlier that an error subroutine is just a simple subroutine that prints an error when something goes wrong. Now you'll learn how to create one.

Type the word **sub**, the name of the subroutine, and an open brace (**{**).

This subroutine requires input, so set a variable to equal the value of the input sent to the subroutine. Type the name of the variable followed by an equals sign.

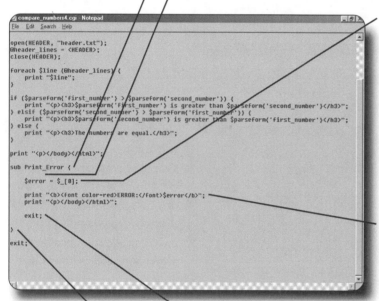

End this line by typing a dollar sign, an underscore, an open bracket, the number **0**, a closed bracket, and a semicolon. Remember that the error message is passed to the subroutine in the special variable @_. The error message is stored as the first element of this array.

Next, print the error message and ending HTML tags using simple `print` statements.

You also need to type the word **exit** followed by a semicolon. This forces the script to exit after printing the error message rather than continue with the rest of the script after the subroutine call.

Finally, close the subroutine with a closing bracket.

Calling an Error Subroutine

Now all you need to know is how to call the error subroutine. To call an error subroutine when there is an error opening a file, add the following code to the line that opens the file.

Replace the semicolon at the end of the line with two pipe symbols (| |). These pipe symbols are another way of saying or. You're telling Perl either to open the file or, when there's a problem opening it, call the error subroutine.

```
compare_numbers4.cgi - Notepad
File  Edit  Search  Help
#!/usr/bin/perl

require "subparseform.lib";

&Parse_Form;

print "Content-type: text/html\n\n";

open(HEADER, "header.txt") || &Print_Error("Could not open header.txt for reading");
@header_lines = <HEADER>;
close(HEADER);

foreach $line (@header_lines) {
    print "$line";
}

if ($parseform{'first_number'} > $parseform{'second_number'}) {
    print "<p><h3>$parseform{'first_number'} is greater than $parseform{'second_number'}</h3>";
} elsif ($parseform{'second_number'} > $parseform{'first_number'}) {
    print "<p><h3>$parseform{'second_number'} is greater than $parseform{'first_number'}</h3>";
} else {
    print "<p><h3>The numbers are equal.</h3>";
}

print "<p></body></html>";

sub Print_Error {

    $error = $_[0];

    print "<b><font color=red>ERROR:</font>$error</b>";
    print "<p></body></html>";

    exit;

}
```

Next, type an ampersand and the name of the subroutine followed by an open parenthesis.

You then type the actual error message in double quotation marks. Finally, type an ending parenthesis and a semicolon.

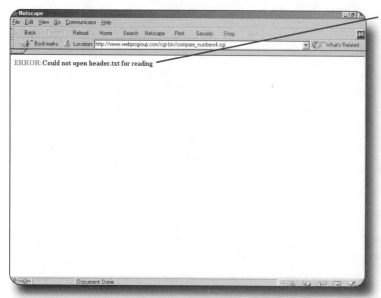

The output of the error subroutine helps you pinpoint any errors when opening files.

To call an error subroutine when a form field is empty, add the following form-validation code. You want this code to be the first line after the form is parsed and after the content header and your HTML header have been printed. If the form input is invalid, there's no need for the script to do anything except go directly to the error subroutine.

Type the word **unless**, an open parenthesis, the name of your first parsed variable, two ampersands (**&&**), the name of your second parsed variable, a closed parenthesis, and an open brace.

Next, type an ampersand and the name of the subroutine followed by an open parenthesis.

```perl
#!/usr/bin/perl

require "subparseform.lib";

&Parse_Form;

print "Content-type: text/html\n\n";

open(HEADER, "header.txt") || &Print_Error("Could not open header.txt for reading");
@header_lines = <HEADER>;
close(HEADER);

foreach $line (@header_lines) {
    print "$line";
}

unless ($parseform{'first_number'} && $parseform{'second_number'}) {
    &Print_Error("Both fields must be filled in before submitting the form.");
}

if ($parseform{'first_number'} > $parseform{'second_number'}) {
    print "<p><h3>$parseform{'first_number'} is greater than $parseform{'second_number'}</h3>";
} elsif ($parseform{'second_number'} > $parseform{'first_number'}) {
    print "<p><h3>$parseform{'second_number'} is greater than $parseform{'first_number'}</h3>";
} else {
    print "<p><h3>The numbers are equal.</h3>";
}

print "<p></body></html>";

sub Print_Error {

    $error = $_[0];

    print "<b><font color=red>ERROR:</font>$error</b>";
    print "<p></body></html>";
```

You then type the actual error message in double quotation marks. Add an ending parenthesis, a semicolon, and an ending brace.

Remember that everything has a true or false value. Variables that have a value assigned to them return a value of true in a true/false test. This `unless` statement tells Perl that unless the first variable and the second variable have values assigned to them, it should call the error subroutine.

Using a combination of form validation and error subroutines prevents empty form submittals.

Summary

Debugging can seem a little overwhelming at first. However, if you learn the skills necessary, you can view it as a challenging, fun, and necessary part of programming. In this appendix, you've learned about the error messages you might encounter, as well as what they mean and how to fix them. You've learned how to debug your code by commenting out lines. You've also learned how to create and use an error subroutine. Don't forget that error subroutines are not only a valuable debugging tool, they are a mark of good programming.

B

What's On
the CD-ROM

Running the CD

To make the CD more user-friendly and take up less of your disk space, we've designed the CD-ROM so that you can install only those files that you desire.

Linux

1. Open the CD-ROM tray and insert the CD.

2. As root, type the following at the command line: **mount/dev/cdrom/** *tmp* (replace */tmp* with wherever you want to mount the CD).

3. Start an X session (*startx* in most cases).

4. Open Netscape Navigator.

5. Choose Open from the File menu, and then click the Browse button.

6. Browse to start_here.html, located in the directory in which you mounted the CD-ROM

Windows 95/98/2000/NT

1. Insert the CD into the CD-ROM drive and close the tray.

2. Go to the Control Panel and double-click the CD-ROM.

3. Open start_here.html (works with most HTML browsers).

The Prima License

The first window you will see is the Prima License Agreement. Take a moment to read the agreement. If you accept the terms of the agreement, click the I Agree button and proceed to the user interface. If you do not accept the license agreement, click the I Disagree button, and the CD will not load.

The Prima User Interface

Prima's user interface is designed to make viewing and using the CD-ROM contents quick and easy. The opening screen contains a two-panel window. The left panel contains the structure of the programs on the disc. The right panel displays a description page for the selected entry in the left panel.

Resizing and Closing the User Interface

As with any window, you can resize the user interface. To do so, position the mouse over any edge or corner, hold down the left mouse button, and drag the edge or corner to a new position.

To close and exit the user interface, select File, Exit (your specific X setup might have a unique graphical means of resizing and closing Netscape).

Using the Left Panel

To view a sample file, click /Chapters. A drop-down menu appears containing each chapter for which there are sample files. Then click on the chapter you wish to view. To view the programs on the CD, click /Programs and then select the desired program.

Using the Right Panel

The right panel displays a page that describes the entry you choose in the left panel. Use the information provided in the right panel for details about your selection, such as what functionality an installable program provides. To download a particular file, follow the directions that appear in the left panel.

Index

License Agreement/Notice of Limited Warranty

By opening the sealed disc container in this book, you agree to the following terms and conditions. If, upon reading the following license agreement and notice of limited warranty, you cannot agree to the terms and conditions set forth, return the unused book with unopened disc to the place where you purchased it for a refund.

License:
The enclosed software is copyrighted by the copyright holder(s) indicated on the software disc. You are licensed to copy the software onto a single computer for use by a single concurrent user and to a backup disc. You may not reproduce, make copies, or distribute copies or rent or lease the software in whole or in part, except with written permission of the copyright holder(s). You may transfer the enclosed disc only together with this license, and only if you destroy all other copies of the software and the transferee agrees to the terms of the license. You may not decompile, reverse assemble, or reverse engineer the software.

Notice of Limited Warranty:
The enclosed disc is warranted by Prima Publishing to be free of physical defects in materials and workmanship for a period of sixty (60) days from end user's purchase of the book/disc combination. During the sixty-day term of the limited warranty, Prima will provide a replacement disc upon the return of a defective disc.

Limited Liability:
The sole remedy for breach of this limited warranty shall consist entirely of replacement of the defective disc. IN NO EVENT SHALL PRIMA OR THE AUTHORS BE LIABLE FOR ANY other damages, including loss or corruption of data, changes in the functional characteristics of the hardware or operating system, deleterious interaction with other software, or any other special, incidental, or consequential DAMAGES that may arise, even if Prima and/or the author have previously been notified that the possibility of such damages exists.

Disclaimer of Warranties:
Prima and the authors specifically disclaim any and all other warranties, either express or implied, including warranties of merchantability, suitability to a particular task or purpose, or freedom from errors. Some states do not allow for EXCLUSION of implied warranties or limitation of incidental or consequential damages, so these limitations may not apply to you.

Other:
This Agreement is governed by the laws of the State of California without regard to choice of law principles. The United Convention of Contracts for the International Sale of Goods is specifically disclaimed. This Agreement constitutes the entire agreement between you and Prima Publishing regarding use of the software.